GOD
FORSAKEN

GOD
FORSAKEN

DINESH
D'SOUZA

Tyndale House Publishers, Inc.
Carol Stream, Illinois

Visit Tyndale online at www.tyndale.com.

TYNDALE and Tyndale's quill logo are registered trademarks of Tyndale House Publishers, Inc.

Godforsaken: Bad things happen. Is there a God who cares? Yes. Here's proof.

Designed by Jessie McGrath

Library of Congress Cataloging-in-Publication Data

D'Souza, Dinesh, date.
  Godforsaken : Bad things happen. Is there a God who cares? Yes. Here's proof. / Dinesh D'Souza.
    pages cm
  Includes bibliographical references.
  ISBN 978-1-4143-2485-2 (hc)
1. Suffering—Religious aspects—Christianity. 2. God (Christianity)—Goodness.
3. Christian life. I. Title.
  BV4909.D84 2012
  231'.8—dc23   2011049946

Printed in the United States of America

18   17   16   15   14   13   12
7   6   5   4   3   2   1

For Lee and Allie Hanley,

whose love of our country

and our Lord

is a great inspiration to me

CONTENTS

My God, my God, why have you forsaken me?

PSALM 22:1

PART 1

Introduction

AN IMMIGRANT'S JOURNEY

The Paradox of Suffering

That to the height of this great argument
I may assert Eternal Providence,
And justify the ways of God to men.[1]
JOHN MILTON, *Paradise Lost*

EACH ONE OF US, at some point in our lives, will find ourselves staring death in the face. None of us can escape that grim reality. Recently, I was reminded of that reality while reading the following e-mail from my friend, Devdas Kamath, who went to school with me in India but with whom I had lost contact over the years.

My elder son Nikhil, a first year student at the Indian Institute of Management, Ahmedabad, died of a rare disorder, Thrombotic Thrombocytopenic Purpura (TTP), at Ahmedabad on Tuesday, September 29. On Monday, September 21, Nikhil complained of fever. Since the fever did not subside with Crocin, he visited the doctor. He did not respond to the doctor's treatment. Hence he was referred to a senior physician on Friday, September 25. He appeared to improve a bit by the same night. The next day, however, his condition had worsened, and he was admitted to SAL Hospital. At that time, I was in Mumbai. I managed to reach SAL Hospital around 7 p.m., while my wife Surekha reached from Chennai around 11 p.m. After a series of blood tests, the doctors concluded that Nikhil had contracted Thrombotic Thrombocytopenic Purpura, a blood disorder which causes blood in small vessels in the body to clot. The clots hamper the flow of blood to key organs. This leads to rapid deterioration and multiple organ failure. By the time the diagnosis was made, Nikhil's condition had seriously deteriorated. He died around 7:20 p.m. on Tuesday, September 29.

I read the e-mail, and I burst into tears. To be honest, I didn't even know why I was crying. Devdas was my best friend in high school, but I hadn't been in touch with him since I came to America three decades ago. Obviously, I had never met his son. As the tears ran down my face, I felt almost embarrassed. Acutely I felt the contrast between Devdas's stoic report of his son's death and my seemingly excessive reaction to it. As I thought about it, I realized I wasn't crying for the young man, but for his father. I was crying for my friend's loss. And it came to me with a shock of discovery that I realized how much I loved this guy. Life had intervened since high school in such a way that I hadn't thought about him in years, yet the hurt I now felt over his loss was a measure of what, deep down, I truly felt about him. Since then we have restored our friendship, at least to the degree possible over a long distance. Remarkably, it was the death in his family that proved to be the catalyst for that restoration—though obviously neither of us would have chosen the suffering.

Suffering is the theme of this book, and it is one that I have been thinking about my whole life, though mine has been a happy life. I grew up in a suburb of Bombay—now called Mumbai—and when I was nine years old, my grandfather died. I remember my grandmother's expression as she returned from the hospital. It was a defeated look, confirming the magnitude of her loss, and yet it was also defiant, as if she would not allow even this to break her dignity. I think this memory stands out for me, not because it was so painful, but because my life was so problem free that death came into it almost as an impostor, a misfit. That's when I began noticing death lurking about, along with its siblings tragedy and suffering.

When I was about thirteen, a group of us went to the beach near my house, not a sand beach but the rocky entrance to the Arabian Sea. As we explored the crevices and small pools leading down to the ocean, one of my friends yelled out. He had spotted a tiny infant, probably only a few days old, floating faceup in the water. Whereas in America our first thought might have been foul play or an accident, as youths in India we had no doubt in our minds that some desperate mother had drowned her child to escape the shame of having him out of wedlock. We stared at the little corpse in horrid fascination, and then we turned and ran away. To this day I wonder occasionally about that young mother, how she must have felt to be driven to do that, and how as a consequence a little life was extinguished even before it had its chance.

I wasn't a complete stranger to suffering as a child—in India I was, after all, surrounded by people who lived on just a few rupees a day—but somehow it didn't make a strong impression. I suppose that's because I was just as likely to see the poor people around me smiling, or even hear them roar with laughter, as I was to encounter their groans and tears. The poor in India take life as it comes, and they seem content to wring whatever happiness they can even out of difficult circumstances. I've often wondered why this is so. I think it's because when you have very little, you typically don't compare yourself to the rich, but to those around you, and you find that by this measure, there is not very much to complain about.

Back then, the person I knew who had suffered the most was undoubtedly my grandfather. That man had stories, and he told them with such gusto that you almost missed the horrific aspect of those life experiences. Never one to dwell on the negative, he only told me his life story once, at my grandmother's insistence.

My grandfather worked in Burma—now called Myanmar—in the 1940s, and when the Japanese invaded the country, he and his family were forced to evacuate. Only women and children were allowed to take the boat, however; the men all had to walk. Walking, in this case, meant going on foot from Burma to India, a distance of hundreds of miles. Some of it was over mountains and across rivers and through malaria-infested jungle. As he described it, there were corpses all along the way. Sometimes the refugees would come upon a massive current, and some were not brave enough to attempt to cross it, so they would just stop and stay put and die.

When my grandfather reached India many months later, he was emaciated and disease ridden, not far from death. Besides his health he had lost his home, his savings—everything except his wife and children. Yet he recounted his hardships with enthusiasm and even humor. He spoke of being on a "compulsory diet" and said he became so weak that "even my sons could beat me up." If you didn't know his story, you would have guessed by his cheerful attitude that he had known little of pain or suffering.

Coming to America

I came to America in 1978 as a Rotary exchange student, and a year later I enrolled as a freshman at Dartmouth College. Dartmouth was a wonderful experience, largely free of suffering, although as a young conservative activist, I tried to impose some suffering on the liberal faculty and administrators. We used to tell the deans that taking on our rebel student group was like wrestling with a pig: not only did it get everyone dirty, but the pig liked it! My idyllic Dartmouth experience, however, took a jolt when one of my good friends, Jeff Lamb, suddenly died. Carbon monoxide had leaked out of a pipe in his apartment overnight and asphyxiated him. Jeff was an atheist, and I remember that the pastor his family rounded up had immense difficulty knowing what to say at his memorial. I recall one of Jeff's family members saying, "God had no right to take that young man," and although I didn't say anything, I thought to myself, *Jeff didn't believe in God, so I wonder what he would have made of this claim on his behalf.* Jeff was a good guy, and he was one of the few married students, so he left behind a grieving wife who was also a Dartmouth undergraduate.

Probably the worst I have personally suffered was the death of my father in the year 2000. My dad died relatively young, in his late sixties. He was a great father, not to mention an inspiring role model. There were hundreds of people at his funeral. By any standard, he lived a successful life. The Greeks used to say, "Count no man happy until his death," and my dad, a good and happy man, died a peaceful death. So what, I asked myself, was I grieving for? Why did his death haunt me months, and even years, later? I realized that I was grieving not for him, but for me. As natural as it was, this suffering was a form of self-pity. I missed him, of course, and his memory and example remain as a guiding inspiration for my life. Still, I realized with his death what a good thing was now gone from my life.

Suffering seems to require from us a balanced perspective, and yet I find that this balance is often lacking, especially in the West. Perhaps the unique horror of the Holocaust is largely responsible for that. When I was working in Washington, DC, I once attended a talk by a Holocaust survivor. Because of her moving testimony, my thoughts were stirred and I bought a book that she recommended, Elie Wiesel's *The Trial of God*. But the book's influence on my thinking about suffering was a bit of a surprise.

Wiesel himself is a Holocaust survivor, but his play wasn't set in Auschwitz. It was set in 1649 in a village in the Ukraine. A traveling group of minstrels come through a village whose Jewish population has been almost completely decimated in an anti-Semitic pogrom. The minstrels offer to perform a play in exchange for food and drink. Appalled, the lone remaining elder of the village asks the minstrels to move along. But when the performers insist, he agrees, with one condition. The theme must be the trial of God: a play indicting God for what he has done to the man's family, to his community, to all the Jews. The performers accept, and the rest of the play is the trial. "Listen," declares the prosecutor, speaking of God. "Either He is responsible or He is not. If He is, let's judge Him; if He is not, let Him stop judging us."[2]

I understand the horror of the Holocaust and the uniqueness of it in history, and I accept Wiesel as a man of unimpeachable moral authority. But as I read his play, I found myself growing very uncomfortable. After all, the pogrom had not been carried out by God; it had been carried out by anti-Semites. The very idea of indicting and trying God, even in fiction, even as a thought experiment, would not have occurred to anyone that I knew growing up. It struck me as very foreign, which is to say, very Western.

Quite recently I was picked up by a car service at JFK Airport. As we drove through Queens, heading to my apartment in Manhattan, the driver suddenly yelled out, "Watch it!" He screeched to a halt. I was mortified to see that he had almost hit a young girl. The girl, who couldn't have been more than twenty, languidly walked up to the driver's window. "Do me a favor," she said, her voice distant and remote. I thought she was going to ask for a lift. But then she clarified what she meant. "Do me a favor," she repeated, "and run me over." I realized that this lovely young girl wanted to end her life. Or maybe this scene was more of a cry for help. Either way, the driver hadn't been careless; the girl had actually jumped in front of the car. We convinced her to go with us to a counseling center. As we rode in the car, the girl not saying a word, staring vacantly into the distance, I thought to myself, *How sad this is. She's well dressed. She isn't hungry. She has her whole life ahead of her. And yet she wants to end it.* Such desperation can come to those who seem to have it all together—but I wondered if that might not be possible anywhere but in the wealthy, enlightened West. I can't imagine anyone leaping in front of a car on the streets of Mumbai, unless it is a scam to extort money from the driver.

There is one group in the West that has been writing eloquently on the subject of suffering, and that is the so-called New Atheists. In the last few years, I have gotten to know several prominent atheists. The late Christopher Hitchens, perhaps America's leading atheist, was a friend. Yet I was still quite surprised to learn in his recent memoir that when he was a college student, his mother eloped with a former Anglican clergyman—and that sometime later, the two of them made a suicide pact and killed themselves.[3] It made me think about his longtime atheism. How could such events not have a profound impact on a young man? How could they not have influenced his thinking about God? Yet was atheism the necessary result? Hitchens's brother, Peter Hitchens, is a believer and has written a book in defense of Christianity. Obviously, emotionally distressing experiences can point people in very different directions.

One who has made clear that experience pointed him in the atheist direction, rather than the Christian one, is Bart Ehrman. A former Christian fundamentalist, graduate of evangelical institutions Moody Bible Institute and Wheaton College, Ehrman has since become an unbeliever. He was raised to believe that "God wrote the Bible" and that the God of the Bible was a fantastic miracle worker who tirelessly intervened in history to help his people, at least the ones who were faithful to him. Later, at Princeton Theological Seminary, Ehrman learned that God didn't write the Bible; humans did. Moreover, the earliest manuscripts that we have of the New Testament are from the second and third centuries. Because the Jewish and Christian Scriptures were hand copied, the books were in some cases altered by the copiers. Ehrman found his confidence in the truth of Christianity being shaken.

Losing Faith

Still, Ehrman says, he didn't give up his faith until he discovered the magnitude of evil in the world. The fact of "unspeakable suffering," Ehrman writes, "was the reason I lost my faith." Ehrman realized that "I could no longer reconcile the claims of faith with the facts of life." I've debated Ehrman several times. He is very eloquent about all the injustice and travails of the world: famines, epidemics, wars, ethnic cleansing, genocide. Ehrman speaks with such passion that one gets the impression that he has just learned about these horrors. Could it really be the case that this fellow in his late fifties has just figured out that the world could be a bad place?

Then I realized that what Ehrman terms his "deconversion"—his rejection of Christianity—didn't come because of his recent discovery of evil. It came because evil forced him to change his attitude toward the God of the Bible. As he put it in one of our debates, "It's not that I don't believe in God. But I came to see that the God that I was raised to believe in, the God of the Bible, this God did not exist." Ehrman writes, "This is the God of the patriarchs who answered prayer and worked miracles for his people; this is the God of the exodus who saved his suffering people from the misery of slavery in Egypt; this is the God of Jesus who healed the sick, gave sight to the blind, made the lame walk, and fed those who were hungry. Where is this God now? . . . But I can't believe in that God anymore, because from what I now see around the world, he doesn't intervene. "

A good question. Watching Ehrman indict God for his failure to prevent suffering, much in the manner of Wiesel's actors, I couldn't help wonder what Ehrman's own experience was of suffering. When I read Ehrman's book on the topic, *God's Problem*, I got my answer. By Ehrman's own account, he has scarcely suffered at all. "I have such a fantastic life," Ehrman writes, "that I feel an overwhelming sense of gratitude for it. I am fortunate beyond words." Then he adds this, "But I don't have anyone to express my gratitude to. This is a void inside me, a void of wanting someone to thank, and I don't see any plausible way of filling it."[4]

What a remarkable situation. Ehrman experiences his own life as a great gift, but refuses to thank God for it. Yet he blames God for the suffering that he has not himself experienced, the suffering of others. Ehrman's special focus seems to be on the sufferings of people outside the West, the people of Asia, Africa, and South America. Yet it is a simple fact that people in those countries don't interpret their suffering as evidence that there is no God. There are very few Bart Ehrman types in Riyadh or Rio de Janeiro.

Historian Philip Jenkins writes that in third-world countries—in what he calls the global south—suffering turns people toward God, not away from him. "Christianity is flourishing wonderfully among the poor and persecuted," Jenkins writes, "while it atrophies among the rich and secure." Jenkins suggests that this is because the world of the Bible, with its lurid accounts of famine, disease, war, and oppression, is a world familiar to those people. We in the West don't typically encounter moneylenders or lepers or people who claim to be possessed by demons and evil spirits. But for many people in third-world cultures, the world of the ancient Israelites, even the milieu in which Christ lived and died, is realistic, and familiar, and a relevant reference point for their own experience.[5]

What's true of non-Western cultures today is also true of the past, even in the West. In previous eras, when general suffering was far worse—horrible diseases, no pain-killing drugs, infants and mothers routinely dying during childbirth—still there was no widespread sense that these counted against God's existence or even turned people away from God. When the bubonic plague swept across Europe, it wiped out one-third of the population. Still, the other two-thirds kept going to church. Indeed, church attendance often increased in times of suffering. What Rudolf Otto describes as the essence of religious experience—a feeling of sublime awe and stupefying dread—was typically enhanced by earthquakes, plagues, and other calamities. Such events convinced people of their complete dependence on God.

Let me emphasize, at this point, that I'm not suggesting that this ancient and now third-world attitude toward suffering is in every respect superior. I mean only that it is anchored in genuine experience. There is something a little off key about Western academics saying, "I have lost my faith because of the suffering of the Rwandans," while Rwandans are saying, "Our faith draws us closer to the only one who can console and protect us, which is God." I recently spoke at a prayer breakfast at the United Nations and had the opportunity to discuss this point with a number of African diplomats. "I am always amazed," one of them told me, "that people in the West always think they know better, even about what we are going through." He then wryly added, "I do believe that we are the world's experts in understanding our own experience."

I agree with him, but there is another side to the story. Outside the West, many people are habituated to suffering. That's because they think it is inevitable. We don't, and that's a sign of progress. We have in our cultures greatly reduced suffering, and this means that we are very intolerant of what suffering still remains. In America and Europe, we have become almost pathologically averse to suffering. Today we can barely stand to read descriptions of torture and public hangings that were, in the past, regarded as public spectacles and even entertainment. Unlike our ancestors, and people in the developing world, we regard suffering as having no legitimate place in the universe. Utopia, for us, is worth striving for.

I mention this outlook not to diminish it; I, too, see things this way. I even have some sympathy for the point of view of the atheists who say, "We don't wait on God to do what he has for centuries, namely nothing. Rather, we deplore God's inactivity and become active ourselves in reducing suffering."

A Christian Solution

This way of thinking, though it seems like atheist propaganda, actually rises out of the Bible. The problem of suffering is first raised in the book of Job, and the vigorous debate about this topic is unique to Christianity. You won't find it in Hinduism or Buddhism or even Islam. I'll say more about this in the next chapter. Christians are the only people who raise the anguished question, Why does God allow this? And consequently Christianity has given rise to more rebellion and unbelief than any other religion. For some reason, it sharpens and deepens our sense and depth of suffering, making the "God question" all the more acute.

This raises a critical question: If suffering is a problem that arises most keenly within Christianity, is there a Christian solution? I believe that there is, and that the depth of the problem and the solution are essentially related. Of course I want to respond to the atheist, to show that there is no contradiction between suffering and the existence of God. But I also want to understand why God permits suffering, and how, as a Christian, I can love and relate to a God who often seems indifferent to suffering. This may be a Western way of framing the problem, but it is one that now preoccupies Christians all over the world.

Since I was raised in India but now live in New York and California, I am, in a sense, between two worlds. I'd like to draw on that experience to tackle the great issues of God, evil, and suffering.

I have thought about these questions for decades, and finally I have something original to say about them. Of the Holocaust victims, Elie Wiesel writes, "Theirs was the kingdom of night. Forgotten by God, forsaken by Him, they lived alone, suffered alone, fought alone."[6] Is it true that we are, like the Jews in the Nazi camps, abandoned and godforsaken? Ehrman and others have concluded that we are. Yet I believe we really cannot answer this question without asking first why the world is designed the way that it is, and the answer to that question will, in part, answer the question of where God is when we need him so desperately. To address the question of suffering, then, requires an inquiry into the mind of God, a search for God's own point of view.

Many before me have contributed to this corporate inquiry. Typically the atheists produce a catalog of crimes and sufferings, and then they demand a divine explanation. Meanwhile, the Christian makes elaborate and ultimately impossible attempts to show the benefit and purpose of all these calamities. This book takes a different approach. While I begin with the debate as it is, I attempt to steer it in a novel direction. Instead of confining myself to philosophical and theological speculation, I propose to draw on remarkable advances in physics, astronomy, brain science, and biology to offer a fresh answer to the problems of evil and suffering, an answer that allows us to see God's providential actions in the natural realm in a fresh light. Incredibly, modern science gives us a new way to think about an ancient philosophical and theological conundrum. In this book, I take one of the greatest recent discoveries of modern science—the discovery of the fine-tuned universe—and apply it in a new way to answer the atheist, the Christian, and anyone else who wonders why God might act in the way that he does. Why do particular evils happen at particular times to particular people? I don't know. Why does an omnipotent, benevolent God permit so much evil and suffering in the world? To this question, I believe I now have an answer.

This answer will not make suffering go away; it will not dry all the tears. In the end, it is an intellectual solution to the problem of suffering; it doesn't solve the immediate emotional problem. People who are hurting still need pastoral counseling, and they need people to commiserate with them and help them get through the pain and the shock. Still, a time comes when sufferers start reflecting on their suffering, on why this has happened, and on what God's role is in causing or allowing it to happen. This book helps to make suffering intelligible, and this, I believe, can provide in the end a profound consolation. We will still mourn, but we won't blame God for it; rather, we will see why he permits it, and we are more likely to draw closer to him.

With this book I am hoping to provide a rational ground for hope, and hope is a very powerful medicine. Though I couldn't do much to help the brokenhearted young lady from Queens that day, I hope this book might help you.

CHAPTER 2

WOUNDED THEISM

The Indictment of God

*If this God of the Christians were proved to us to exist, we
should know even less how to believe in him.*[1]
FRIEDRICH NIETZSCHE, *The Anti-Christ*

THERE IS A TIME in every debate when your opponent drops his guard
and states the real basis for his position. Not long ago in Florida, I
debated the atheist Michael Shermer, the editor of *Skeptic* maga-
zine and author of *Why Darwin Matters*, on the existence of God.
For most of the debate, he had been telling us how he became an
atheist. Shermer recounted that he had been raised as an evangelical
Christian. He attended Pepperdine University, a Christian institution, where he even participated in evangelism in the Los Angeles
area, handing out Christian literature. But now, Shermer quipped,
he'd liked to go from door to door and get that stuff back! It was at
Pepperdine, Shermer said, that he lost his faith.

It wouldn't be the only time, alas, that a Christian stopped being
a Christian at a Christian college. More interesting was Shermer's

account of how it happened. Basically, Shermer said that he discovered science. He claimed that he saw that science, based on reason, is simply a better way of getting truth than Christianity, which is based on faith. Darwin showed that there is a natural explanation for how life forms evolved, one from the other; we don't need to posit a creator. As I heard all of this, I nodded wearily. I've heard this story many times before.

Still, I've never found this kind of explanation to be a convincing one for the new atheism that Shermer represents. Think about it this way: if you don't believe in something because there isn't any evidence for it, what do you do about it? You ignore it. You go about your life as if that something, for which there is no proof, does not exist. Case in point: I don't believe in unicorns, but you'll notice that I haven't written any books disputing the existence of unicorns. I am not the author of, for example, *The Unicorn Delusion* or *The End of Unicorns* or *Unicorns Are Not Great*. I don't attend conferences on the fallacy of unicorns, nor do I go around debating people on whether there are unicorns.

Now admittedly I might be roused to do something if our society were besieged by advocates of unicorns. But still, I would have a hard time responding with anything other than dismissive humor. I certainly wouldn't spend much time trying to win over unicorn enthusiasts, or raging against the unicorns themselves. This is in sharp contrast to the New Atheists, who are obsessed with God. They probably spend just as much time thinking about God as religious believers do. In fact, they expend great efforts to win young people over to their position. They have become atheist missionaries or, if you will, evangelical atheists.

What's going on here? At a crucial point in our debate, Shermer provided the answer. Almost unprovoked, he narrated an episode from his college years in which he was dating a young woman who ended up having a terrible accident that paralyzed her. Shermer movingly described the days that the two of them spent at the hospital, in which he prayed fervently to God for a healing that never came. I looked over at Shermer, and I saw that he was shaking a little. But then he stopped, and a look of firm resolve came across his face. "That was it," he told the audience. "I was done with God." (He didn't say whether he was also "done" with the woman.) That's when I realized the roots of Shermer's atheism. Shermer didn't reject God merely because he found an alternative explanation for the universe. His atheism seems to have had more to do with disappointment with God.

The cognitive psychologist Steven Pinker is not merely disappointed with God; he is downright angry at God. In his book *How the Mind Works*, Pinker alludes to the tragedy and suffering in the world: the wars, the famines, the epidemics, the natural disasters, the Holocaust. Citing a Yiddish proverb, he explodes, "If God lived on earth, people would break his windows."[2] In the same vein, philosopher Bertrand Russell ranted that the horrible events in the world seem to indicate not a benign sovereign but rather a vicious dictator. "If the world in which we live has been produced in accordance with a plan," he wrote, "we shall have to reckon Nero a saint in comparison with the author of that plan."[3]

The same notes of sarcasm and bitterness are evident in the writings of Richard Dawkins. Dawkins, a biologist, has written numerous books, such as *The Blind Watchmaker* and *The Ancestor's Tale*, arguing that evolution supplies an adequate explanation for the development of life on earth. Dawkins's atheism seems founded on his discovery, via Darwin, of an alternative account of Creation. Natural selection, not God, deserves all the credit. Or, as Dawkins also suggests, sometimes it deserves the blame. Dawkins eloquently describes the ruthlessness of evolution. A female wasp, he informs us, lays her eggs inside the body of a caterpillar so that her larva can feed on the caterpillar, eating it from the inside out.[4] Dawkins seems horrified; in fact, he is so taken by this example that he cites a letter that Charles Darwin wrote to Asa Gray on the subject of the ichneumon wasp: "I cannot persuade myself that a beneficent and omnipotent God would have designedly created the Ichneumonidae with the express intention of their feeding within the living bodies of caterpillars."[5]

One might think, given these examples, that Dawkins's main objections to God arise from his contemplation of evolutionary design and from his compassionate concerns for wasps and caterpillars. But in his book *The God Delusion* we read this: "The God of the Old Testament is arguably the most unpleasant character in all fiction: jealous and proud of it; a petty, unjust, unforgiving control-freak; a vindictive, bloodthirsty ethnic cleanser; a misogynistic, homophobic, racist, infanticidal, genocidal, filicidal, pestilential, megalomaniacal, sadomasochistic, capriciously malevolent bully."[6] What a list! Not only is God a mass murderer, but he's also an anal-retentive guy who has far too high an opinion of himself. I'm struck by Dawkins's tone, which to put it mildly departs from the scientific. Setting aside for now the merits of Dawkins's indictment, clearly the man has a deep personal grudge.

With Dawkins, as with these others, we are not dealing with ordinary atheism; we are dealing with wounded theism. The wounded theist is distinguished from the atheist in that the atheist doesn't believe in God; the wounded theist is angry with God. In some cases the wounded theist hates God; his atheism is a form of revenge.

Consider the case of Dawkins's mentor, Charles Darwin. Many people think that Darwin became an unbeliever due to evolution. True, Darwin attributed the diversity of life on this planet to chance and natural selection, not divine providence. Even so, Darwin, who was raised as an Anglican and at one time considered a career in the clergy, did not lose his faith over evolution. Rather, he became an agnostic when his beloved daughter Annie unexpectedly became ill and then died. Darwin's biographers Adrian Desmond and James

Moore write, "Annie's cruel death destroyed Charles's tatters of belief in a moral, just universe. Later he would say that this period chimed the final death-knell for his Christianity. . . . Charles now took his stand as an unbeliever."[7] But it wasn't his daughter's death alone that pushed Darwin into the camp of the unbelievers; it was also his response to the Christian doctrine of hell. As Darwin himself put it, "I can indeed hardly see how anyone ought to wish Christianity to be true; for if so, the plain language of the text seems to show that the men who do not believe, and this would include my Father, Brother, and almost all my best friends, will be everlastingly punished. And this is a damnable doctrine."[8] This is Darwin rejecting the kind of God who would take from him a daughter in childhood; he is also damning the God of damnation. Here again we have wounded theism, rooted in frustration with God and rage at perceived divine injustice.

Indeed, wounded theism is perhaps more common than ordinary atheism, as we can see from the candid statements of some leading philosophers and writers. One of them, Owen Flanagan, says that he rejected Christianity because "I came not to like or respect the God I was taught to believe in. I still don't like or respect the image of *that* God." Thomas Nagel writes in *The Last Word*, "I want atheism to be true and am made uneasy by the fact that some of the most intelligent and well-informed people I know are religious believers. It isn't just that I don't believe in God. . . . It's that I hope there is no God! I don't want there to be a God; I don't want the universe to be like that." Physicist Victor Stenger candidly writes of God, "If he does exist, I personally want nothing to do with him."[9] And Christopher Hitchens said in several of our debates that, assuming there was a heaven, he had no interest in going there. God, he said, is a celestial dictator like the now-deceased North Korean despot Kim Jong-il—only worse. "If you are living under Kim Jong-il," Hitchens said, "then at least at some point you die, and the tyranny is over. But with God it goes on forever. I cannot imagine a more terrifying place than heaven. For me, it would be hell."

This is deep atheism, the kind that interested the novelist Dostoyevsky. In *The Brothers Karamazov*, Ivan, one of the brothers, has become an atheist. Ivan is horrified by the suffering in the world, by soldiers who coldly drive their bayonets through innocent victims, by the suffering of children most of all. Oh, Ivan says, we could justify these things in terms of ultimate salvation or some higher harmony, but for him this will not do. Of children he says, "It is quite incomprehensible that they too have to suffer, that they too should have to pay for harmony by their suffering. Why should they be the grist to someone else's mill, the means of ensuring someone's future harmony? I don't want harmony. The price of harmony has been set too high, we can't afford to pay so much for admission. And therefore I hasten to return my ticket. And it is my duty, if only as an honest man, to return it as far ahead of time as possible. It's not that I don't accept God, Alyosha; I just most respectfully return him the ticket."[10]

The Believer's Anguish

Christians, too, can be wounded theists. When things are going well, it is easy to proclaim God's sovereignty and submit to it. Some of us even seek to comfort those who are suffering with anodyne assurances: "I'm really sorry to hear that, but you know, God has a plan." Or, more insensitively, "I realize this has been a terrible loss for you, but maybe God needed another angel." When you are the one who is suffering, however—when you are the one who has been raped, or whose legs have been severed in an accident, or whose child has been kidnapped, or whose beloved spouse is deteriorating from Alzheimer's disease—then these explanations offend more than they console. "God has a plan to kill my wife?" "God has lots of angels in heaven; was it also necessary for him to take my only child?"

The eminent theologian Nicholas Wolterstorff lost his

twenty-five-year-old son Eric in a mountain-climbing accident. For a long while after the burial, Wolterstorff writes, the whole world became surreal to him. "I walked into a store. The ordinariness of what I saw repelled me: people putting onions into baskets, squeezing melons, hoisting gallons of milk, clerks ringing up sales. 'How are you today?' 'Have a good day now.' How could everybody be going about their ordinary business when these were no longer ordinary times? I went to my office and along the way saw the secretaries all at their desks and the students all in their seats and the teachers all at their podiums. Do you not know that he slipped and fell and that we sealed him in a box and covered it with dirt and that he can't get out?" While Wolterstorff and his family were surrounded by Christians giving reassurances—"What a full life he lived," "Look how he blessed your life," and so on—he didn't find them consoling. The pain of what we have lost, he says, outweighs our gratitude for what we once had. "Don't say it's not really so bad," he urges his would-be sympathizers. "Because it is. . . . If you think your task as comforter is to tell me that really, all things considered, it's not so bad, you do not sit with me in my grief but place yourself off in the distance away from me."[11]

So while atheists frequently cite the problem of evil and suffering to discredit religious belief, Christians, too, recognize the problem, for it is one that they face as well. Indeed, there seems to be an inconsistency at the heart of the Christian response to God. Christians praise God when good things happen to them, so should they also blame God when bad things happen to them? Moreover, thoughtful Christians recognize that evil and suffering—not merely the existence of evil and suffering but the extent of evil and suffering—raise serious questions about God's omnipotence and benevolence. "The fact of suffering," John Stott writes, "undoubtedly constitutes the single greatest challenge to the Christian faith." So much so that theologian Hans Küng calls it "the rock of atheism."[12]

The Christian problem of evil and suffering is, in a way, more difficult than the atheist problem. Partly this is because for Christians, the category of evil and suffering is wider. Christians, for instance, believe in sin as an important category—the most important category—of evil. Atheists don't. Christians and other religious believers also speak of a distinctively spiritual type of suffering, what John of the Cross famously termed the "dark night of the soul." This is the inward torment of the believer who is being purged of earthly attachments, who is, in a sense, being purified for God by suffering the absence of God. As we know, Mother Teresa, whose life was spent alleviating the suffering of others for Christ's sake, experienced the most profound sense of being abandoned by God for nearly half a century.[13] There is no point discussing this with atheists; they won't know what you are talking about. Christians also believe in hell, while atheists don't; consequently, Christians must answer the question of why finite sins merit infinite punishment at the hands of a God who supposedly loves us and wants us to be united with him. So if God is responsible, even in part, for permitting evil and suffering, the Christian must hold him responsible for more evil and suffering than the atheist would. That's because there is more evil and suffering in the world, from the Christian viewpoint, than there is from the atheist viewpoint.

Moreover, the atheist problem of evil is mostly confined to the question of whether God exists. The magnitude of evil and suffering provides a reason to doubt God's presence, and perhaps in some cases to express hostility to a God who rules the world in this way. For the Christian, however, things aren't so simple. The Christian believes in God. At the same time, he or she is horrified by the evil that has just happened. There seems to be no way to reconcile it with who God is. It is as if I have a rich and powerful father who says he loves me and will be there for me. Yet when I encounter a desperate situation, he refuses to help, even though I know he can. My response is not unbelief. I don't say, "I no longer believe my dad exists." Rather, I say, "My dad does not seem to be the person I thought he was." I now have to reevaluate my father's character and reexamine the basis for my relationship with him. So the Christian must now reconsider how to love and worship a God who stands aside and allows terrible things to happen even to those who are dedicated to him. While the atheist merely uses suffering to confirm disbelief in God, the Christian who is suffering feels betrayed by God. The atheist is intellectually triumphant—*See, I told you there is no God!*—while the Christian is heartbroken . . . godforsaken.

In respect to suffering, most Christians are in the position of Job. In this famous story in the Bible, Job is a righteous man whose prosperous and happy life is ruined when he becomes the object of a bet between God and a character called "the Satan." This character may not be Lucifer; he seems to be a member of God's imperial court, and God converses with him in cordial, if sometimes adversarial, banter. The Satan taunts God that Job's righteousness is mercenary; he is good only because of the blessings that God has bestowed on him. Remove his good fortune, the Satan tells God, and Job will curse you. So God accepts the wager and permits the Satan to take away Job's possessions and kill his family and eventually afflict Job himself with debilitating ailments. Even Job's wife unhelpfully advises him, "Curse God and die." But Job doesn't. Still, as his predicament worsens, he becomes bitter and even accusatory against God. Job's three friends—Zophar, Eliphaz, and Bildad—all seek to help Job in the situation, dubious though that help may seem in the end.

Over the centuries the book of Job has been recognized as one of the deepest, most candid examinations of the problem of evil and suffering. Yet remarkably, it never occurs to Job or to anyone else in the story to question God's existence. What Job questions is the character of God. Job's problem is not a generic one, as in, Why does God allow such horrible things to happen to the good and the innocent?

Instead it is intensely personal: "Why are you, God, allowing this to happen to me, Job, a righteous man?"

Not Their Problem

If Christians and atheists alike confront this question, there seems little doubt that it is a universal conundrum. Therefore, it comes as a shock to discover that in other religions the conundrum is simply absent. They find another way to deal with the problem of suffering, and it's worth looking at how they do it.

In ancient times, no one wrestled to reconcile the travails of the world with divine omnipotence and benevolence. Historian Rodney Stark writes that "ancient civilizations did not regard their gods as necessarily just or loving." Anger and fickleness were characteristic of the gods; there was no point in asking why. Ancient civilizations, Stark writes, focused on offering sacrifices to appease the gods, to keep them from getting enraged and sending drought or famine to afflict us puny humans.[14]

That's because the ancient Greeks and Romans didn't believe in divine omnipotence. In fact, they were polytheists—they believed in multiple gods, each of them very powerful, but none of them all-powerful. Classical historian Mary Lefkowitz notes that the ancients had no difficulty in believing their gods to be capricious and even cruel. "The gods of traditional Greek and Roman religion do not exist for the benefit of humankind, and they do not always take an interest in what mortals are doing. The gods do not always agree with one another . . . and innocent human beings who are caught up in the conflict suffer or die and are not always avenged. . . . It is a religion from which it is possible to derive little comfort. . . . The myths, as the ancient authors relate them, do not offer hope." In a sense the gods reflect rather than transcend the capriciousness and cruelty of life. Shakespeare summed up the way many ancient Greeks and Romans thought of their deities: "As flies to wanton boys, are we to the gods. They kill us for their sport."[15]

Islam regards God as so above human comprehension that it is presumptuous, even blasphemous, to question his divine plan. The very term *Islam* means "submission," and the Islamic solution to the problems of evil and suffering is simply to accept human ignorance and acquiesce in God's greater wisdom and goodness. Seyyed Hossein Nasr writes in *The Heart of Islam*, "In contrast to the modern West, in which many people have turned away from God and religion because they could not understand how a God who is good could create a world in which there is evil, in the Islamic world this question . . . has hardly ever bothered the religious conscience of even the most intelligent people or turned them away from God."[16]

Buddhism and Hinduism view suffering as the core of the human condition; it is the way of the world. From this indubitable premise, both Buddhism and Hinduism offer a surprising philosophical solution: the world itself is not real. What this means is that the entire material world—the world of our experience—does not really exist. We think it does, but that's because our minds are playing a kind of trick on us. Suffering is not caused by the world but by our minds, and the remedy for suffering, quite literally, is to change our minds. To overcome suffering we need enlightenment, the enlightenment to realize that the world is an illusion and suffering is also an illusion. In this view, we can transcend suffering by recognizing its illusory quality, by seeing through its veil. If we can do this, Buddhism promises "nirvana," a release not only from suffering but also from the world itself.

Hinduism shares many of the same views of suffering as Buddhism, but it also adds a further ingredient. While in Buddhism suffering has no merit or justification, in Hinduism all suffering is entirely deserved. Hindus understand suffering in terms of reincarnation, the idea that the sins of one life are requited in the next life. Thus if you are a wicked person in this life, after you die you may be reincarnated as a beggar or a cockroach. Reincarnation, however, also implies that people who are suffering and starving today must have done terrible things in their former lives. So it is appropriate that they are in this situation; reincarnation is a philosophy of just deserts, where those who suffer now are considered guilty of previous sins. Hinduism, in a sense, does away with the problem of innocent suffering by doing away with innocence itself.

In contrast with the Eastern religions, which treat suffering as either illusory or deserved, the Bible portrays suffering as very real and unequivocally bad. No one can say that Scripture evades the topic of suffering. On the contrary, it records just about every crime and suffering, from cruelty to torture to poverty to disease to war. One of the central themes of the New Testament is, of course, the suffering of Christ the Messiah, what John Hick terms "an evil than which no greater can be conceived."[17] The Bible also typically portrays suffering as bad thing; for instance, Jesus cures the blind and the lame without ever suggesting that there are positive aspects to being blind and lame. Finally, the Bible is very familiar with the subject of wounded theism, which is in fact a consistent theme in the psalms. For instance, Psalm 44:23 says, "Wake up, O Lord! Why do you sleep? Get up! Do not reject us forever." Psalm 82:2 says to God, "How long will you hand down unjust decisions by favoring the wicked?" Again, divine neglect would be understandable if the petitioner had rejected God, but this is not the case. These are the pleas of the faithful servant who feels betrayed by God.

While Scripture portrays evil and suffering with ruthless honesty, it does not offer a direct and consistent explanation for why God allows so much evil and suffering in the first place, and herein lies the problem. The human attempt to give such an explanation is called "theodicy," a term coined by the philosopher and mathematician Gottfried Wilhelm Leibniz. Literally, *theodicy* means "God's justice," and it refers to a project to vindicate God by showing that there is no contradiction between God's attributes and the magnitude of evil and suffering on earth. Despite the centrality of this problem in Christianity, no Christian church has ever officially endorsed any particular theodicy. But intelligent Christians over the centuries have offered a variety of ways to reconcile God's power and goodness with all the bad stuff that goes on in the world.

In this book I offer a solution to the problem of evil that, to my knowledge, has not been offered before. It is not a solution that displaces existing answers; it is one that complements them and integrates them into a persuasive whole, considering both the atheist and the Christian perspective of the problem. Here I'd like to offer a preview of where I am going, so that you can get some idea of the building in advance of its construction.

The crux of the problem of evil and suffering is that it is a complaint about the divine architecture of the universe. Why, the atheist asks, did God build the world in this way? Couldn't God have given me, and other humans, a better world? Christians and other believers also wonder the same thing. The basic assumption here is that God could have constructed the universe in many ways, perhaps an infinity of ways, and yet he chose this particular way. I call this the Many Ways assumption.

This assumption underlies the position not only of the critics of God but also of the defenders of God. Given the options available to God, the defectiveness of his architecture raises in the atheist's mind the question of whether there is a God, and in the Christian's mind the question of what kind of a God this is. Meanwhile, those who seek to answer these objections and vindicate God's existence and his goodness also share the premise that God had multiple choices in making the universe. These champions of God try to show that God chose the best option. Leibniz, for instance, famously argued that God made "the best of all possible worlds." In his view, God reviewed the many ways he could have constructed the universe and then, being omnipotent and infinitely wise, chose the best option.

The Only Way

The thrust of my argument is to deny that premise. In this book I will argue that God is the divine architect, the Cosmic Designer. He wanted to make a lawful universe containing human beings. More broadly, God wanted to create conscious, rational agents who could understand his creation and also freely relate to him. Given God's objective to make humans, God constructed the universe not in the best possible way, but in the *only* way that it could be constructed. In other words, God chose the sole option available to produce the result that he wanted. Did God have other options available to him? Yes. God could have abstained from creating in the first place. He could have created lifeless worlds, and perhaps he did. Alternatively, he could have chosen a different formula—a different universe with different laws—in which case he would have gotten a different creation with other types of creatures in it. As we will see, this is not outside the realm of possibility, even though ours is the universe we know about. If God did make other universes, however, I will show that those other universes would have their own constraints. For instance, death and dissolution are inevitable features of all physical worlds. Moreover, if God created other worlds with some sort of space aliens who are conscious, rational, and free, as we are, then their world would also contain a good deal of evil and suffering, as ours does.

Most complaints about God, however, do not focus on his alleged mistreatment of space aliens. Consequently, the focus of this book is on how God could have improved the world for us human beings. Could God have made this universe differently and still have us in it? No. God intended us to be here to marvel at his architecture and get to know the architect and enter into an intimate relationship of mutual love with him. Consequently, he built the universe in the appropriate way—indeed the only way—to get this result. I call this the Only Way argument.

By way of analogy, consider a maze, the kind that you might have been challenged to find your way through as a child. There are two basic characteristics of a maze: numerous wrong ways to get from start to finish and one correct way. So for our purposes, think of the maze as representing God's options. God is standing at the starting point of the maze. His destination is a universe containing rational creatures like us. What does God do? Being omniscient, God knows the best way through the maze, and being omnipotent, he has the power to get from here to there. So God unerringly finds his way through the maze. In other words, he takes the appropriate path to get to his desired destination. And with the universe, as with the maze, there is one and only one road that leads to the finishing point.

Now, like all analogies, this one isn't perfect. I am not suggesting—as this analogy may lead one to believe—that God is constrained by the laws of nature. Those laws are human descriptions; they are our way of understanding the coherence of God's creation. Natural laws do not precede the universe, and they do not make the universe. Rather, the universe comes first, and the laws are a system of human understanding that makes sense of the existing universe. We comprehend the world by describing its regularities and built-in parameters in law-like, generally mathematical, form. If God had chosen to make a different universe, obviously the laws describing that universe would be different also. The point of the maze analogy, however, is to say that there are some outcomes that can be obtained in only one way, and my contention is that the universe resembles a maze in being such an outcome.

At first glance, this Only Way argument seems to place restrictions on God's omnipotence. If God is God, we may think, surely he can do *anything*, can't he? I will discuss this question later in the book, but the short answer is no. For instance, God cannot make two plus two equal five, nor can he make married bachelors, nor can he wish himself out of existence, nor can he tell lies. There are all kind of limits on God's omnipotence, but they are limits that arise out of a wrong understanding of what omnipotence means. As we will see, omnipotence does not mean the ability to do anything, but rather the power to do what is possible. If there is only one possible way to make a universe containing creatures like us, then omnipotence implies that God has the power to do that if he chooses.

But who says that there is only one possible way to make a universe containing creatures like us? The remarkable answer to this question is modern science. In fact, this is perhaps the most important discovery of modern science in the past half century. This is the discovery of the fine-tuned universe, sometimes called the Anthropic Principle. *Anthropic* refers to man, but the principle has a wider reference: it includes man but refers more broadly to life itself. And the discovery of the Anthropic Principle rivals in importance Einstein's discovery of relativity in the first half of the twentieth century, or Darwin's discovery of evolution in the second half of the nineteenth. I will show later in this book that the anthropic or fine-tuned universe is not only required for human beings to exist on the earth; it is even required in order for evolution to have taken place. Consequently, the argument of this book is immune to Darwinian attack. Most important, the fine-tuned universe explains how there are creatures around to ask the question, Why does God permit so much suffering?

A Big Surprise

When the Anthropic Principle was first discovered in the 1970s, it came as a surprise. That's because for a couple of centuries scientists had subscribed to the Copernican principle, which arose out of Copernicus's discovery of the heliocentric universe. Copernicus showed that the sun doesn't go around the earth; the earth goes around the sun. This was understood to mean that our planet is nothing special, and we humans are not special either. Astronomer Carl Sagan expressed the Copernican principle in its classic form, "We live on a hunk of rock and metal that orbits a humdrum star in the obscure outskirts of an ordinary galaxy comprised of 400 billion stars in a universe of some hundred billion galaxies. . . . We have not been given the lead in the cosmic drama." Paleontologist Stephen Jay Gould put it even more bluntly: man, he said, is a "fortuitous cosmic afterthought."[18]

Today, however, these sentiments no longer command universal assent. In fact, many leading scientists no longer subscribe to the Copernican principle. Here, for instance, is the Nobel prize-winning cosmologist Joel Primack: "We humans are significant and central to the universe in unexpected and important ways." Primack adds, "Intelligent life is neither incidental nor insignificant but has a place in the universe so special it could not even have been imagined before the invention of modern cosmological concepts." Physicist John Barrow writes, "The large size and great age of our visible universe is not coincidental; it is a necessary condition for the existence of biochemical complexity of the sort that we call life. . . . The existence of complex structures in the universe is made possible by a combination of apparent coincidences regarding the values of the constants of nature. Were those values to be slightly changed, the possibility of conscious observers evolving would disappear." And physicist Paul Davies asserts, "Through my scientific work I have come to believe more and more strongly that the physical universe is put together with an ingenuity so astonishing that I cannot accept it merely as a brute fact. There must, it seems to me, be a deeper level of explanation. . . . Furthermore, I have come to the point of view that mind— i.e., conscious awareness of the world—is not a meaningless and incidental quirk of nature, but an absolutely fundamental facet of reality. . . . We human beings are built into the scheme of things in a very basic way." Biologist Christian de Duve, another Nobel laureate, notes that "life and mind emerge not as the results of freakish accidents" but rather are "written into the fabric of the universe." De Duve adds, "I view this universe . . . as a meaningful entity, made in such a way as to generate life and mind, bound to give birth to thinking beings."[19]

In the past couple of decades, the Anthropic Principle has been the subject of intense debate involving scientists, atheists, and religious believers. This debate, however, is not over the principle's validity but instead has focused almost entirely on what its implications are for the existence of God. Basically, religious people say that fine tuning proves that there must be a fine-tuner, and atheists deny this, with scientists occupying positions across the spectrum of this debate. My approach, however, is to introduce an altogether new debate. I want to apply the Anthropic Principle to the problem of evil and suffering. My argument is that if there is only one way to make a universe with rational, conscious creatures like us, then all the evil and suffering in the universe is completely necessary for us to exist in this world in the first place. It is both senseless and futile to deplore this evil and suffering unless we would prefer not to exist. To affirm our own existence, however, is to approve the required conditions for us to be here. Of course we may continue to be unhappy about evil and suffering, but we can now, for the first time, understand that it is an intrinsic part of the formula that produced us.

Of course, this is not the end of the story; there is much more to be said, and fortunately I have found both in modern science and in the Christian intellectual tradition the resources to say it. I am not arguing in this book that God had to go with an imperfect plan because this was the only mechanism to produce humans. God's plan is indeed perfect. But the perfection of the plan required God to situate his plan for the universe within a larger plan. The "lower providence" of God's creation was therefore embedded in a "higher providence" that redeemed this creation. This is all that I am going to say about that subject here. But I want to assure the atheist of getting an argument here that resolves the alleged contradiction between God's attributes and the evil and suffering in the world. I also want to assure the Christian that I am not merely confounding the atheist but offering a real answer to the question of why God permits so much evil and suffering, even in the lives of those who love him. I invite both to join me in considering the argument.

PART 2

A Universal Conundrum

CHAPTER 3

THE LIMITS OF THEODICY

Why the Usual Answers Don't Work

God's in his heaven
All's right with the world![1]

ROBERT BROWNING, "PIPPA'S SONG"

FOR TWO THOUSAND YEARS, Christian thinkers, writers, and pastors have been engaged in theodicy, which is the task of reconciling divine omnipotence and goodness with the existence and extent of evil and suffering in the world. The church fathers Irenaeus and Augustine, the medieval thinkers Anselm and Aquinas, and the reformers Luther and Calvin were all participants in the grand enterprise of defending the honor of God. This is what theodicy is mainly concerned with—not proving the existence of God but vindicating the character of God.

Why? Because for most of human history, there were no atheists around to question God's existence. This is not to say that for most of human history no one considered difficult theological or philosophical questions, that there was nothing but blind belief. Indeed, in churches and monasteries and universities, intelligent Christians have long debated questions about God at the most fundamental level. They were not reluctant to play "the devil's advocate," in other words, to raise objections from the skeptical point of view. But their goal was "faith seeking understanding," which is to say, they believed certain things but they wanted to see if those beliefs could survive the most exacting rational scrutiny. This book is in that tradition. It is written by a professed Christian, yet its purpose is to examine the problem of evil and suffering *not* primarily on the basis of revelation or sacred authority but on the basis of reason, science, and experience.

Christian tradition supplies some well-reasoned and ingenious solutions to this problem. Christians have given the same degree of careful thought to why there is evil and suffering as atheists have; in fact, atheists have little to say on the topic that Christians haven't already thought of. Even so, the Christian answers explored in this chapter have not in general proven persuasive to atheists. Truth be told, they have not been found fully satisfactory by most Christians either. They contain nuggets of truth, but there is always something missing. My objective in presenting these traditional Christian arguments is to incorporate their nuggets of truth while moving beyond them.

One might expect that the primary vehicle for Christian theodicy would be the book that Christians affirm to be God's inspired Word, the Bible. It is on this assumption that atheist and Bible scholar Bart Ehrman recently wrote a book called *God's Problem*, the subtitle of which makes his position clear: *How the Bible Fails to Answer Our Most Important Question—Why We Suffer*. In this book Ehrman gives us an informed tour through the precincts of Scripture, listing several biblical positions and then showing us why each of them fails to answer our questions. Ehrman's book is simply one in a long line of books he has written to refute and discredit the Bible. And like the others, despite Ehrman's scholarship, this one does not hit the target.

It makes no sense to discredit the arguments in the Bible, because the Bible doesn't make any arguments. Think about it. Does the Bible seek to prove that God created the world? Does the Bible offer reasons why Jesus is the Son of God? Actually, the Bible doesn't attempt to *prove* anything; it merely asserts things, such as, "In the beginning God made the heavens and the earth." Consequently we should hardly be surprised to find no explicit theodicy in the Bible.

What we can find in the Bible, though, are narratives and stories, and from them we can certainly infer what Scripture seems to be saying about theodicy. We'll begin by taking up some of the biblical teachings that Ehrman presents and then attempts to debunk in *God's Problem.*

Blame It on Adam and Eve

In the early chapters of Genesis we read that God created man and woman and placed them in the Garden of Eden to enjoy God's bountiful provision with just one exception: they were commanded not to eat from a single tree, the tree of the knowledge of good and evil. Yet when Eve was tempted by the serpent with a series of inducements, including the assurance that she could be like God, she ate the forbidden fruit. So did Adam, in part out of solidarity with her. Because of their disobedience, God expelled them from the Garden. Adam and Eve were the original humans, and therefore their sin was the original sin. We, their descendants, live with the consequences of their sin and, in some sense, we inherit their sin. We are all now born with original sin. And it is this original sin that brought death and suffering to the world.

It is worth noting at this juncture that the concept of original sin is not directly mentioned in the Bible. Many Eastern Orthodox Christians do not accept the doctrine, and it is even controversial among Protestants, some of whom regard it as unbiblical. Even so, this teaching is the most mainstream way in which the Genesis account has been read for two millennia, and it does seem to offer one account for the existence of evil and suffering in the world. Ehrman is quick to dismiss this account, which he finds incredible and, not surprisingly, unpalatable. Leaving aside issues of whether there was a real Adam and Eve, the main problem he sees is how the sins of two people could automatically pass to all their descendants.

Some books on theodicy say that in feudal times people believed in inherited blame and inherited hardship, while we in the modern world do not. But this is not true. Historically people have always recognized that the *consequences* of the parents' actions are visited upon the children and their children—so if the father loses the farm, his progeny may become itinerant laborers. Even in the twenty-first century, we recognize that the actions of one generation influence the lives of those who come later. The real issue is whether blame and guilt can be inherited.

Today we have trouble seeing how future generations can be faulted for what someone else did. How can we be held responsible for Adam and Eve's transgression? We may endure the effects of their sin, but it seems preposterous to say that their sin becomes our sin. Even the great Christian apologist Blaise Pascal, in his *Pensées*, writes that "nothing shocks our reason more than to say that the sin of the first man made guilty those who, so far from that source, seem incapable of having taken part in it. This contamination seems not only impossible to us, but also quite unjust."[2]

Moreover, there is a deeper problem, one concerning the Christian notion that the first human sin adversely affected all creation. Geology tells us that the earth is very old, and biology tells us that there were other living creatures on the earth for hundreds of thousands of years before the arrival of *Homo sapiens*.[3] So, taking modern science at its word, if human beings are relative latecomers to the scene, how can human transgression, however grievous, explain the pain of the other animals? Modern biology seems to challenge the very basis of the Garden of Eden story. That story tells of a state of innocence, which was subsequently corrupted by the deeds of the first man and woman. But the facts seem to show that there was no such pure state and that predation, violence, suffering, and death were defining features of life all along.

Christian apologist and literary scholar C. S. Lewis recognized that many species of animals lived on the earth before man, and he offered a surprising theological explanation for animal suffering: the other fall. What other fall? Well, the fall of Lucifer and his legion of wicked angels. This fall is alluded to in several passages in the Bible. It happened when God first created the angels, long before he created humans. Some angels wanted to be like God, and so led by Lucifer they mounted a martial assault on God's authority. God hurled the bad angels into hell, but the Bible tells us that God also made Lucifer—also known as Satan—the ruler of the earth. Jesus calls him "the prince of this world,"[4] and John's epistle affirms that "the world around us is under the control of the evil one."[5] Lewis suggests that Satan is the one responsible for the natural conditions that produce animal suffering, that he "may well have corrupted the animal creation before man appeared."[6]

The beauty of this argument is its simplicity—it unifies the fall of the angels and the fall of man and holds the two rebellions responsible for all suffering in the world—and a few contemporary thinkers, notably the philosopher Alvin Plantinga, have embraced it.[7] Yet I cannot go along with this argument, which is not actually consistent with the biblical thinking it attempts to be reconciled with. First, the idea that Satan has sovereign authority over the earth makes no sense from the perspective of the Bible itself: it contradicts the notion that God gave man dominion over the earth; and besides, how can God call his creation "good" and "very good," as he does upon completing the job, if Satan has been continually corrupting that creation? Second, the authority of Satan must, in the Christian view, be subordinate to the authority of God. We see this in the book of Job, with God entering into a bet with Satan and giving Satan leave to afflict Job. It is inconceivable that Satan could do this unless God allowed it.

More broadly, the attribution of animal suffering to Satan's nefarious actions is open to the same objection that is raised against the attribution of human suffering to the sin of Adam and Eve. Why should the bad actions of an angel who inhabits one order of creation, namely the immaterial realms of heaven and hell, destroy the lives and happiness of animals that inhabit a completely different order of creation? If God created things this way, isn't God himself responsible for this perversion of justice?

Suffering as Punishment for Evil Deeds

A second biblical explanation for suffering that Bart Ehrman cites is the idea that suffering is due punishment for man's evil deeds. The basic idea is one of just deserts: do good and God will reward you; do evil and God will punish you. Notice that this explanation for suffering only applies to humans; clearly it cannot account for animal suffering. But within its domain it is an old and powerful claim. The prophets of the Old Testament are repeatedly warning people to repent and stop their sinful ways, lest they kindle the punitive wrath of God. The clear message, Ehrman writes, is that "God . . . is punishing his people when they have gone astray."

In the same passage Ehrman adds, "I should stress that the prophets themselves never state this as a universal principle, as a way of explaining every instance of suffering. The prophets, that is, were speaking *only* to their contemporaries about their specific sufferings." Even so, he says, the general principle is repeatedly affirmed throughout the Bible. "It is the point of view of the majority of authors who produced the biblical texts."[8] For example, we read in Isaiah 3:10-11, "Tell the godly that all will be well for them. They will enjoy the rich reward they have earned! But the wicked are doomed, for they will get exactly what they deserve." The same theme is stressed in Proverbs 12:21: "No harm comes to the godly, but the wicked have their fill of trouble."

Even secular people affirm this principle of cosmic justice when they say things like "what goes around comes around" or when they ask themselves, when confronted by personal tragedy, "What did I do to deserve this?" This link between suffering and wrongdoing is built into the English language: our word *pain* derives from the Latin *poena*, which means "penalty" or "punishment." Yet we all know, believer and unbeliever alike, that the pain and hardship of this world are not directly attributable to our virtues and vices. In fact, there is no clear correlation between the two. This becomes obvious to us when some unthinking preacher says that AIDS is God's punishment for homosexuality. Is homosexuality an offense that merits the death penalty? And if so, what about the many homosexuals who do not have AIDS, or the children who got AIDS from their mothers, or the adults who got it from a blood transfusion? Consider the cholera-stricken infant in Bangladesh; who will have the temerity to say that it is being duly chastised for its sins? Earthquakes and tsunamis seem to make no distinction between the just and the unjust. It is simply a fact, as Rabbi Harold Kushner puts it in the title of his bestselling book, that "bad things happen to good people."

Some Christians assert that there is no need to explain why bad things happen to good people, because there are no good people; we are all bad in various ways. I know there are some people who deny this, but I think it is clearly true. The philosopher Immanuel Kant put it very well: "One cannot fashion something absolutely straight from wood which is as crooked as that of which man is made."[9] This is a secular restatement of the Christian doctrine of original sin. In other words, human nature is a bit bent or warped, and this corruption is manifest in the way we live. Still, this realism about the human condition hardly solves our problem. That's because there are various degrees of good and bad in people, and their quota of suffering in life rarely matches what they deserve under the circumstances. Sometimes people who are paragons of goodness, compared to their fellow man, suffer greatly, while others who are the nadir of humanity seem only to prosper. Even if we look at ordinary folk, neither spectacularly good nor bad, some have it relatively easy and others have it woefully tough. The distribution of hardship and pain is unrelated to the virtue of the people who are afflicted.

In the book of Job in the Bible, Job's sufferings are attributed by his friends to wrongs that Job is presumed to have done. The key word here is *presumed*, because Job has the reputation for being a just and righteous man. And that is what his friends think about him as well. But when Job turns bitter and accuses God of wronging him by sending so many afflictions, Job's friends turn on him and say, in effect, "Job, you had us fooled. You come off looking like an upright and religious man, but when bad things happen, you show your true character." It's clear why Job's friends are so harsh in his time of suffering: their assumption is that God is in the right, and they are trying to defend God's actions against Job's strident accusations.

The marvelous thing about the book of Job is that while the friends are lambasting Job, we get, in a sense, an insider view of the action. That's because we know that God himself considers Job to be a righteous man. God's first statement about Job is that he is not only upright but also blameless. And God never wavers in this assessment, even in the face of Job's indictment of divine justice. We know that Job is suffering, not because of anything he has done, but because he is the object of a test. As it turns out, Job passes the test. Later in the story God admonishes Job's friends and says that they are not true friends and that they deserve punishment; only Job's prayers can save them. So here we have, through the story of Job, confirmation that the afflictions of life are not necessarily the just deserts of human action. They may, and in Job's case they do, have other causes.

Suffering as a Benefit to All Involved

We now consider, before moving on, the third and final justification of evil and suffering that Ehrman locates in the Bible: the idea that suffering is good for you, or at any rate, that it is good for the people around you. At first glance this idea seems completely preposterous; if suffering is good for us, then we should constantly be trying to get more of it. In fact, we do everything we can to avoid pain and suffering. So how can a claim like this even begin to make sense?

It makes sense when we consider G. W. F. Hegel's famous maxim, "The owl of Minerva flies at night." What Hegel means is that we gain wisdom and understanding only in retrospect, when a particular period of time comes to an end. Things that seem one way when they occur are later understood very differently through the benefit of hindsight. We find several examples of this principle in Scripture, one of which is the story of Joseph, son of Jacob. Joseph is sold by his brothers into slavery, a clear case of evil on their part, which imposed suffering on him. But captivity launches Joseph on a journey that will result in his becoming a very important figure in Egypt, able to protect an entire nation from famine and to rescue his family from calamity. In the process, he is reconciled to his brothers. The story has a happy ending, and it is just one biblical illustration of the possibility that good ends can stem directly from evil and suffering.

We know this from our own experience as well. Tim Keller, the pastor of Redeemer Presbyterian Church in New York City, writes about a man in his parish who lost most of his eyesight after being shot in the face during a drug transaction that went bad. The man had lived a selfish and cruel life, but the loss of his sight humbled him and made him change for the better. "It was a terrible price to pay," he told Keller, "and yet I must say it was worth it." Keller comments,

"With time and perspective most of us can see good reasons for at least *some* of the tragedy and pain that occurs in life. Why couldn't it be possible that, from God's vantage point, there are good reasons for all of them?"[10]

A few years ago I was reading Tom Brokaw's book *The Greatest Generation.* The book is a celebration of the virtues of a unique generation that lived through the great events of the twentieth century and is now passing away. I asked myself, "How did the greatest generation become so great?" Its virtues, I realized, were the product of the Great Depression and World War II. It was through extreme danger and hardship that this generation learned the virtues of frugality, deferred gratification, hard work, and courage. However, the greatest generation failed in replicating itself, because it tried to give its children all the things it had lacked, such as peace, security, and comfort. Consequently it produced the spoiled children of the 1960s. Here is a clear case where character was forged through suffering, while the absence of suffering seems to have produced self-indulgence and decadence.

We can all recall situations in which suffering turned out to be good for us, and others in which suffering produced benefits in the people around us. Think of the way in which 9/11 rallied the American people and generated a rare sense of community and solidarity. This unity may have been short lived, but it was real. I have seen the way in which a death in the family brought together siblings and relatives who had become not merely distant from each other but in fact bitter enemies. We all know that suffering can enhance character by bringing forth love, compassion, wisdom, courage, forbearance, and sacrifice.

Some religious leaders argue that suffering is God's way of drawing us closer to him. The Muslim thinker Al-Ghazzali writes that illness is a "cord of love" that connects us to our Maker. "Illness itself is one of those forms of experience by which man arrives at the knowledge of God."[11] The Christian evangelist Billy Graham writes that "suffering can give us opportunities to witness. The world is a gigantic hospital; nowhere is there a greater chance to see the peace and joy of the Lord than when the journey through the valley is the darkest."[12] Certainly it seems the poor and the wretched are more attracted to religious teachings than the successful and the prosperous. That's because prosperity gives one a sense of self-sufficiency; we are doing well and feel that we don't really need God. By contrast, the poor feel a constant sense of vulnerability, and consequently a need to depend on God. No wonder religious faith and practice are much higher in third-world countries than in the West.

In his book *Theodicy*, Gottfried Leibniz makes a philosophical point that is worth considering. Imagine, he says, a world without evil and suffering—in other words, a world that is completely painless and good. How would we even recognize such a world for what it is and appreciate its benefits? Leibniz's contention is that we need suffering in order to recognize and cherish joy, just as we need the night in order to recognize and celebrate the morning sunrise. Often in music, such as in Bach's *The Well-Tempered Clavier*, one encounters discordant notes that would be unpleasant if played by themselves. But they contribute to the loveliness of the whole, and the whole would be impoverished if they were removed. Leibniz concedes that evil and suffering seem by themselves to be ugly spots on the canvas of God's creation. But, he says, that's because we are focusing on them exclusively and up close; if we could step back and view the canvas as a whole, we would see how they make the overall painting even more beautiful.[13]

All these points are true as far as they go, but how far do they really go? Conceding the benefits of suffering and sorrow as moral and spiritual instructors, it still remains unclear why God would choose these vehicles to produce the desired benefits for the individual and the community. A good friend of mine, Stan Oakes, who founded The King's College in New York City, has brain cancer.

Recently he surprised me by saying, "I have come to believe that this is the best thing that has happened to me." How could he possibly say such a thing? Is he a masochist? Does he feel no pain? Of course not; he feels chronic pain, and unlike most of the rest of us, he knows his time is limited. But Stan believes that he is a different and better person because of his cancer. His marriage is better, he is closer to God, and he is actually happier. Incredibly, he does not wish it never happened to him. For Stan the suffering, painful as it is, is producing good that outweighs the suffering.

But why couldn't God have produced the desired benefits without the accompanying suffering? I'm not God, but if I had the power, I think I could have found a way to improve Stan's life without destroying a part of his brain, or humbled the drug dealer in Tim Keller's church without costing him his eyesight. Moreover, in that particular case, suffering turned the man to God and toward a reformed life. But in other cases, suffering turns people away from God and morality. Albert Camus explores this idea in his novel *The Plague*, in which a plague in the French town of Oran causes many people to lose their faith and their moral inhibitions. Promiscuity, not piety, is the consequence of suffering in that situation, as is sometimes the case in reality.

God is supposed to be omnipotent; thus he has resources available to him that we do not. When we as human beings make choices, we often do so out of a limited menu of options. The Civil War surgeon had no choice but to operate without anesthetics, yet a successful operation was considered worth the intense pain it caused. No one would lightly choose such deadly actions as the bombing of German cities and the dropping of the atomic bomb on Hiroshima and Nagasaki, yet the defeat of such devastating evils as Nazi tyranny and Japanese imperialism might not have been possible without them. The terrible human cost of those actions, if it can be excused, is excused by the greater good of preventing a global takeover by the Nazis and the Japanese with an even higher cost in human suffering. But if God is all-powerful—if he is truly Almighty God—then he doesn't have to make these trade-offs. Surely he could find a way to get the result he wants without suffering, or at least with a minimum of suffering.

Is evil really necessary to appreciate the good things in life? Perhaps it is, but philosopher Peter van Inwagen notes that this only explains the fact of evil in the world; it does not explain the amount of evil. For instance, let's say that because of war and concentration camps we come to a greater appreciation of the horrors of war, and therefore we are inspired to work harder to prevent war. But van Inwagen writes that surely God could have produced this awareness in humans without so many wars in which so many millions have died and so many horrors perpetrated. Perhaps a single war would have made the point much more frugally, and if there is a danger that people living much later would forget, then perhaps God could produce in them vivid and convincing nightmares that would re-create the experience. A world of recurrent nightmares would not be a world free of suffering, but surely it would be a better world than one in which the nightmares of war and its atrocities were actually realized.[14]

Not only could God produce results at a lower cost, but sometimes it seems that the cost is so high that the resulting benefits aren't worth it. The Great Depression may have improved the character of a whole generation, but did we need economic devastation to achieve this moral uplift? If so, maybe we are better off without either. Certainly we don't hear anyone now arguing, "Let's drive the world economy into another Great Depression so that people will have their character improved as a result." Young people ought to be careful, but no parent would want his or her child to be hit by a car in order to learn to look both ways before crossing the road. No one wants more hurricanes and airplane crashes in order to give people opportunities to learn and display heroism.

Rabbi Harold Kushner wrote *When Bad Things Happen to Good People* in response to the death of his son Aaron, who died of a degenerative disease called progeria. Kushner recognizes that his son's tragedy deepened his own sense of compassion and understanding. Without Aaron's death, Kushner would not have been able to minister as effectively to his congregation, or to help others through his writing. Yet Kushner reflects that, despite all he has learned from his son's death, he would much rather have his son. "I am a more sensitive person, a more effective pastor, a more sympathetic counselor because of Aaron's life and death than I would ever have been without it. And I would give up all of those gains in a second if I could have my son back."[15]

Notice that Kushner, for all his generosity of spirit, is only considering the cost and benefit of his son's death from his own point of view. He informs us that he would be better off if his son were living rather than dead. What about the benefit, however, from Aaron's point of view? Here the case seems more clear cut. Too often we consider how evil or suffering imposed on one person may benefit others or even society. But why should one human being be harmed or sacrificed so that others can gain from it? If suffering has redemptive value, it would seem that this value should accrue not just to others, or to the group as a whole, but to each individual creature that is required to bear that suffering.

While we have so far been weighing the benefits of suffering against the cost, there is a whole category of evil and suffering that appears to have no benefit at all. This is what Marilyn McCord Adams calls "horrendous evil." In her book *Horrendous Evils and the Goodness of God*, Adams defines this as evil so great that it destroys faith in the value of life itself. The Jewish Holocaust would obviously fit into that category, despite the fact that it eventually generated support for the formation of the state of Israel, allowing the Jews who remained to return to their ancestral homeland.

Around the time I was reading Adams's book, I came across news accounts of Jaycee Dugard, a missing girl who had finally been found. At first her parents were relieved—she had been missing for almost two decades. Dugard's stepfather even said, "I've actually won the lotto." But then it emerged that Jaycee had been kidnapped by a convicted rapist named Phillip Garrido. Garrido had abducted Jaycee when she was eleven years old, and he had held her against her will for eighteen years. She was kept confined in the back of Garrido's yard. Garrido had renamed her Allissa and had two children by her. The children were kept in a shed, and neither had ever been to school or a doctor. As he learned what happened, Dugard's stepfather broke down. "This is so horrific, I don't believe it."[16]

Adams gives her own examples of horrendous evil: a woman is raped and her arms chopped off; a prisoner is tortured both physically and psychologically so that his entire personality disintegrates; a child is systematically abused and sexually violated by its parents; a woman is forced by terrorists to choose which of her children will live and which will be executed; a group of captives is made to watch its loved ones being maimed and disfigured; a man discovers that through his own unwitting actions, his wife and child have suffered a slow death by starvation.[17]

Horrendous evils don't merely deform people; they crush and degrade them. Far from making people better, such evils produce self-loathing and defilement. While in some cases such evils may turn people to God, this seems like a very sadistic way to win them over: "I'll smash them completely so that they have nowhere else to go and will come crawling back to me." Moreover, it seems that horrendous evils are just as likely to turn people away from God. Reduced to despair, some people give up hope, even in God, and say, "How can I worship and trust a God who would let this happen to me?" On the balance, it is hard to reconcile horrendous evil with the goodness of God. It seems that there are no positive results that come close to justifying or redeeming these horrendous evils.

Evil Isn't Real

Next we turn to an argument that seems ridiculous at first. This is the church father Augustine's argument that evil isn't real. By this Augustine does not mean that evil is not experienced by us as real; of course it is. He is saying, however, that when we think about it, evil isn't a real thing. If we want to be blunt about it, evil doesn't exist.

Augustine arrived at this astonishing conclusion by considering the question, If God created everything, isn't God responsible for creating evil? God made rocks and trees and the rest of what exists in the world, so it seems that he must also have made evil. Augustine's solution was to say that God did indeed create everything, but evil is not a thing. Evil is the absence of a thing. Therefore God is not responsible for creating evil.

"There is no such entity in nature as 'evil,'" Augustine writes in his *City of God*. "'Evil' is merely a name for the privation of good."[18] For Augustine, evil results when good is absent, or when good things are corrupted or misused. Consider the example of a knife. A knife is a good and useful object, yet knives can be used to murder people. So there is nothing intrinsically wrong with a knife, but there is something wrong with using a knife to stab someone in the chest.

A good way to think about Augustine's point is to think about a hole in a shirt. Now, a hole isn't just an opening or gap in the shirt; after all, there are two holes in the place where we insert our arms, and those are called sleeves. Augustine's argument isn't concerned with that kind of a hole, but rather a hole in the shirt where there ought to be cloth. Here the hole isn't a thing; it is the absence of a thing. By analogy, evil is simply the "hole" where goodness ought to be. Augustine's own example is that of blindness. What is blindness? It is not a thing in itself; it is simply the absence of sight. Similarly, cold is just the absence of heat, and darkness the absence of light. Augustine notes that all our terms for evil presuppose a good that has been corrupted. Impurity presupposes purity, wickedness presupposes righteousness, transgression presupposes a boundary that has been violated. Augustine isn't merely saying that evil is parasitic on good. He is saying that everything that exists is good.

I do not think Augustine's metaphysical point is valid on its own terms. I'm not sure hatred is merely the lack of kindness, or that cruelty is only the absence of love. Technically, we can view pain as merely the absence of pleasure, but we know that we feel the hurt of pain as intensely as we feel the elation of pleasure. In any case, Augustine's solution doesn't really help our situation very much. Yes, a hole in my shirt may not be a thing, but I still have to get it fixed. So, too, we have to deal with the powerful consequences of evil in human experience; these are real enough for us.

What consolation can we derive from Augustine's argument? Imagine telling the children of Auschwitz, "We understand your feelings of pain and loss, but you will be consoled to discover that the evils you are experiencing are not real. They are not things in themselves, but merely the absence of a thing." As physicist and Christian writer John Polkinghorne writes, after the terrible events of the twentieth century, Augustine's solution to the problem of evil "seems to me to be an impossible stance to adopt."[19]

The Best of All Possible Worlds

Finally we consider an argument no less audacious than Augustine's. This is Leibniz's idea that we live in the best of all possible worlds. In his book *Theodicy*, Leibniz argued as follows: we fault God because we think that his creation is somehow defective. We believe this because we survey the world we live in and find in it instances of evil and suffering. But we cannot condemn God without considering the options available to him. These are the alternative worlds that God might have instead created.

Leibniz maintained that God, being omniscient, started out by considering all possible worlds. Then God compared them in all respects to figure out which was the best world. That's the one God created, and we know that he must have created it, because he is God, and God would not content himself with anything less than the best.[20] The power of Leibniz's argument is not that Leibniz knows how or what God actually did. Rather, it is that Leibniz is daring us to show that we can do better than God in actually creating a world superior to this one.

The philosopher Voltaire took up the challenge and ridiculed Leibniz's position in his novella *Candide*. Yet Voltaire seems not to have been familiar with Leibniz's actual thesis; instead, he parodies the version of it given in Alexander Pope's "Essay on Man," in which Pope summarizes Leibniz as arguing that "whatever is, is right."

Voltaire's *Candide* gives us the character of Pangloss, a professor of metaphysics in the employ of the Baron of Westphalia. Pangloss contends that everything around him is for the best: the Baron's castle is the best of all possible castles, and the Baron's wife the best of all possible baronesses. Pangloss also insists that pigs exist to make pork available year-round, and that noses were designed to support spectacles. The absurdity of Pangloss is that he puts a positive spin on events even when they are obviously deteriorating. At one point Pangloss informs Candide, "All events are linked together in this, the best of all possible worlds; for after all, if you had not been driven out of a beautiful castle, with hefty kicks on your backside, because you loved Miss Cunégonde, if you had not been arrested by the Inquisition, if you had not crossed America on foot, if you had not thrust your sword through the baron, if you had not lost all the sheep you had obtained in the good land of El Dorado, you would not be sitting here eating roasted pine nuts and pistachios."[21]

It's all good fun, but has very little to do with Leibniz's real argument. Leibniz never claims that everything in the world will turn out the best for Pangloss or Candide or anyone else. Rather, he claims that this design of the world is the best overall scheme. "God," he writes, "chooses what is best on the whole."[22] Leibniz urges that we understand this by looking beyond appearances to the underlying harmony of the universe. For instance, the extremes of heat and cold may seem pointless and painful until we recognize that they are inevitable as a consequence of the earth going around the sun, which is very beneficial for our planet. As we better understand the natural order, Leibniz concludes, we will come to appreciate more fully the supreme handiwork of God.

However sympathetically we approach Leibniz's argument today, we have a hard time going along with it. That's because there seems to be so much unnecessary and avoidable evil and suffering in the world. Start by taking the world as it is. Now think about some evil that could have been prevented, however small. Let's say, for instance, that instead of punching his wife in anger, a certain man redirected his aggression and punched the wall instead. Now that would be a small improvement in the world, so why didn't God create our exact world but with this one modification? And if he could have done this, then we can continue the experiment. Now imagine that world with one less rape or one less epidemic; surely an omnipotent God could have arranged for these tragedies not to have occurred, and this would be a further reduction in human suffering. And we can keep going in this way, all the while improving on the world as it is, and proving that what we have now is emphatically not the best of all possible worlds, because any of us can think of massive improvements for God to make.

Thus we have come to the end of the major theodicies considered in the past. I do not mean to suggest that those outlined here are without value or have been fully refuted, by myself or anyone else. I don't think that either Augustine or Leibniz would be convinced by the counterarguments given in this chapter, for example. My point is rather to suggest that in the wake of the travails of the world these traditional defenses of God do not work for us today. Something, some underlying framework, is missing that would give context and new force to these ancient arguments. This framework is what I will attempt to provide, and to that project we now turn.

CHAPTER 4

ATHEIST DELUSIONS

Contradictions of Unbelief

There is nothing that cannot be understood.
There is nothing that cannot be explained.[1]
PETER ATKINS, *The Creation*

IN THIS BOOK I offer a new answer to the problem of evil and suffering and a refutation of the atheist claim that no good, all-powerful God could have made a world like the one we have. Before the atheist can be persuaded, however, he or she has to be willing to listen. And here we face a problem: many of the atheists are very arrogant. I encounter them all the time, and even atheist undergraduates typically approach me with a know-it-all tone: "Mr. D'Souza, has it occurred to you . . . ?" And then they ask me a question that I have been asked a hundred times before. Reason itself becomes a casualty when people have so high an opinion of their own cleverness. In this chapter, therefore, I intend to show that even the best of the atheists are not so clever. Ultimately, however, I turn this argument on myself as well. I will show, with the help of reason, that we humans are not as smart as we often think. Once we understand our limits, and the limits of reason itself, we can all approach this topic with greater humility, and then we might actually be ready to learn something.

Atheist arrogance, however, is somewhat understandable in this case. We can see this once we recognize that, from the atheist perspective, evil and suffering in themselves do not pose any kind of intellectual problem. If the world were completely full of evil and suffering, that fact alone would not require explanation; it would simply represent the way things happen to be, no more surprising than other facts about the world. Even the distribution of evil and suffering is not inherently puzzling. Why should we be astonished, for instance, that birth defects, natural calamities, unconscionable crimes, and other forms of suffering afflict the virtuous and the vicious alike? These things may perturb us, but so far there is no intrinsic philosophical or theological problem. Philosophically, we could explain such things as the inevitable result of chance or blind evolution. Theologically, we could explain them as the result of God being indifferent, or malignant, or nonexistent. Everything changes, however, when we posit that the world is under the sovereign rule of an almighty, benevolent God. Now there is a problem—the problem of reconciling disaster, evil, and unmerited suffering with the belief in a God who is both all-powerful and all-good.

The Burden of Proof

Standing behind a podium before three thousand people at Biola University in Los Angeles, the atheist philosopher Peter Singer grinned in triumph. He and I were there to debate the issue of whether God is the author of morality, and Singer began his speech by informing the audience that there was nothing to debate. God couldn't be the author of morality because there was no God. And we know that there is no God, he argued, because the world doesn't look like it is under the governance of an omnipotent and wise deity. Singer gave his own list of evils that undeniably plague our planet. He focused not only on human suffering but also on animal suffering. Religious believers, he said, must account for why their God would allow these horrors, and that, he insisted, is something that they have never done. Atheists, he said, have nothing to explain.

Here we see the great strength of the atheist position. On most points of contention between atheists and believers, there are two positions, and each side must argue the merits of their own position. Here, however, the believer faces a daunting challenge—to demonstrate not only God's existence but also his goodness—while the atheist seems to have nothing whatsoever to explain. Assuming atheism, we can make no firm prediction about how the world ought to be. Therefore if the world is unjust and full of suffering, *c'est la vie*.

The point was made somewhat differently two centuries ago by the skeptic David Hume. Imagine, he said, a house in which the rooms are ill-sized and ill-constructed. The windows, doors, and passageways are all sources of darkness, noise, and confusion; and the whole place is vulnerable to the extremes of heat and cold. According to Hume, we would automatically blame the architect. Sure, the architect may give excuses or even propose how this or that flaw might be corrected. Even so, Hume writes, the overall deformity of the structure would raise serious questions about whether a competent architect is in charge. Hume asks, "Is the world, considered in general, and as it appears to us in this life, different from what a man or such a limited being would, *beforehand*, expect from a very powerful, wise, and benevolent deity?" Hume's conclusion is that we would not expect God to have built such a defective structure. Therefore, he writes, from the flawed design of the world we may infer that there is no designer; we may even suspect an evil or an indifferent designer, but we can never infer an omnipotent and benevolent designer.[2]

In one of my early debates with Christopher Hitchens, he advanced an argument that stunned me and one that I was not able then to answer. I call this the argument of the Absentee God. Hitchens said, in effect, that Christians affirm there is a wise and good God who cares about us and wants to have a relationship with us. But now look at how this God of yours operates. Man has been on the planet for a very long time. Estimates differ, but let's say that *Homo sapiens* has been around for one hundred thousand years. For most of human history, Hitchens said, man lived in conditions of indescribable horror, with fratricidal war, devastating disease, high rates of infant mortality, and of course no medicines to alleviate his plight. So what, Hitchens asked, was your God doing all this time? Evidently he was indifferent. This Absentee God was partying in his tent. And this went on for between eighty thousand and ninety-five thousand years. Then, a few thousand years ago, God finally decided to get involved. Still, he didn't bother to tell the whole world his message, contenting himself with whispering it to a few itinerant Hebrews. That message didn't get to places like China and India for another thousand years. Now, Hitchens scornfully asked, what kind of God acts like this? Only a capricious, irresponsible, and cruel one. Hitchens concluded that God, if he exists, is surely some kind of a monster.

Of course, in making this case against God, the atheist still has to explain why so many people in the world believe in a wise and all-powerful God. After all, the world is full of such people. They know the same facts about evil and suffering as Hume, Singer, and Hitchens. So is the human race simply stupid, unable to see what atheists so clearly see? No, say the atheists, the vast majority of people aren't necessarily dumb. They are just wishful thinkers who want something to be true that isn't true. So they believe against the evidence because they are driven by hope rather than facts.

Here's the argument as Sigmund Freud first put it in *The Future of an Illusion*. Life is tough, as we know from the debilitations of old age and sickness. We are all awaiting the grave digger. We don't like to face death, and we don't want to live with life as it is, so we make up another life. We imagine a God who is a father figure, and we invent a world in which there is no suffering and no death. Religious belief is an illusion produced by what Freud famously called wish fulfillment. This is the argument Hitchens echoes in his book *God Is Not Great*, and we find the same sentiment in Sam Harris's *The End of Faith*.[3]

My purpose in this chapter is to take on some key elements of the atheist worldview and show that atheist confidence in it is largely misplaced. The objective isn't to refute atheism per se, but rather to show that in considering evil and suffering in the world, the atheist position has its own serious limitations. Contrary to first impression, this is not a case in which atheists have nothing to explain and theists have everything to explain. Rather, both positions require a defense, and in choosing we have to compare the merits of each side.

Let's begin with Freud's argument, resurrected by Hitchens, that religious belief is a product of wish fulfillment. Certainly this would explain one-half of religious belief. Most of the great religions of the world, Christianity included, have some notion of heaven—and certainly heaven meets Freud's criteria for wish fulfillment. It is a realm without suffering, without death. But heaven is only one part of the story. The great religions also believe in another place, which in the Abrahamic religions (Judaism, Christianity, and Islam) is called hell. Now, hell poses an insuperable difficulty for the Freudian scheme. That's because hell is a lot worse than disease or even death. Death by itself is simply a terminus, a case of turning off the computer. But hell portends eternal separation from God, the ultimate expression of evil and suffering. How is that a product of wish fulfillment? Why would man invent a scheme more terrible than the forces of nature that provoked man to invent a scheme in the first place? As Hitchens himself conceded when I raised this point against him, atheism has no good answer to this question.

The Great Leap Forward

Now consider Hitchens's case against the Absentee God who sat in his tent for eighty thousand to ninety-five thousand years. When Hitchens first made this argument, I was flummoxed, but then I looked into the matter, so that in a subsequent debate I was able to offer my rebuttal. I reproduce that rebuttal here, and you can be the judge of its merits. I claimed, first, that Hitchens had his math precisely inverted and, second, that his argument backfired on atheism. For the first argument I'm indebted to Erik Kreps of the Survey Research Center of the University of Michigan's Institute for Social Research. An adept numbers guy, Kreps notes that it's not the number of years but the levels of human population that are the issue here. The Population Reference Bureau estimates that the number of people who have ever been born is approximately 105 billion. Of this number, about 2 percent were born in the one hundred thousand years before the birth of Christ. "So, in a sense," Kreps notes, "God's timing couldn't have been more perfect. If he'd come earlier in human history, how reliable would the records of his relationship with man be? But he showed up just before the exponential explosion in the world's population, so that even though 98 percent of humanity's timeline had passed, only 2 percent of humanity had previously been born, so 98 percent of us have walked the earth since the redemption."

These numbers undermine Hitchens's argument, but its plight is even worse than this. To see why this is so, let's apply a secular analysis and go with Hitchens's premise that there is no God and man is nothing more than an evolved primate. Well, biologists agree that man's basic frame and brain size haven't changed substantially during his terrestrial existence.[4] So here is the problem. *Homo sapiens* has been on the planet for one hundred thousand years, and yet apparently for the vast majority of those years he accomplished virtually nothing. No real art, no writing, no inventions, no culture, no civilization.

The science journalist Nicholas Wade illustrates the point very clearly in his book *Before the Dawn*: go back in history five thousand years, he says, and written records completely disappear. Go back fifteen thousand years, and there are no archaeological markers whatsoever. "Before that time, people lived a nomadic existence based on hunting and gathering. They built nothing and left behind almost nothing of permanence." Wade calls this eighty-five-thousand-year period "the long darkness before the dawn."[5]

Then, in the blink of a historical eye, everything changes. Somehow around thirty-five thousand years ago, savage man gives way to historical man. Suddenly primitive man gets his act together. Now there are wheels and agriculture and art and culture. In short order we have dramatic plays and philosophy and an explosion of inventions and novel forms of government and social organization. Pretty soon we have the Chartres Cathedral, space travel, and the iPhone. Anthropologist Jared Diamond has dubbed this transition from barbarism to civilization the Great Leap Forward. If we compare the human trajectory on earth to an airplane on a runway, we see a long, long stretch of the airplane faltering on the ground, and then suddenly, a few thousand years ago, takeoff!

How to explain this successful flight, after such a long period of idling? Were ancient human creatures, otherwise physically and mentally indistinguishable from us, such complete idiots that they couldn't figure out anything other than cave drawings and the art of primitive warfare? And how did *Homo sapiens*, heretofore such a slacker, suddenly get so smart? It is a serious question, one that scholars have made strenuous efforts to account for. One explanation is the development of language. Another is the use of increasingly sophisticated tools. Perhaps the most common explanation is the agricultural revolution. In his book *Human Accomplishment*, Charles

Murray aptly notes that "the beginning of agriculture . . . opens the way for all the rest of human accomplishment."[6] But all of this only raises the question, How did it take more than eighty-five thousand years for man to figure out that he could effectively communicate, make useful tools, and settle in one place and grow crops?

Well, there is one way to account for this historical miracle. It seems as if some transcendent being or force reached down and breathed some kind of a spirit or soul into *Homo sapiens*, because after accomplishing virtually nothing for 98 percent of its existence, abruptly in the past 2 percent of human history humans produced everything from the pyramids to Proust, from Newton to nano-technology. So paradoxically Hitchens's argument becomes a boo-merang. It raises a problem that atheism cannot easily explain and one that seems better solved by the biblical account of Creation.

An Atheist Conundrum

Atheists like to show how evil and suffering pose a problem for believers; let us turn the tables and show that evil and suffering pose no less of a problem for unbelievers. Normally the argument is made in the way that C. S. Lewis did in *Mere Christianity*. Lewis argued as follows: atheists invoke objective evil in order to undermine the existence of God, but this implies that there are objective standards by which we identify good and evil. Well, where do those standards come from? What is the source of the moral law that enables us to distinguish good and evil? According to Lewis, objective moral laws presume a moral lawgiver. So ironically the atheist case against God relies on a premise that, upon reflection, itself points to the existence of God.

I find this a tantalizing argument, but I'm not sure the inference is as obvious as Lewis suggests. Many philosophers from Plato to Kant have attempted to uphold objective morality without reference to God. This is not, however, the subject I want to consider here.

Rather, I intend to go in a different direction and show that atheism cannot easily account for the variety and magnitude of evils that we find in the world. This is the atheist conundrum of evil, and I have yet to see an atheist even attempt to solve it.

Most atheists affirm that there is such a thing as objective evil. Here is a typical statement, this one from atheist Kai Nielsen: "It's wrong, God or no God, to torture little children just for the fun of it."[7] But let us consider this question: On atheist grounds, could human beings derive satisfaction from so pointless an enterprise as torturing little children? Look at things from the unbeliever's perspective: there is no God, and the best way to understand human behavior is to recognize that we are evolved primates. Since nature has shaped our genes in this way, our evolutionary mandate is to survive and reproduce. Consequently, the broad objectives of survival and reproduction are the imperatives that guide our actions, and this is precisely what we observe in the animal kingdom.

Now, there is plenty of cruelty in the animal kingdom, at least if we want to use the term in an anthropomorphic sense. We can say, for example, that lions are cruel in eating antelopes. But animal cruelty is limited by necessity. A lioness will kill an antelope so that she and her cubs can feed on it. But whoever met a lion that would torture an antelope for the sheer fun of it? Certainly no one has ever found a genocidal lion that wants to wipe out every antelope from the face of the earth. Anthropologist Jane Goodall said in a recent interview that while chimpanzees, supposedly our nearest genetic relatives in the animal kingdom, will fight each other for territory and access to mates, they are incapable of the kind of evil that humans perpetrate. "Humans are capable of evil, of real and deliberate torture." Chimps, she adds, never plan to mutilate their fellow creatures or to "twist someone's thumbs."[8] Torture, like genocide, seems to be a distinctively human proclivity.

So I turn Hume's question on the atheist: if all we know is that humans are evolved primates, formed with attributes that enhance survival and reproduction, would we expect, *beforehand*, to see genocide and torture among the qualities of this group? Certainly not! Therefore, a purely evolutionary account of *Homo sapiens* cannot account for a degree of human evil that radically surpasses biological necessity.

The Limits of Reason

Finally in this chapter let's consider what may be the most serious defect of the atheist argument about evil and suffering: the problem of local knowledge. By this I mean knowledge that is limited in scope and capacity; in short, human knowledge. To see why this is a problem, let's recall what the atheist is saying about God. Basically the contention is that there is no good reason for an omnipotent, benevolent God to allow so much evil and suffering. But the atheist is being a little hasty here. When the atheist claims that "there is no good reason," what he or she really means is, "I can see no good reason." In a famous article, William Rowe considers the case of a fawn dying in agony as the victim of a forest fire. "Is it reasonable to believe," Rowe asks, "that there is some greater good" to justify this suffering? Rowe answers his own question. "It certainly does not appear reasonable to believe this. . . . So far as we can see, the fawn's intense suffering is pointless."[9]

The key terms here are "does not appear" and "so far as we can see." Philosophers call such claims Noseeum arguments. This term can be easily understood from the following exchange. I say that there are millions of bacteria in your nose, ears, and mouth. You say, "I no see um." Your position is that, since you don't see them, there can't be millions of bacteria in your nose, ears, and mouth. Viewed on this small scale, the position seems pretty foolish, yet this is not far from the atheist position on God and suffering.

Noseeum arguments aren't always wrong; sometimes they work.

But what must be the case in order for them to be convincing? Basically, such arguments presume that you have comprehensive access to the information necessary to make your Noseeum claim credible. Imagine that we are in the parking lot of a shopping mall and we see a vehicle with its passenger door open. Inside there is an infant strapped in a car seat. No mother is in sight. Certainly it seems to us that it is unsafe to leave a child exposed like this, and besides, it is dangerous in the summer heat. Since we can think of no good reason why a mother might do this, we conclude that the mother must be an evil, negligent person who is clearly unfit to raise children.

Does this Noseeum argument make sense? It doesn't, because we don't know enough about the situation. We know almost nothing of the character of the mother. We have no idea what circumstance may have caused her to leave her child unattended. Perhaps the mother had to chase after her other small child, who ran out of the car without warning into the parking lot. Or perhaps she rushed into the grocery store upon receiving a frantic call from her husband who, while picking up some items inside, suddenly collapsed from a stroke or heart attack. Given our extremely limited perspective, it is premature to leap from "I can't see the reason" to "There is no reason." We cannot condemn what we don't fully understand. In this situation we would be better off suspending judgment and watching the child until the mother's return rather than assuming parental incompetence and calling child protective services.

Here's another example, this one borrowed from philosophers Bruce Russell and Stephen Wykstra. Imagine a student who finds a philosophy manuscript in the library. It has many sections that seem utterly meaningless. (I certainly hope that this example does not apply to this book.) The student is about to dismiss the paper as nonsense, until it occurs to him that a distinguished philosopher may have written it. Philosophers are known to write specialized papers that are intelligible only to a small group of their peers. So the student's Noseeum case fails. There is no warrant for the student to say, "I don't see the merit of this paper, therefore it doesn't have merit." If the paper did have merit, the student is not likely to have seen it anyway! Notice that the Noseeum case fails even if we aren't sure that the paper was in fact written by a distinguished philosopher. The mere possibility that it was is enough to defeat the student's presumption that "there is no merit to this paper."[10]

Now let's apply what we have learned from these examples to the case at hand. If there is a God, then we can assume that his range of knowledge and wisdom is vastly greater than ours. Here *vastly* is an understated term: the distance between God's understanding and ours would be much greater than, say, the distance between our adult understanding and that of a two-year-old. Now if the two-year-old is taken by her parents to the doctor, and she cannot understand the reason why she is being given an injection and being made to suffer pain, we don't consider her incomprehension to be a decisive refutation of the good sense and compassion of her parents. Why? Her parents are so much wiser than she is. Even if they were exercising good sense and compassion, we wouldn't expect the two-year-old to recognize it. The same can be said of God. Since God alone understands the overall design and purpose of creation, we would expect that creation to be fully comprehensible only to him. If finite creatures who inhabit a tiny corner of the universe don't understand why things are structured a particular way, their objections cannot carry much authority. That's because they have such a limited understanding of God's overall scheme, and also because if God had a purpose in permitting particular evils, we would not expect them to be always in a position to comprehend that purpose.

Philosopher Walter Sinnott-Armstrong, a prominent atheist, attempts to salvage the atheist position in the face of this critique. "Suppose," he writes, "your neighbor lets his child suffer and starve. . . . If he *gives* no adequate reason when he could and would give one if he had one, then you would be justified in concluding that he *has* no adequate reason."[11] True enough, but there is a flaw in the reasoning here. We are in a good position, being fellow humans and living in close proximity, to judge the value of our neighbor's actions. Between God and us, however, there is an epistemic distance that is nearly infinite. If God had a good explanation for each and every event, what is the chance that we would be able to figure it out in each case? There is no chance. That's because we are not omniscient. Consequently atheists whose arguments rely on the presumption "If I were omniscient, I would have done things differently" can easily be answered with the riposte, "Sorry, buddy, but you aren't omniscient."

Note that in countering the atheist in this way, we are not saying that God's purposes are a mystery and therefore people should not ask questions. A mystery is something that is literally "beyond explanation." The argument here is not that evil and suffering have no explanation. They do, but it is not always comprehensible to us. So evil and suffering may be a mystery as far as we are concerned. They may not, however, be a mystery as far as God is concerned. They may have perfectly rational explanations, but these explanations are known only to God. That's because one needs the "God's-eye view" to see creation as a whole. Our knowledge, by contrast, is always local. We see things in a limited way from a narrow perspective. So something that appears senseless to us may still make a whole lot of sense when viewed in a larger context that is unavailable to us.

It is extremely important to recognize that this is not an attack on reason. It is simply a demonstration of what Hume called "the narrow compass of human reason."[12] Hume's point is that human reason has its limits, and reason itself can help us see what those limits are. The mathematician and philosopher Pascal put the point a different way. "Reason's last step," he wrote, "is to recognize that there is an infinite number of things which surpass it."[13]

We see Hume's and Pascal's point dramatized at the conclusion of the book of Job, in which God himself appears to answer Job's litany of complaints. And here are some of the things God says: "Where were you when I laid the foundations of the earth?" "Do you know the laws of the universe?" "Is it at your command that the eagle rises to the height to make its nest?"[14]

This is not, as Bart Ehrman alleges, a despicable case of God using his "raw divine power" to silence Job. Ehrman accuses God of showing up "to overwhelm Job with his presence and cow him into submission in the dirt."[15] Actually, God is there to remind Job of the very narrow circle of his knowledge. The issue here is not only the power of God but also the incomprehensibility of the world. God is not simply claiming the right to do whatever he wants; he is also pointing out how little Job understands of the natural order.

Now Job certainly understands what is happening to him. He knows that he is a just man and that he doesn't deserve his suffering. God completely agrees with this. But there may still be a purpose to Job's suffering that is not evident to him but only evident to God. The beauty of this story is that in this case we know the purpose of the suffering: to test Job's fidelity and to quash the accusations of the Satan. Ignorant of the goings-on in God's realm, Job cannot be expected to know any of this until God finally shows up and tells him. Then Job submits. "I was talking about things I knew nothing about," he admits, "things far too wonderful for me." And finally, "I take back everything I said, and I sit in dust and ashes to show my repentance."[16] God rewards Job's insight, and his submission, by restoring his family, health, and prosperity.

The Role of Humility

Let's sum up. We have learned in this chapter that the atheist case against God is weaker than it first appears. Atheists offer confident diagnoses about how belief is an illusion based upon wish fulfillment, but these diagnoses fail to explain important aspects of belief, such as the belief in hell, something no believer wishes for. While atheists raise legitimate questions about God's inscrutable purposes—Why did he intervene in history when he did? Why did he choose the Jews as vehicles for his revelation?—the atheists also have some explaining to do. Their evolutionary perspective cannot account for the Great Leap Forward, or for extreme forms of human malevolence, such as genocide and torture, that seem to serve no evolutionary purpose whatsoever. Finally, the atheist is a victim of his own arrogance. He thinks that because he can't figure out God's purpose in allowing suffering, therefore there cannot be a purpose. God is declared to be deficient because the atheist somehow "doesn't get it." This carries all the intellectual authority of the six-year-old declaring his parents incompetent because they have subjected him to the dentist's drill for no reason that is evident to him.

I began this chapter with Peter Singer's triumphant assertion that the facts of the world don't make sense if you assume that there is a God. I have tried to show that this is equally true of atheism. Atheism, too, cannot adequately explain the world as it is. In subsequent chapters I take up Singer's challenge and seek to show that his central claim is wrong. Not only is the existence of an all-powerful, loving God compatible with the facts of the world; it is only through God that we can make sense of those facts. Here, however, my task has been more modest: to level the playing field between the atheist and the believer, and to call both groups to an openness and modesty that enables us to converse with each other, to our joint objective of understanding, and to deal with the misery that we all endure in this vale of tears.

PART 3

Moral Evil

CHAPTER 5

FREE TO CHOOSE

Omnipotence and Human Freedom

Never shall I forget those moments which murdered my God and my soul and turned my dreams to dust.[1]

ELIE WIESEL, *Night*

IT'S TIME TO STATE the problem of evil in its classic form, given many centuries ago by the philosopher Epicurus: "God either wishes to take away evils and is unable; or he is able and unwilling; or he is neither willing nor able; or he is both willing and able. If he is willing and unable, he is feeble, which does not agree with the character of God. If he is able and unwilling, he is malicious, which is equally at odds with God. If he is neither willing nor able, he is both malicious and feeble and therefore not God. If he is both willing and able, which is alone suitable to God, from what source then come evils and why does he not remove them?"[2]

Here is a more modern way to frame the indictment:

1. God is omnipotent, so he has the power to eliminate gratuitous evil and suffering.
2. God is benevolent and good, so he has the desire to eliminate gratuitous evil and suffering.
3. The world contains innumerable cases of gratuitous evil and suffering.
4. Therefore an omnipotent, good God does not exist.

This is the strongest argument that can be made against God, and its strength lies in the sturdy intellectual scaffolding of the case. The argument seems rock solid: it begins with premises that hardly anyone could doubt, and then it moves by steps that seem dictated by reason itself to the conclusion that God does not exist. So we have here an actual disproof of God's existence

Most atheist arguments aren't like that. Atheists may say that there is no evidence, or not enough evidence, that God exists, or they may offer an alternative way to account for the diversity of life on the planet, making it superficial to posit a supernatural creator. But none of this refutes God. At best such arguments show that belief in God is not obligatory. Here, however, we have a different kind of argument. As philosopher J. L. Mackie writes, this is an attempt to show it is impossible for an omnipotent, benevolent God to exist. If this is true, then belief in such a God would be, in Mackie's words, "positively irrational."[3]

What a remarkable situation! It has God on trial, as in Wiesel's play. C. S. Lewis writes, "The ancient man approached God (or even the gods) as the accused person approaches his judge. For the modern man the roles are reversed. He is the judge: God is in the dock."[4] Even when God is put on trial, though, obviously he doesn't show up to defend himself. Consequently the religious believer sometimes finds himself in the position of being God's advocate, or perhaps God's court-appointed defense counsel. His job—and part of my job in this book—is to get God off the hook. There are two easy ways to do this—neither one of which I am going to use.

The first easy method of "excusing" God on the problem of evil is to deny the premise that God is good. As far as I know, no one engaged in the task of theodicy does this. The reason is obvious: this way of saving theism would answer the question but do so by removing the attraction of believing in God. We may fearfully submit to a wicked God, but we could never love or worship him. The second method is to deny that God is omnipotent. This is the position that Rabbi Kushner takes in *When Bad Things Happen to Good People*. Kushner's view is that God doesn't stop the bad things because he can't. So he does what he can to reduce evil and suffering, and he identifies with the victims. Kushner concludes that we can still turn to God for help "precisely because we can tell ourselves that God is as outraged by it as we are."[5]

Remarkably there is a whole branch of theology, so-called process theology, that takes a similar view of God. The basic idea here is that God is himself learning as he goes along, in a sense improving and perfecting his creation. I suppose that all of this is supposed to endear God to us, by showing him to be a fellow sufferer. But I for one cannot worship this pathetic, bungling God. For me, and I think for most people, a God who isn't omnipotent scarcely deserves the name God. So let's jettison these easy theodicies and face the atheist challenge head-on.

In the early part of this book I intend to play the role of defense counsel and dismantle the atheist case against God. Please understand that in this role I am not directly addressing the aggrieved believer, whose concerns I will take up later. Now, as a self-appointed counsel for God, I realize I do have one advantage: the burden of proof is on the accuser. The atheist must prove his case, if not beyond a reasonable doubt, then at least by a preponderance of the evidence.

Meanwhile, if we take the position that God is really being put on trial, the defense does not have to prove anything. It merely has to show that the case against God doesn't hold up. If this can be done, then God must be pronounced "not guilty."

But how to secure this "not guilty" verdict? Let's go back to the original atheist syllogism: God is omnipotent. God is benevolent. Evil exists; therefore, God does not exist. Notice that the conclusion relies on an assumption that an omnipotent, benevolent God could have no good reason to allow gratuitous evil and suffering. If he did, he would not still be both powerful and good. So the task of the defense is to show that there could be morally sufficient reasons for the existence and magnitude of evil and suffering in the world. In particular, I intend to argue that evil and suffering are necessary in order to secure a vastly greater good, a good that even an omnipotent being could not obtain without it. I cannot account for each and every case of evil and suffering, but there is no need for me to do this. I merely have to show that, in general, God is justified in creating and sustaining a universe that has an observable level of evil and suffering as part of its ingredients. I intend in this book to do a lot more than this, but if I have done only this, the defense has won its case.

So let us preview the defense, with my answers to the charges in italics.

1. God is omnipotent, so he has the power to eliminate gratuitous evil and suffering. *Yes, he does, but he may have morally sufficient reason not to do this.*
2. God is benevolent and good, so he has the desire to eliminate gratuitous evil and suffering. *Yes, but God intends to produce a greater good that requires him to permit both evil and suffering.*
3. The world contains innumerable cases of gratuitous evil and suffering. *True, but some of it is necessary for humans to exist, and the rest is caused by those humans themselves and not by God.*

4. Therefore an omnipotent, good God does not exist. *This conclusion no longer follows.*

Let's begin with the prototype of modern evil, the starting point for just about every discussion of the subject of theodicy. As Bart Ehrman puts it, "How can we fathom the heartless extermination of six million Jews? The Jews were to be God's chosen people, elected by God to enjoy his special favor in exchange for their devotion to him. Were the Jews chosen for *this*?"[6]

Ehrman is raising a specific question: Why did God allow the Holocaust? But there is a broader issue here. In history, as in modern life, we see examples of the horrific things that humans do to one another. The twentieth century was stained not only by the crimes of Hitler but also by those of Stalin and Mao. Pol Pot, a Little League tyrant compared to the Big Three, nevertheless managed through his Khmer Rouge regime to kill two million people in Indochina. In our own century, we have the tribal massacres in Africa and the depredations of Osama bin Laden and other Islamic terrorists. To all that we can each add our own examples of real and harmful evil that is perpetrated on a regular basis in this sad world of ours, from abandonment of a child to the violent crime that takes a loved one.

Why does God allow evil? Why doesn't he stop it? These questions carry an understandable sense of bewilderment and even outrage. Yet the answer is staring us in the face. Of course God didn't perpetrate the Holocaust; that was Hitler and the Nazis. Stalin and Mao committed their own crimes, as did Pol Pot. In case after case, we find that human beings are the ones responsible for crimes against their fellow creatures and, in some cases, against God's creation itself. So why did they do these monstrous things? The simple answer is that they chose to. In perpetrating these outrages, human beings exercised their free will. It is free will, not God, that makes possible all the moral evil in the world and all the suffering that results from it.

I recognize, of course, that there is enormous suffering that is produced by disease and natural disasters and other events that have nothing to do with human action. I am not discussing those yet. The focus of this chapter is moral evil, which is the exclusive prerogative of human beings. You see, it makes no sense to call the workings of nature "evil," except in a loose, metaphorical sense. Hurricanes aren't evil, although they do cause suffering. Even predatory animals aren't evil; they are merely doing what nature programmed them to do. The free will defense is not intended to cover all suffering, but it is intended to cover all evil. It vindicates God by blaming humans, not God, for what humans freely choose to do.

Why Free Will?

Obviously the next question is this: Why did God create man as a free creature? What are the benefits of free will, to man, and perhaps even to God? One possible answer—in fact, the Christian answer—is that God wanted to create a special type of creature that could relate to him and love him. While God loves all his creatures, he sought to create one in particular that could reciprocate his love. Now, it is in the nature of love to be free: love cannot be compelled. Consequently, God made humans free so that he could love them and they could love him in return.

All very good for God, you might say, but what value does free will bring to us? Theologian John Hick gives an interesting answer to this question. Free will, he argues, enables us to make of the world an arena for self-improvement and self-perfection, a project he calls "soul-making." Hick got his phrase from the poet John Keats, who once described the world as "the vale of soul-making." In establishing his point, Hick cites the biblical statement that God made man in his "image" and "likeness."[7] God himself is free, and in making us in his image, he made us free. This alone gives us human dignity, which is the source of human self-worth and human rights and so much else. But if dignity is conferred by the Creator, respect and esteem are things we have to earn for ourselves. We do this by exercising our free will—this is the key—on behalf of virtue. For Hick, this is how we come to resemble God, to be in his "likeness."

In reciprocating God's love and also performing acts of love in the world, with the help of grace, we start living our calling as imitators of a loving and holy God. So freedom is much more than the right to do what we want; it is the God-given ability to learn from the workshop of life and to make of ourselves a finished work that our Creator would be proud of. Why do we need free will to do this? Because freedom is the necessary prerequisite for virtue: coerced actions have no moral value, so without free will, there is no virtue. More than this, freedom is also a vehicle for human development.

Sometimes we make bad decisions, but we can learn from them, and in this way we can progress and grow.[8] While Hick frames his argument in religious vocabulary, it can also be understood in a secular way. Freedom is a school of responsibility for human beings. We all understand this very well when we send our children out into the world, allowing them freedom so that they can grow up and learn to be responsible adults. We don't want to keep them in perpetual childhood, choosing the good for them; we want them to be good choosers themselves.

Hick's contention is that without freedom, we would be incapable of evil; but without freedom, we would also be incapable of good. I think this is inarguable, but I want to go further than this. Without freedom, I would argue, we would not be human at all. Freedom is not an incidental characteristic for humans. One can give paint to a building, but one cannot give roundness to a circle. That's because roundness is an intrinsic characteristic of circles; without it, circles would cease to be circles. Freedom for humans is like roundness for circles: without it, we would lose our humanity.

Let's think for a moment about what freedom requires. Human

freedom requires consciousness, and if we didn't have consciousness, we would be, in effect, robots or zombies. Zombies, as least in the construction of Hollywood movies, are creatures without consciousness. They move around and act as humans do, but they have no inner life. Presumably God could have created a world of zombies, but I assume that this is not a world that we would prefer to our own. Now many animals, unlike zombies, are conscious, but their choices seem to be governed almost wholly by instinct. In other words, they do not make free choices in the way that humans do, and that is why they are not held morally accountable or morally worthy in their actions. Again, God could have created a world made up wholly of such animals, or he could have made humans who acted solely on the basis of biologically programmed instinct. But again, this is presumably not a world that we would choose—that is, neither the atheist nor the Christian—because it's certainly not one in which we would remain recognizably human. In fact, in none of those worlds could we even consider questions like, Is God being unfair in creating a world with so much evil and pain?

Free Will and Foreknowledge

Now, free will may be an undisputed good, but do we actually have it? For centuries, this question was examined from a theological perspective. Now it is considered from a scientific one. We have two schools of thought, one ancient and the other modern, that deny the possibility of free will. Let's consider first the ancient objection, according to which free choice is inconsistent with God's foreknowledge. The argument goes like this: God is omniscient, and so he knows everything. If he knows everything, then he knows what is going to happen in the future. But if God knows the future, then the future is fixed—it cannot be different from what God knows it to be. And if the future is fixed, then humans have no choice. We simply have to do what God knows we are going to do. We cannot choose differently; therefore, free will is an illusion.

The church father Augustine considered this objection in several of his works, including *On Free Choice of the Will*. Augustine argued that God's foreknowledge imposes no restrictions on free will. The mere fact that God knows you are going to do something doesn't compel you to do it.[9] Here's an example that illustrates Augustine's point. Let's say that, based on my special knowledge of my daughter Danielle's character and tastes, I know that she is going to major in English. I also know that she will marry a guy who likes to travel and knows how to dance. The fact that I know all this about her—and even if I knew it with certainty—in no way cancels out her freedom to choose. These are her decisions to make; I simply happen to know how she will decide.

A second example: let's say that you are standing on the terrace of a tall building and watching the people below. You see two cyclists approaching each other from perpendicular streets. You realize that, given how fast they are going, they are sure to run into each other. Still, your knowledge of this imminent occurrence does not make the accident occur. The riders are going to bump into each other anyway, and the fact that you are aware of this imposes no conditions or restrictions on the event. Both riders are fully in charge of their own actions, and they are freely maneuvering their own vehicles. Your foreknowledge in no way limits their freedom. And so it is with God, who knows what we are going to choose, even though the choices themselves are made by us and not him.

Augustine's argument, valid so far as it goes, fails to consider the time element that is part of the objection to free will. True, foreknowledge doesn't make anyone do anything, but the very concept of knowing something in advance places irremovable restrictions on what can be done in the future. Think about it: if God truly has foreknowledge, how is it possible for us to choose differently? If God knew at the beginning of Creation that at a given point in time, I am going to write this book, then it seems that I cannot choose at that particular time to write a different book instead. This deeper challenge to free will was taken up by the philosopher Boethius. In his book *The Consolation of Philosophy*, Boethius addressed the problem by drawing on one of Christianity's central propositions, that God is a being who is outside of time. This concept of a timeless God—a God beyond time—was known to Augustine and was in the mainstream of Christian philosophy. Boethius's originality is to give this understanding of God a new application.

Boethius writes that, because God is not time bound, he does not experience the world the way that we do. He doesn't live in the present, recall the past, and anticipate the future. Rather, for God, past, present, and future are all equally present. Everything for God happens in an eternal now. If we think of time as a flowing river, then God isn't riding with the current; rather, he is standing on the riverbank, watching the river go by. So God knows the past and the future in the same way, and with the same clarity, that he knows the present. The significance of this conception of God is that God doesn't have *foreknowledge*; he merely has knowledge. No longer do we have to worry that God, in knowing the future, is in some sense controlling the future. God is omniscient, but this does not prevent free creatures from making their own choices that God knows about but does not dictate.[10]

The Scientific Objection

Today we hear less about theological objections to free will than about scientific objections. We are products of heredity and early socialization. Freud has shown us the operations of unconscious drives that continue to affect us. Moreover, we are unable to control the very operation of our bodies, not to mention the external circumstances of everyday life. Yet these constraints on free will are not decisive; they do not remove completely the possibility of free will. Certainly our experience is that, with all the limitations taken into account, we still have some hope to make choices in the world. Free will may be limited, but it still feels very real.

Some physicists, however, argue that this felt experience of free will is an illusion. Free will, they say, contradicts the modern scientific view of causation. The basic idea is that the universe is deterministic, a case first made by the physicist Pierre-Simone Laplace in the eighteenth century. Laplace argued that living creatures are no different from inorganic matter. The same laws of physics, he insisted, govern everything on earth and in the entire universe. But if this is the case, then there is no room for free choice. Why? Think about it this way. In science, there is no effect without a cause. But if this is true, then our will also has causes. In a very obvious sense, our will is moved by the operation of neurons in the brain. Obviously, we don't have control over those neurons. Therefore, however much it feels like we have free choice, in reality we are merely responding to physics promptings in the brain.

This is a serious objection, one that is especially relevant to my central argument. While much of the argument of this book depends on the idea that free human beings are part of the laws of nature and arise in the world as a consequence of those laws, it is also important for my case that human freedom be real. Yet the determinists contend that the very laws that make humans possible also make free choice impossible.

Some philosophers say that the situation is not as bad as it looks. We can still, they contend, salvage free will even within the context of determinism. After all, these philosophers say, we do make choices among alternatives—in that sense, we are free. Freedom, in this view, simply means that there are no external constraints preventing us from doing what we want to do. It does not mean, however, that there are no internal constraints. Our minds and wills continue to be shaped by physical forces that are beyond our control—in that sense, we are not free. Perhaps a better way to put it is that we are free to *do* what we will; we are not, however, free to *will* what we will.

To my way of thinking, this halfway concept of free will is hardly satisfactory. How can we be truly free if something outside our control is causing us to make all our choices? Imagine if I am acting under the influence of a hypnotist. I am going where I want and doing what I want. No one is stopping me. So I seem to be free, at least in the sense of not facing external restrictions. And yet what kind of freedom is this? My will itself is being manipulated by someone, in this case the hypnotist. I am doing what he wants me to do rather than what I want to do, or more precisely, what I want to do is being largely controlled by what he wants me to do. This hardly seems to be freedom in any meaningful sense.

The philosopher Immanuel Kant agreed; he said there is no freedom without voluntary control over the decisions that we make. And Kant offered an ingenious philosophical argument that we actually have this kind of freedom. Kant's argument begins with our human recognition that we are moral creatures. We know not only that we do things, but we also know that we ought to do things. Morality is as much a fact in the world as any other; it is as fundamental a part of human experience as the experience of rocks and trees. Yet if this is true, according to Kant, then it follows that we have genuine free will. Why? Because if I ought to do something, it means that I am free to do it.

If a parent tells a child, "You ought not to tell lies," obviously this instruction would make no sense if the child did not have the power to decide not to tell lies. If the child's will were determined in such a way that she had no free choice in the matter, then not only the parent's moral rule but all moral rules would make no sense. There would be no point in instructing anyone that he ought to do anything. All our wills would merely be acting under the influence of forces outside their control.

Philosophically, this may be convincing, but is there also a scientific argument for free will? Actually, there is. It is not as much an argument proving free will as a refutation of the deterministic scientific critique of free will. Remarkably, nineteenth-century determinism has been discredited within science itself, although some people continue to argue as if this were not the case. As physicist Stephen Barr points out, determinism was felled by the discovery of quantum mechanics, one of the most important and revolutionary discoveries of twentieth-century science. Quantum physics shows that, at the subatomic level, the motion of particles is not only unpredictable but also undetermined.

Barr concedes that quantum mechanics doesn't prove or even explain free will; rather, he argues, it "provides an opening for free will." It does so by proving determinism, the most serious objection to free will, false. The proof is very simple: Determinism says that everything is in principle predictable and determined; quantum mechanics shows that everything is not predictable and determined; therefore determinism is wrong. Scientists today speak of "quantum indeterminacy," and the term itself is confirmation that determinism has been falsified.[11] So scientific determinism can no longer be used to prove there is no free will.

I regard these philosophical and scientific arguments, taken together, as having adequately answered the objections to free will. Thus I hold, simultaneously, that we live in a lawful universe, and that we are free creatures in that universe. Of course you are free to disagree, but notice that in disagreeing you are confirming my argument by exercising your free will!

The Meaning of Omnipotence

So far we have shown that moral evil is the result of human choice and free will, and that free will is genuine, valuable, and also intrinsic to our humanity. But if free will has an upside, it also has a downside.

The same free will that enabled Mother Teresa to serve the orphans enabled Hitler to kill the Jews. Free will not only corrupts the soul of the person who misuses it, but it can also impose suffering on innocent people. Why should the Jews have to pay the price for Hitler's misdeeds? We can ask this question of God because he is omnipotent, and omnipotence brings with it infinite resources. So why couldn't God have figured out a way to have free will without evil and without suffering? That may seem like a tall order, but tall orders don't intimidate omnipotent beings. A God that can do anything should surely be able to figure out a way.

I want to conclude this chapter by showing that there is no way. The assumption that there must be a way is based on a confusion about the meaning of the term *omnipotence*. We think that omnipotence means the power to do anything, but actually it does not and cannot mean that. If omnipotence means that God can do anything, then God should be able to make one and one equal five, or draw a four-sided triangle on a flat plane. But God can't do those things. If God can do anything, then God should be able to tell a lie. But it is impossible for a perfectly good being to lie, and therefore we know that God can't do that.

To understand why some of these claims about God are senseless, and to figure out what omnipotence really means, it is helpful to consider a classic puzzle. The puzzle is known in philosophy as the paradox of the stone. The question is a simple but baffling one: Can God make a stone so heavy that even he can't lift it? Framed this way, it is a maddening question, because whatever answer you give, it seems that God isn't omnipotent. If God can make such a stone, then he isn't omnipotent because there is a stone he can't lift. And if he can't make such a stone, well, then he can't be omnipotent because we have identified something that God can't do. In his book *God: The Failed Hypothesis*, Victor Stenger cites the paradox of the stone as a refutation of the idea that God is omnipotent.[12]

Actually, the refutation doesn't work, and indeed the paradox of the stone is based on a muddled conception of omnipotence. We can get around these muddles very easily by clarifying our terms. Omnipotence doesn't mean the ability to do *anything*. Rather, omnipotence means the possession of unlimited *power*. In God's case, omnipotence means having unlimited power to do what God wants to do. So can God tell a lie? No. God has unlimited power, but since it is not in his nature to lie, that power is only used for doing what God actually intends. God cannot draw four-sided triangles because the very idea of a four-sided triangle is nonsense. Omnipotence does not mean the ability to do what is impossible and nonsensical. A sign of this is that no amount of additional power would make a triangle four-sided. Can God build a stone so heavy that he can't lift it? The answer is no, and here's why: because God has unlimited power, there is no stone he can't lift; and as there is no stone God can't lift, God obviously cannot build a stone so heavy that he can't lift it. So the puzzle of the stone has been solved, and now we can see that God's inability to make a stone so heavy that he can't lift it is no refutation of his omnipotence; rather, it is the result of his omnipotence.

Thus we come back to our earlier question: Could an omnipotent God create a world with free will but no evil? The clear answer to this question is no. That would be like asking for a four-sided triangle. The very definition of free will includes the real capacity to choose evil, in the same way that the very definition of a triangle includes three-sidedness, and in both cases, we realize that no amount of added power would make impossibilities into possibilities. As philosopher Alvin Plantinga puts it, "God can create free creatures, but he cannot *cause* or *determine* them to do only what is right. For if he does so, then they are not significantly free after all; they do not do what is right *freely*. To create creatures capable of *moral good*, therefore, he must create creatures capable of moral evil, and he cannot leave these creatures *free* to perform evil and at the same time prevent them from doing so. God did in fact create significantly free creatures; but some of them went wrong in the exercise of their freedom: this is the source of moral evil. The fact that these free creatures sometimes go wrong, however, counts neither against God's omnipotence nor against his goodness; for he could have forestalled the occurrence of moral evil only by excising the possibility of moral good."[13]

Moral evil is not the only vehicle of suffering, but it is clearly one of the main forms of human suffering in the world. God permits such suffering because it is a worthwhile price to pay for a world in which there are conscious, rational, and free creatures called humans. In choosing to create humans as he did, God had to figure out whether giving us one of his own distinctive attributes, free choice, was worth the risk and the cost. Evidently God decided that it was, and as difficult as it may be for us to accept the cost, if we value our dignity and humanity, we will have to agree that he was right.

CHAPTER 6

CHOICES AND CONSEQUENCES

Why a Lawful Universe

If there is a God, it is a pity He didn't provide
conclusive evidence of His existence.[1]
BERTRAND RUSSELL, *Russell on Religion*

IN THE PREVIOUS CHAPTER we have examined why God created a world with free will. In this chapter we explore a different, though related, question: Why did God create a lawful world—that is, a world conforming to discoverable and predictable laws? Astronomer Carl Sagan calls it a "deep and extraordinary fact" that "laws of nature exist and are the same everywhere." Sagan notes that "laws of nature . . . apply not just in Glasgow but far beyond: Edinburgh, Moscow, Beijing, Mars, Alpha Centauri, the center of the Milky Way, and out by the most distant quasars."[2]

Obviously, an omnipotent God didn't have to create such a world. God could have created a world where gravity sometimes works but sometimes doesn't, or a world where physical causes sometimes have predictable effects and sometimes don't. Physicist Paul Davies writes,

"There are endless ways in which the universe might have been totally chaotic. It might have had no laws at all, or merely an incoherent jumble of laws. . . . One could imagine a universe in which conditions changed from moment to moment in a complicated or random way, or even in which everything abruptly ceased to exist. There seems to be no logical obstacle to the idea of such unruly universes. But the real universe is not like this."[3]

Instead of creating this whimsical or discretionary world, God seems to have created a world that operates according to general and universal laws. Physicist James Trefil terms this the "principle of universality." It means, in Trefil's words, that "the laws of nature we discover here and now in our laboratories are true everywhere in the universe and have been in force for all time." Trefil admits that "there is no logical reason why the same laws should hold everywhere in the universe."[4] Yet science is based on the assumption that they do. And every time science tests this assumption, for instance by measuring the force of gravity in outer space, or on the moon, it proves to be correct. Gravity is not something that happens just on earth; it is a universal force.

Here we will discover a powerful reason for why God may have chosen to make such a world. A lawful universe, it turns out, is necessary for humans to be able to exercise their free will. Without such a universe, free will would be useless because choices would not have predictable consequences. Neither morality nor science would be possible in a whimsical or discretionary universe.

We begin our inquiry into this topic by considering a serious deficiency in the free will defense. This deficiency was first pointed out three centuries ago by the philosopher Pierre Bayle. Bayle was not directly addressing the free will issue; he was responding to Leibniz's famous claim that this is the best of all possible worlds. Bayle responded that God could have done better. "If man were the work of an infinitely good and holy principle, he would have been created not only with no actual evil but also without an inclination to evil."[5] Bayle's point is a simple one: if God made a better type of human being, he would have gotten a better world. So this is not the best of all possible worlds, because we can easily envision one that is better.

Writing a half century or so later, philosopher David Hume expressed a similar complaint. In his *Dialogues Concerning Natural Religion,* Hume offers his own suggestions for how God could have created a better world: "In order to cure most of the ills of human life, I require not that man should have the wings of the eagle, the swiftness of the stag, the force of the ox, the arms of the lion." Hume would be content if the creator had provided "the endowments of superior penetration and judgment, of a more delicate taste of beauty, of a nicer sensibility to benevolence and friendship. . . . Let the whole species possess naturally an equal diligence with that which many individuals are able to attain by habit and reflection." Basically Hume wants all of humanity to share in the admirable attributes that he observes in himself.

Yet Hume goes further. Why, he asks, did God insist on building nature according to general laws? "This seems nowise necessary to a very perfect being." Certainly, laws may make the organization of the universe simpler, but Hume notes that God could use "particular volitions" to correct all the anomalies and catastrophes of nature. For example, "A fleet, whose purposes were salutary to society, might always meet with a fair wind," and good rulers may be granted "sound health and long life," while tyrants like Caesar and Caligula might be sent to early deaths or, better, converted in infancy into caring and public-spirited people. Hume isn't just calling for miracles here and there; he wants to know why miracles aren't the norm; why God made a lawful world in the first place, and then let things run their course without his direct and continual interference to correct evident evils.[6]

More recently, the philosopher J. L. Mackie writes, "If God has made men such that in their free choices they sometimes prefer what is good and sometimes what is evil, why could he not have made men such that they always freely choose the good?" Mackie argues that this is not inconsistent with granting humans free will. "If there is no logical impossibility in a man's freely choosing the good on one, or on several, occasions, there cannot be a logical impossibility in his freely choosing the good on every occasion." The social critic James Wood offers a concrete case to prove Mackie's point. In heaven, he says, the angels and saints supposedly have free will. Yet in heaven there is no sin. So if saints and angels can have free will and yet not sin, why didn't God make humans on earth the same way? The free will defense, Wood says, is "unraveled by the very idea of Heaven." Christopher Hitchens says that God is always objecting to human thoughts of evil, but this is the way that he made us. "If God really wanted people to be free of such thoughts, he should have taken more care to invent a different species."[7]

Critics of free will theodicy are making a very powerful point here that can be illustrated by means of an example. Let's say that we know a fellow who is basically a good guy, but he has a strong and virtually irresistible proclivity to alcohol. Now let's say that we dispatch this fellow into an alley that is lined on both sides with bars. Then when our friend shows up drunk, we say, "It's entirely your fault! You had free choice, and look how you have abused it." In such a case, however, part of the blame would surely lie with us, because we knew that he had this weakness and yet we sent him into an environment where he was likely to succumb. Our blame would be even greater if we, with godlike power, created a being susceptible to alcohol and then faulted him for freely exercising this proclivity that we implanted in him at the outset.

Now consider, by contrast, me and my attitude toward drugs. I do not regard it as a statement of virtue, only of fact, that I have never used drugs. I don't take any moral credit for this because I have never been tempted to use drugs. The whole idea of inhaling cocaine or injecting myself with some sort of drug is entirely unappealing to me. I simply don't see the point of frying my brain in this way. Notice, however, that I have the free choice to use drugs. So just as I have free will in using drugs but no inclination to do so, why couldn't God have created all humans with free will but no inclination to do any evil or harm anyone else? There seems to be no reason for God's decision to make inferior creatures bent on wicked and destructive behavior. Herein lies the fatal flaw in the free will defense that this chapter seeks to address.

But there is a second problem here that is worth teasing out at this point. I argued in the previous chapter that God wants us to have free will so that we can love him back, but where is God? Sure, we can reply that God is everywhere and God is within us, but what does it mean to love a being that is everywhere and inside you at the same time? Certainly God is not available for a normal kind of relationship with us. Typically if we love people, we can see them and touch them. When we talk to them, we get a direct and audible response. Not so with God. We relate to him through a kind of interior monologue, and even then we can't apply the usual standards to confirm that he is actually listening or even there. As Catholic philosopher Michael Novak points out in the title of his recent book: *No One Sees God.*

These are important philosophical questions, but of course God's absence is felt even more acutely when we are confronting hardship and pain. Recall that in an earlier chapter I noted the limits of human reason and argued that God may have reasons for us to suffer that we don't know but he does. I gave the analogy of the parent taking the child to the doctor to administer a painful treatment whose benefits are apparent not to the child but only to the parent. Still, in that situation it's easier for the child to endure the treatment if the parent is standing there, holding the child's hand and reassuring the child that everything is going to be all right. Where, then, is God when we are suffering, when we don't know why we are suffering and desperately need his reassurance? Surely God can at least make an appearance, as he did with Job, but he usually doesn't.

God's Disappearance

This is the puzzle of the hiddenness of God. In a marvelous book, *The Disappearance of God*, Richard Elliott Friedman shows how, even in the Bible, God progressively disappears. In the early books of the Bible, God is conspicuously present. "It is not a world of belief in God but of *knowledge* of God." Adam and Eve enjoy a kind of direct communication with God. God also speaks in a clear and intimate way with Noah, Abraham, and Moses, although not one of them sees his face. But in subsequent books of the Hebrew Bible, God hides himself from man. This very phrase, Friedman writes, occurs more than thirty times in the Old Testament. For example, in Deuteronomy 31:17, God tells Moses that when the people break their covenant with God, "I will abandon them, hiding my face from them." In the Psalms, there are frequent laments about God's hiddenness. "Wake up, O Lord! Why do you sleep?" "Why do you turn your face from me?" "Why do you hide when I am in trouble?"[8] Such cries will not be unfamiliar to those who suffer for any length of time. In the latter books God uses prophets as mediators for his messages, and not even the prophets always talk to God directly, as Moses did. Finally, Friedman writes—and here he may be referring to the Christian Scriptures—God disappears altogether. The God of the Old Testament makes no direct appearance in the New Testament. As Friedman puts it, "The initial biblical depiction of a world in which the deity is intimately involved has gradually transformed into a picture of a reality not so different from the one we know." In God's absence, Friedman writes, "Humans are left in control of their destiny."[9]

But Friedman never resolves the issue of why God hides himself in this way. The elusiveness of God, or at least his reluctance to show himself as directly as he once did, is baffling to believers because of the biblical promise: seek and you shall find. And some atheists argue that the hiddenness of God is itself an argument against the existence of God. A good God, philosopher J. L. Schellenberg argues, would never want to prevent people who genuinely seek him, or are open to him, from eventually finding him and experiencing his love. Yet, Schellenberg writes, there are surely many people in the world in this situation. They possess what Schellenberg calls "reasonable nonbelief." From this fact, Schellenberg concludes, "We can argue from the reasonableness of nonbelief to the nonexistence of God." In other words, God does not exist because, if he did, he would make his presence more obvious to all who seek him or are open to him.[10]

Schellenberg's point is affirmed in a less rigorous way by astronomer Carl Sagan. Sagan writes that God shouldn't have contented himself with "making enigmatic statements to ancient sages." He should have gone for more obvious signs of his existence. For example, "God could have engraved the Ten Commandments on the Moon." Sagan's other suggestion is "a hundred-kilometer crucifix in Earth's orbit." His point may be crude, but it is very clear: "Why should God be so clear in the Bible and so obscure in the world?"[11] This chapter, I believe, can answer Sagan's question and account for the general hiddenness of God.

The best way to answer this question is to seek God's own answer, as revealed in the Bible. We are going to focus on the biblical account of Creation and the Fall, as portrayed in the first three chapters of Genesis. Somewhat surprisingly we find Bart Ehrman insisting that "this standard explanation that God had to give human beings free will and that suffering is the result of people badly exercising it plays only a very minor role in the biblical tradition."[12] But free will is what the first three chapters of Genesis are all about!

There is theological debate over how literally the biblical account of the Fall should be taken. I have no doubt that historically there was a first human couple that sinned and, as a consequence, introduced sin into the world. But this is not crucial to my argument. So we will leave the historicity of the Fall aside to focus on the more important issue of what the biblical account of the Fall means. It is interesting and significant to note that many early Christians, including Augustine, interpreted biblical passages symbolically; they did not think that such an approach detracted from the veracity or reliability of Scripture.

Atheists often ignore this. Cognitive psychologist Steven Pinker in his book *The Blank Slate* states, "The modern sciences of cosmology, geology, biology, and archaeology have made it impossible for a scientifically literate person to believe that the biblical story of creation actually took place."[13] Yet the Bible has some profound things to say about origins: the origin of the universe, the origin of man, and the origin of evil.

In this sense, the biblical account resembles the account of the early modern philosophers, such as Thomas Hobbes, John Locke, and Jean-Jacques Rousseau. These philosophers envisioned man in a "state of nature" and discussed how men, through a "social contract," moved from a nomadic, largely solitary existence into political and social community. Even "rights" are presumed to derive from this original contract. And yet, as Pinker knows, no one has ever found such a contract. Indeed the early modern philosophers didn't claim that there was one. Rousseau in his *Second Discourse* even writes, "Let us . . . begin by setting all the facts aside, for they do not affect the question. . . . This subject must not be taken for historical truths, but only for hypothetical and conditional reasonings better suited to clarify the nature of things than to show their true origin."[14]

Pinker knows all this, for he writes, also in *The Blank Slate*, "Of course, humans were never solitary . . . and they did not inaugurate group living by haggling over a contract at a particular time and place. . . . But the *logic* of social contracts may have propelled the evolution of the mental faculties that keep us in these groups."[15] In other words, Pinker concedes that while the actual contract may be fictional, there is considerable value, perhaps even scientific value, in understanding the genesis and identity of social groups in this way.

Yet it never occurs to Pinker to understand the book of Genesis in this intellectually broad-minded way. So I am going to do that. Now, Pinker might object: Wait a minute! Isn't Christian apologetics supposed to be conducted in the vocabulary of reason? Why are we hearing about the Bible? Ordinarily this objection would be valid, and my other books make the case for God, immortality, and Christianity without appealing to revelation or sacred texts. In this book and in this section, however, a discussion of what the Bible has to say about evil is entirely legitimate.

Here's why. The core of the atheist argument is that there is a contradiction between what Christians believe about God and the existence and magnitude of evil and suffering in the world. But when it comes to discussing what Christians actually believe about God, the atheist confines himself to noting two of God's attributes: God is omnipotent, and God is benevolent. Christians, however, have a much fuller and more detailed understanding of God than this. So obviously the atheist account is inadequate if all that it can do is show a clash between two of God's attributes and the facts of evil and suffering. Possibly some of God's other attributes would clear up the contradiction. Therefore the atheist has to show that there is a contradiction between evil and suffering on the one hand and the whole Christian worldview on the other. Meanwhile, the Christian has every right to draw on the entire Christian perspective to dissolve the contradiction and reconcile God's character with the evil and suffering in his creation.

Indeed it is not incumbent on the Christian to even prove that

God did things this way or that way. Remember that the atheist is the one who has to prove the case. The atheist is the one who says it is *impossible* for an almighty, benevolent God to permit so much evil and suffering. But we can fully refute the claim that something is impossible merely by showing that this something is possible. We find the same strategy employed by defense counsels in murder cases; when the prosecution says that the accused did it in this way and that way, the defense only has to prove that the same facts can be interpreted differently, that things could have happened another way. If the defense can do this, then there are sufficient grounds for acquittal.

That's what we're going to do here: through a careful examination of the biblical account of the Fall, we're going to inquire into some fundamental questions. How did human beings become the way they are? What is the origin of evil? Where do conscience and morality come from? Why are we so dissatisfied with the world? Why is God hiding even from those who seek to know him better? In examining these questions, I am not confining myself to what the Bible says; I am also going to draw on a deep and ingenious interpretation of another fall—the fall of Satan—by the medieval philosopher Anselm. And in the end, I think a lot of these muddles will have been cleared up.

The Fall has nothing to do with eating an apple, of course; the Bible refers merely to the forbidden fruit. Nor does Genesis portray the snake as Lucifer in disguise. We find this imagery in *Paradise Lost*, and we can see that it represents subsequent elaborations on the biblical story. One modern elaboration, indulged by Christian and secular scholars alike, is to understand the first sin as involving sex. How predictable that we would seek to impose our own obsessions on the Bible! But sex is irrelevant to Adam and Eve's original transgression, even though they experienced the effects of that transgression in terms of guilt and shame over their nakedness.

The Original Transgression

So what was the original transgression? The biblical account focuses on a prohibition imposed by God. In Genesis 2:16-17, God says, "You may freely eat the fruit of every tree in the garden—except the tree of the knowledge of good and evil. If you eat its fruit, you are sure to die." Given the scope of God's allowance, the prohibition is absurdly minor. God tells Adam and Eve to enjoy the whole bountiful Garden, but just don't eat from this one tree. The tree is not one that brings life or happiness; it is the tree of the knowledge of good and evil. Apparently God doesn't want Adam and Eve to know good and evil. And what reason does God give for why man should not eat from this particular tree? He gives no reason. God intends that man obey simply because he says so.

Is God being unfair here? I don't think so. He is basically saying to Adam and Eve, "You can either live my way or you can live your own way. I have made you to be in relationship with me and to love and worship me. I have a plan for you, and for you to be perfectly happy, you should follow my plan. You should be willing to do this because I am your creator, and therefore you ought to know that my plan for you is the best plan, even if you, a creature, cannot understand why this is so. So I am not going to give you a reason why you shouldn't eat from this tree. If I were to give a reason, then you would be acting on the basis of your reason, not on the basis of my prescription. My plan is better because it is mine and because I am God, perfectly wise and perfectly benevolent. However, even though it is better for you to do things my way, I will not force you to do so. I am free, and I have made you free. So you have the option to choose your own way."

The message of the Fall is not only that Adam and Eve chose their own way over God's way, but also that all of humanity chooses its own way. Adam is a description of the prototypical man. (The very name Adam means "man" or "mankind.") In a sense, Adam and

Eve are stand-ins for humanity, and their choice as portrayed in the Bible is the same choice that every other human being would make and indeed has made. The choice is one of going our way instead of God's way, of following our plan for our lives instead of God's plan for our lives. We opt, in other words, for freedom—knowledge of, and choice between, good and evil—over subordination to God's supreme will. And the rest of the story is about God's reluctant acquiescence in the human decision, and the logical and necessary consequences of that decision.

But why is the human choice for freedom over subordination described in the Bible as "sin"? Why shouldn't we know about good and evil? What's wrong with choosing our own way over God's way? The answer is that this is what sin means: going with our plan over God's plan. The tree is described as a tree of the knowledge of good and evil because, upon eating from the tree, Adam and Eve are choosing their own understanding of good and evil over God's understanding. God's understanding is very simple: something is wrong because I prohibit it; something is right because I allow it. But the tree offers humans a different framework: God's explicit prohibition is ignored, and we decide for ourselves what is right and wrong.

The Fall is a sin of disobedience, because it represents infidelity to God's way. It is also a sin of pride, because it takes extreme arrogance for a finite creature to prefer its own plan to the plan of its wise and infinite creator. Randy Alcorn writes, "Any attempt to liberate ourselves from God's standards constitutes rebellion against God. In replacing his standards with our own, we not only deny God but affirm ourselves as God. Evil is always an attempted coup, an effort to usurp God's throne."[16]

But can the pursuit of knowledge by itself be regarded as a usurpation? Knowledge seems to us a very good thing, so what's wrong with knowing good and evil? Actually, knowledge by itself *is* good, and Adam and Eve had all the knowledge they needed. They knew what their creator wanted of them, and that's all that they needed to know. The problem is that what Adam and Eve sought was not intellectual knowledge but a different kind of knowledge. They sought to know good and evil so that they could decide for themselves whether to do one or the other. In particular, they desired to know whether what was forbidden by God as evil was really evil when it appeared to be good. And the message of the Fall is that this knowledge comes with a high cost. Not only is innocence lost, but Adam and Eve now know evil in a completely different way than before. Previously they knew evil only through prohibition; now they know it through experience.

It's important to understand that Adam and Eve don't fall by figuring out the meaning of evil; they fall by doing evil. The knowledge they gain isn't merely the intellectual kind; rather, they "know" evil in the same way that many biblical characters "know" their wives. Here "know" is used in the Hebrew to signify a kind of intimate knowledge, a knowledge borne of *experiencing* evil and *becoming* evil.

That's why the penalty for sin is death. God warns Adam and Eve that, if they eat of the forbidden fruit, they will die. They do eat, and of course they don't die right away. But they do become aware of their own mortality. Not only mortality but also anticipation of mortality is shown as a consequence of the Fall. Even more significant, the disobedience of Adam and Eve brings spiritual death, which is alienation from God. Humans' relationship to God is severed when they decide to go their own way rather than follow his way.

All of this today may strike us as "over the top," an overreaction by God. So corrupted are we by sin, so like Adam and Eve in our own proclivities, that we have difficulty appreciating the gravity of their offense. Adam and Eve, however, have a different reaction. They both immediately recognize the scale of their transgression. That's why they feel shame and hide themselves. The Bible portrays this as the moment when man became morally self-conscious. Adam and Eve are now fully aware of what they have freely chosen, and this choice brings shame rather than happiness. The shame of Adam and Eve is not due to their physical nakedness—they were naked before and not even conscious of it—but to their full recognition that they have opted for their own will over God's. They now know sin from the inside, as it were, and they experience shame and remorse—shame because of their guilt, and remorse in experiencing alienation from God as the immediate effect of their disobedience.

So the Fall is an account of how humans came to be sinners by cutting themselves off from God. And the Bible tells the story as a "fall" from an original state of happiness and innocence because it wants to communicate that this is how God originally meant for us to live. God intended man to be innocent and happy, but man chose instead to be free. Man was resolved from the beginning to choose good or evil based on what seemed best to him, according to his own finite judgment rather than in freely choosing to obey God's divine, benevolent wisdom.

The Motive for Sin

Still, a deep mystery remains: what was man's motive for sinning in the first place? The surface-level answers are that man wanted to be like God or to find out whether God was telling the truth or simply that man wanted to be independent of God and "do his own thing." But these answers only beg the question, Why did man, created by God and happy in Eden, want to break with his Maker in such an act of flagrant disloyalty and disobedience? To put it differently, who is to blame for man's decision to rebel against God—man or God? The traditional Christian answer is, of course, man. A case can be made, however, that the correct answer is God.

Augustine was perhaps the first to recognize the problem, and he begins one of his books with an astounding question: Is God the author of all evil? The question being raised is a simple but startling one: From where did Adam and Eve get the desire to sin? If God is the creator, and all things come from God, doesn't it follow that Adam and Eve's desire to sin must also have come from God? If this is so, then God, not man, is the author of evil.

Augustine labored ingeniously to resolve this problem, but with limited success. In my view, the most profound treatment of the issue is in Anselm's "On the Fall of the Devil." At first it may seem strange that Anselm is addressing not the fall of humans but the fall of Lucifer. The reason Anselm focuses on the fall of the devil is that he wants to get to the core of who is responsible for rebellion against God. In the Garden of Eden, one can ascribe some responsibility to the cunning snake. But in the case of the first fall—the fall of Lucifer and the rebel angels—there are no third parties. There are only the angels and God. Some of them fell and some of them stayed on God's side. Anselm's discussion of how this happened and who's responsible for it applies equally to angels and to human beings. In this way his solution to the first fall also illuminates the second.

"On the Fall of the Devil" is written as a dialogue between a student interlocutor and a teacher who is Anselm himself. The interlocutor begins by citing a passage in Paul's letter to the Corinthians. In 1 Corinthians 4:7, Paul writes, "What do you have that God hasn't given you?" The implied answer is nothing. And we know this is the answer because Paul follows his question with "if everything you have is from God, why boast as though it were not a gift?" Paul seems convinced that God is truly the source of everything that we have. Yet, Anselm's interlocutor says, this gives rise to a serious problem. If everything we have comes from God, then from where do we get the inclination to sin?

The student cites the case of Lucifer and the rebel angels. If they sinned, he says, that must be because they turned away from God. If they turned away from God, that must be because they lacked steadfastness, which in Christianity is called "grace." But if they lacked steadfastness or grace, that can only be because God didn't give it.

The student emphasizes that he is not questioning God's authority to punish the rebels—as creator, God has full rights over his creation. Still, the student wonders how we can blame the rebel angels for lacking something that God chose not to give them.

The question raised in this dialogue applies equally to Adam and Eve: How can they be faulted for thwarting God's original plan if God did not give them the strength and grace to stick with that plan? Where did man get the idea of rebelling against God except from God? It is no answer to say that man got it from the serpent, because the serpent itself is part of God's creation, under the sovereignty of God. So why did God permit the serpent to corrupt man? It would seem that, however we look at the matter, the ultimate responsibility for everything, and therefore for evil also, falls squarely on God.

Anselm replies by saying that God gave all the angels, as he gives all men, the grace and the power to resist evil and choose his will. But the rebel angels used that power badly and thus fell, while the good angels used it well and remained steadfast. Anselm's originality is in showing why some fell and others didn't. Anselm says that angels, like humans, have basically two motives for whatever they do: the first is self-interest or happiness, and the second is justice or morality. Happiness here means doing what benefits you, and morality means doing what God wants you to do. Even as an account of human motives, this seems sound. It's hard to think of any decision we make that is not motivated either by the desire to be happy or the desire to do right.

Anselm claims that God gave the angels happiness but not perfect happiness. He withheld something from them that, if they had it, would have made them even more happy. Since God is the creator, he has every right to do this, and it is appropriate that the angels gratefully accept what God has given them. The good angels, Anselm says, were content. Even though they were not perfectly happy, they were happy enough, and they were willing to forgo the extra happiness that God did not want them to have. The good angels chose morality over happiness. In Anselm's words, they "loved the justice that they had, rather than the happiness that they did not have." The bad angels, in Anselm's account, went the other way. They chose happiness over morality. Anselm writes that not only did they will what God did not want them to will, but they willed themselves to be equal to or even greater than God, because they sought to put their own will above God's will. Under Satan's leadership, these rebel angels mounted a rebellion, although an unsuccessful one, against God. Anselm ends his story with an ironic twist. God punished the bad angels who chose happiness over morality by taking away all the happiness that they had until then enjoyed, and he rewarded the good angels who chose morality over happiness by giving them the happiness that he had until then withheld.[17] There is a message here for us: in our own lives, far from the heavens, perhaps one benefit of our suffering is greater happiness as a result of choosing God's way than we would have ever had while choosing our own way.

Anselm has given us not only a powerful account of motivation, showing why created beings rebel against their creator. Anselm also gives Christians the resources to reply to the atheist who asks how there can be free will and no sin in heaven, while there cannot be free will without sin on earth. The answer is that in heaven, unlike on earth, no one has a motive to sin. The creatures there are perfectly happy and, as Anselm puts it, they have "progressed to the point where [they do] not see what more [they] could desire."[18] Anselm also answers the question we raised earlier: Is God the author of evil? Anselm's answer is an emphatic no. God gives us the grace and the power to do what is right, but any actual choosing to do what is evil—that doesn't come from God; it comes entirely from us. If we are honest with ourselves, we will admit that God hasn't forsaken us; rather, we are the ones who have forsaken him.

The Consequence of Freedom

So far we have focused on the meaning of the Fall, and the reason for the Fall; now we turn to the consequences of the Fall. As a consequence of man's choice, God, in a sense, revised his original plan. Adam and Eve couldn't remain in the Garden of Eden because that was a place that operated according to God's will. Reluctantly, God went with a sort of secondary creation. God sent humans out into a new world, a world that would enable them to live by their own plan and to apply their newfound knowledge of good and evil. That is, instead of taking their light directly from God's wisdom, they would have to struggle to understand good and evil, learning from tough experience rather than acting on simple trust.

In some sense this is a "curse," because it involves a wider degree of separation between man and his Maker, and it also involves hardship, both for the man and for the woman. God declares that both childbirth for the woman and work for the man will involve effort, pain, and hardship; truer words were never spoken. Still, man is not entirely abandoned to his own devices. We read in Genesis 3:21 that "the LORD God made clothing from animal skins for Adam and his wife." This is symbolic of God's continuing solicitousness for his human creation. He grants Adam and Eve independence, but he also gives them the means to fend for themselves.

We might be tempted to ask what this new world, this second creation, might look like. But we don't have to ask, because we are living in it. We know that such a world would have to contain, as it does, free human beings, which is to say, humans with free will. But we should also recognize that such a world needs to be physically and materially independent of God's direct control. In other words, we need a world that operates through laws of nature rather than by God's discretionary command.

The reason for this was given two centuries ago by David Hume.

"If everything were conducted by particular volitions," he wrote, "the course of nature would be perpetually broken, and no man could employ his reason in the conduct of life." Martin Gardner puts it another way: "It is not possible for human beings with free wills to exist except in a physical world with an environment structured by natural laws."[19] Imagine living in a world where events are truly random, unpredictable, and indescribable through laws. Obviously science would become impossible and so would most of modern technology. Moreover, freedom would lose most of its moral significance. Certainly virtue and vice would become meaningless in a world where actions don't have foreseeable consequences. Murder, for instance, takes on an entirely different meaning when bullets sometimes kill and sometimes don't. Thus, in order to give man freedom and enable human choices to have consequences, God creates for man an independent, lawful universe. The freedom of man requires, it turns out, the self-limitation of God as well as the independence of the world.

Hiddenness of God

A further consequence of the Fall is that this new world has to be one in which God largely hides himself. The reason is that, if God made his presence obvious, then humans would be, in a sense, forced to believe in him. God's presence would be so overwhelming and controlling that agnosticism, let alone atheism, would not even be an option. Even those who didn't want to submit to God would, as a practical matter, be forced to do so. Clearly God didn't want this. He gave freedom, and he wanted this freedom to count for something. So God made himself invisible in the world so that his presence would be obvious only to those who desire to meet him. God wanted to ensure that if we seek him, we will indeed find him; but if we don't, we will have plenty of excuses for ignoring or rejecting him. In Pascal's words, "There is enough light for those who desire to see, and enough darkness for those of a contrary disposition."[20]

In a recent essay, philosopher Paul Moser further explains divine hiddenness by arguing that God doesn't just want us to know him; he wants us to know him in a particular way. As Moser puts it, there is propositional knowledge of a thing, and then there is filial knowledge. Propositional knowledge is knowing about someone, as when we know that God exists. Filial knowledge is actually knowing that person, coming into a relationship with him, and in the case of God, placing ourselves under his divine jurisdiction. Moser contends that God is not interested in our merely knowing about him; he wants us to relate to him. Divine concealment is a necessary strategy to seek out those who are open to a filial relationship with God.[21]

Scholars of the Old Testament have long identified the two Creation accounts in the Bible. Sometimes these two accounts are portrayed as contradictory, or at least about very different things. The first portrays God's act of creation, beginning with the world and culminating in man; the second portrays man's rebellion against God and the consequences of that choice. Now we can see why there are two accounts, and that there is no contradiction between them: the first represents the way things ought to be, and the second represents the way things are.

No wonder there is so much evil in a world where evil is determined not by God's will but by human choice. No wonder nature operates by laws that can themselves be the source of hardship and suffering. No wonder God is hidden from us. No wonder the world in which we live contains so much anxiety, and that we pine for, almost as a forgotten memory, another world where everything operates through an infallible master plan, and where we are happy. At first glance the Fall is such a preposterous story, yet upon reflection it reveals so much: how we became human; how we inherited the world that we have; why we feel the way we do about the world.

Theodicy does not have to pretend, as Leibniz did, that we live in "the best of all possible worlds." We don't. But theodicy can help us understand how we lost that world. We lost it not because God denied it to us but because we chose not to live in the place where his will is supreme. We opted, rather, for a place where our will is supreme. God went along with our choice, but of course we also have to live with the consequences of that choice. Having said no to God's world, we are now living in a different world, a world of our own preference and, in that sense, a world of our own making.

PART 4

Crimes of Nature

CHAPTER 7

ACTS OF GOD

The Reason for Earthquakes

Say what advantage can result to all,
From wretched Lisbon's lamentable fall?[1]

VOLTAIRE, "THE LISBON EARTHQUAKE"

ON NOVEMBER 1, 1755, a massive earthquake struck Lisbon, Portugal—at the time, one of the richest cities in Europe, with one of the most active ports in the world. The quake occurred midday on All Saints' Day, when many people were in church. Many churches and homes were razed; museums and libraries were leveled; priceless paintings and manuscripts were destroyed; and thirty thousand people died instantly. Later accounts would put the number of deaths around fifty thousand, one-fourth the population of the city. Contemporary chroniclers noting the ruins also observed that the sky turned black with dust. The quake was followed by fires raging across the city and causing more death and destruction; then a series of tidal waves smashed the port, drowning hundreds of people in coastal areas.

Historians note that the Lisbon earthquake produced a convulsion in Europe unrivaled since the shock produced hundreds of years earlier by the fall of Rome.[2] Following the disaster, Voltaire wrote a poem in which he challenged the prevailing idea that earthquakes were a divine punishment for human evil. "Whilst you these facts replete with horror view," he wrote, "will you maintain death to their crimes was due?" Voltaire concedes that there was plenty of vice in Lisbon. Still, "Was then more vice in fallen Lisbon found, than Paris, where voluptuous joys abound?" Moreover, "Can you then impute a sinful deed, to babes who on their mother's bosoms feed?"[3] Voltaire goes on to blame God for the Lisbon disaster. Certainly, he writes, a God who can do miracles could have prevented it. And if God was not inclined to do miracles, he could certainly have designed the world in such a way that tragedies like earthquakes don't happen.

We recognize here the problem of evil in its modern form—Voltaire's protest against God sounds a lot like those addressed in chapter five. But there we were discussing the problem of moral evil; now we must look at the problem of natural disasters. In fact, on this issue we are at a turning point historically. Why? Because for centuries natural disasters like earthquakes, hurricanes, famines, and fires do not seem to have provoked reactions of this sort. The Lisbon earthquake was especially destructive because Lisbon was a heavily populated city—yet Lisbon was also a wealthy city, with the resources to recover from the disaster. Prior to that time, by contrast, natural disasters wreaked havoc on people who were much poorer, yet far from challenging God, those people viewed such events as a reason to turn to him. For them, the tumultuous movements of the elements were a sign of God's power, a power that produced stupefaction and, in its aftermath, humble devotion.

The Lisbon earthquake occurred during the Enlightenment, when a new kind of thinking was sweeping across Europe. This way of thinking spread among the intellectual classes; ordinary people responded to the Lisbon earthquake with the same religious fervor as had people in the past. The new intellectual current, however, emerged in opposition to the old order of things, in which the world was viewed as evidence of God's grand design. The great thinkers of the Enlightenment—Hobbes, Locke, Hume, Voltaire, and so on—did not deny that the world had been made by some kind of god. But, they began to wonder, was this the caring, paternal God of the Bible? Or was it rather a supreme though indifferent force, akin perhaps to Aristotle's prime mover, who set the laws of nature into motion and then went on an extended vacation? Voltaire's questioning can be understood as part of this debate. Voltaire isn't defending atheism; rather, he is asking what kind of a deity would design the world in this apparently faulty way.

In our time, natural disasters continue to ravage the planet. On March 11, 2011, a cataclysmic earthquake in Japan was followed, as the Lisbon earthquake was, by tsunamis. The toll by the end of the month was eleven thousand dead, seventeen thousand missing. Japan's already-sluggish economy took a further blow, and the economic reverberations were felt around the world. We can only speculate how much worse the devastation would have been if a nuclear disaster had followed the meltdown of Japan's reactors. Just a few years earlier, in December 2004, an earthquake measuring 9.1 on the Richter scale unleashed a tsunami that swept across Southeast Asia, wrecking the coastlines of Sri Lanka, Burma, and India and leaving more than two hundred thousand casualties. The *New York Times* profiled Santosh Selvam, "a charismatic, mammoth man with a flowing black beard," a bodybuilder whose great strength was insufficient to prevent four of his five children from drowning. "He recited the boys' names, oldest to youngest, like a descending scale. Shankar Das, 12. Sadishwaran, 10. The younger the son, the harder the name was for Mr. Selvam to say. At Tara Singh, 6, he began to choke up. By the time he reached King Kong, a 4-year-old who was already trying to lift weights like his father, he was crying."[4]

In addition to earthquakes, the world regularly has to contend with hurricanes, tempests, famines, epidemics, diseases, floods, fires, droughts, avalanches, mudslides, and other natural calamities. Plagues and diseases can be especially virulent, and tens of millions suffer and die each year from tuberculosis, leprosy, malaria, stroke, and heart disease, while others are incapacitated by blindness, deafness, misshapen limbs, mental deficiency, and insanity. Beyond these disasters there are rare but potentially cataclysmic threats in nature: in 1996, for example, an asteroid about a third of a mile wide passed within three hundred thousand miles of the earth, very close by astronomical standards.[5] We live, it seems, on a dangerous planet.

Insurance companies typically refer to natural calamities as "acts of God." The term is revealing because it conveys the idea that human beings are not responsible for such disasters. They are outside our control, which means that if we didn't do them, God must have. Consequently the suffering produced by natural disasters cannot be directly explained by free will. In the previous chapter, however, I argued for an indirect connection. As a result of the Fall, produced by man's decision to go his own way instead of God's way, God dispatched humans into a world where they could function as free and responsible creatures, a world governed by regular and predictable physical laws, woven within which are pain, toil, and death. Such laws, I argued, are the necessary precondition of choices that have foreseeable consequences, that is to say, the precondition of human responsibility. They are the laws that define a world in which God is not directly present, and in which his ordering power is known, at best, indirectly through these laws. And it is within this world that we struggle to discern for ourselves what is good and evil.

This argument, however, does not solve the quandary of "acts of God." It answers the question of why God made a lawful world, but it doesn't answer why God made a world with these particular laws. The philosopher Bertrand Russell raises the question of why God created a world with so much disease, and in particular why he allows even children to suffer. "I would invite any Christian," he writes, "to accompany me to the children's ward of a hospital, to watch the suffering that is there being endured, and then to persist in the assertion that those children are so morally abandoned as to deserve what they are suffering. In order to bring himself to say this, a man must destroy in himself all feelings of mercy and compassion. He must, in short, make himself as cruel as the God in whom he believes."[6]

A similar argument was raised by David Hume around the time of the Lisbon earthquake. Hume raised the question of why nature is so parsimonious. True, he said, nature supplies us with useful things like land and air and fire and water. But the same land that we need for agriculture can also rupture and cause earthquakes; the same air and water so essential for life also conspire together to produce hurricanes. Hume also noted that humans must constantly endure sickness and disease, often accompanied by pain of the emotional as well as physical variety. In his *Dialogues* he writes, "Were all living creatures incapable of pain, evil never could have found access into the universe." Finally, Hume considers the "hostile and destructive" attitude that so many living creatures bear toward each other. He is referring here to predation—one species essentially feasting on another—and also the bitter rivalries that occur within animal species. "The whole," he concludes, "presents nothing but the idea of a blind nature . . . pouring forth from her lap, without discernment or parental care, her maimed and abortive children!"[7]

Hume seems to write as though natural suffering is entirely outside human control. He assumes a clear line between moral evil and natural suffering. But, in fact, the distinction is not clear cut. Human action can contribute to or exacerbate natural suffering. For instance, habitual smoking and drinking can increase the risk of cancer. Christopher Hitchens, who had cancer of the esophagus, admitted that his chronic smoking and drinking clearly didn't help. Drought can cause famine, but governments can make the problem worse by refusing to plan for such contingencies, or by stealing the food aid that is sent by international relief agencies. Shoddy building practices and even poor urban design can increase the destructive effects of earthquakes. Following the Lisbon earthquake, Rousseau wrote a letter to Voltaire, in which he said, "Most of the physical evils we experience are . . . of our own making. . . . In Lisbon . . . it was not nature that piled up there twenty thousand houses of six or seven floors each." Had the inhabitants of the city been more spread out, Rousseau added, the destruction would have been much less.[8]

Even so, in many cases of natural suffering the human role is negligible, or even when we have factored out human action, there remain other forces of nature that are outside human control. To use Hitchens's example again, had he no affection for his cigarettes or whiskey, he might still have gotten cancer because his family has a history of cancer. Given the obvious role of natural forces in causing the 2004 tsunami, columnist Barbara Ehrenreich published an article in *The Progressive* titled "God Owes Us an Apology." She wrote, "If we are responsible for our actions, as most religions insist, then God should be too, and I would propose, post-tsunami, an immediate withdrawal of prayer and other forms of flattery directed at a supposedly moral deity—at least until an apology is issued."[9] Ehrenreich's tone suggests to me that she wasn't doing much praying even before the tsunami, but still, her challenge is one that believers should take up. Does God owe us some penitence of his own for the natural suffering he seems to inflict on us?

In the next three chapters, I investigate this question by asking why there are earthquakes, tsunamis, disease, predation, and other forms of natural suffering. Why is the natural world the way it is? Could God have made a lawful universe containing human beings in some other way? It seems like I am looking for the cause of natural suffering, as opposed to moral evil. Incredibly, however, the answer that we are going to find will help us to account for both natural suffering and moral evil. Humans, after all, are also part of nature. In accounting for the construction of the natural world, therefore, we are also going to inquire into how free and rational creatures called humans became part of that world. To my knowledge, for the first time in the history of theodicy, we are going to uncover a unified explanation for natural suffering and moral evil, an explanation that makes both more intelligible and endurable, while exonerating God from the culpability that atheists seek to place upon him.

The Benefits of Plate Tectonics

Let's begin by asking a simple question: why are there earthquakes? By extension, we can also ask why there are volcanoes and tsunamis and hurricanes. For many centuries, the only answer to this question was that the gods were angry. Even during the Enlightenment, the cause of earthquakes was not known, so it was natural for Voltaire, Hume, and others to portray earthquakes as somehow pointless and gratuitous. In a way, Voltaire and Hume agreed with the ancient primitive consensus—earthquakes have no other purpose than arbitrary divine action—except that Voltaire and Hume turned the argument around. If there is a good and wonderful God, clearly he wouldn't allow earthquakes, and therefore we suspect that the planet is not governed by a good and wonderful God. Now, however, we ask whether there is a good reason for God to permit earthquakes. If there is, then Voltaire and Hume's argument collapses. Picking up Voltaire's line quoted at the beginning of this chapter, we would be able to specify "what advantage can result to all, from wretched Lisbon's lamentable fall."

In the last century, modern science has discovered that earthquakes are the consequence of plate tectonics, the movement of giant plates under the surface of the earth and the ocean floor. When the concept of plate tectonics was first proposed in the 1920s by meteorologist Alfred Wegener, scientists dismissed it as preposterous. But the evidence for Wegener's thesis continued to grow until it was widely accepted by the 1960s; today it is beyond dispute. We know that the earth's crust is divided into plates, and that old crust is destroyed and new crust is formed at plate boundaries. Very generally, plate boundaries are of two categories: ridges and trenches. New crust is produced at the ridges by the upsurge of liquid rock from the earth's mantle below, and old crust is dissolved at the trenches by sinking back into the mantle. Theoretical physicist Freeman Dyson writes, "The action of plate tectonics ensures that the geography of the earth is constantly changing. New continents such as Australia and Antarctica are formed by splitting up old ones. New chains of mountains such as the Himalayas rise where the formerly separate continents India and Asia collide. And new chains of islands such as Japan and the Aleutians are created by volcanoes rising from the edge of a descending plate."[10]

As the giant plates move and rub against each other, they sometimes rupture the crust at the surface, cracking and splitting it. That's how we get earthquakes. Volcanoes occur when scalding materials from the earth's interior are coughed up and spewed out. When the cracking and rupturing happens on the ocean floor, huge quantities of water can get displaced, and this is how we get seaquakes (earthquakes at sea) and tsunamis. In the important book *Rare Earth*, published in 2003 by Peter Ward and Donald Brownlee, the authors—one a paleontologist, the other an astronomer—make the striking observation that "ours is still the only planet we know that has plate tectonics." Earth is also the only planet known to have life. Obviously these are claims based on current knowledge; who knows what future discoveries will show? Even so, Ward and Brownlee ask, is there a connection? What does plate tectonics have to do with the apparent uniqueness of life on earth?

The authors show that plate tectonics is a "central requirement for life on a planet." Plate tectonics is also largely responsible for enabling differences in land elevation and thus separating the land from the water. Without plate tectonics, the authors write, "the oceans contain enough water to cover the spherical Earth to a depth of about 4,000 meters. If the surface of the planet varied only a few kilometers in elevation, Earth would be devoid of land." Keep in mind that, while two-thirds of the earth is covered by water, over two-thirds of all animal species live on land. Fish might survive in such an environment, and perhaps birds, but not armadillos or antelopes or us. Plate tectonics also helps explain the biodiversity we find on land because it causes the breaking up of land into continents, each with its own distinctive topography and climate, and thus each enabling the flourishing of different forms of life. So plate tectonics is responsible for earth's stunning variety, and if we appreciate that variety, we must admit that earthquakes and volcanoes have helped to generate it.

But we shouldn't be misled into thinking that if we subtracted tectonics, we'd still have, at least, oceans swarming with fish. Quite possibly without tectonics there would be no life at all. Life, after all, is highly dependent on having carbon dioxide in the atmosphere. Today we hear that the atmosphere contains too much carbon dioxide—the supposed cause of global warming—but whatever the merits of this claim, the fact is that we need carbon dioxide; without it, the earth would most likely resemble Antarctica. It is the tectonic system that recirculates carbon dioxide into the atmosphere, keeping the level of greenhouse gases (and hence the earth's temperature) stable. The whole tectonic system serves as a kind of "planetary thermostat," helping to regulate the earth's climate and preventing the onset of scorching or freezing temperatures that would make mammalian life, and possibly all life, impossible. Plate tectonics also helps the formation of minerals on earth and their recirculation to the surface through tectonic activity. Without our vast, rich storehouse of available minerals, it's hard to envision complex life and even harder to envision the development of any kind of complex civilization. Tectonics also maintains the proper chemical balance of the sea, allowing for its rich biodiversity. If that weren't enough, plate tectonics makes possible the earth's magnetic field, without which "earth and its cargo of life would be bombarded by a potentially lethal influx of cosmic radiation."[11]

Other prominent scientists agree with Ward and Brownlee. Following the 2004 earthquake, William Broad of the *New York Times* interviewed prominent scientists and discovered a consensus that earthquakes and other such events, despite their tragic effects, were absolutely vital for life on earth to exist in the first place. "The type of geological process that caused the earthquake and the tsunami is an essential characteristic of the earth," said geochemist Donald DePaolo. "It doesn't occur on any other planetary body and has something very directly to do with the fact that the earth is a habitable planet." Geophysicist Robert Detrick said, "There's no question that plate tectonics rejuvenates the planet." Frank Press, past president of the National Academy of Sciences, said, "On balance, it's possible that life on earth would not have originated without plate tectonics, or the atmosphere, or the oceans." And environmental scientist William Schlesinger added, "Having plate tectonics . . . is absolutely essential to maintaining stable climate conditions on earth. Otherwise, all the carbon dioxide would disappear and the planet would turn into a frozen ball."[12]

So plate tectonics, the process that gives us earthquakes, is also a process that is vital to enable and sustain life on earth. From a scientific point of view, we owe our existence to plate tectonics. Where, then, is the logic of bemoaning earthquakes? Certainly they create havoc and devastation when they occur near civilization. But if we consider the evidence of the overriding benefit of earthquakes, decrying them wholesale is about as persuasive as cursing the sun. The sun can cause heatstroke, or even cancer—terrible maladies, surely—but where would humans be without the sun? In fact, we would not be at all. Not only do we need the sun, but we also need the sun to be positioned precisely where it is, eight light minutes away from the earth. If the sun were only a little farther away, we'd freeze; if it were even a little closer, we'd bake.

And on the subject of overheating, fires (such as those that occurred after the Lisbon earthquake) can be devastating—but on the other hand, where would civilization be without fire? Complex technological advances simply could not have occurred without the ability to smelt metals. Even forest fires, we now know, are help-ful in maintaining the balance of the ecosystem, which is why we frequently allow them to burn unchecked and even start them in a controlled manner. Moreover, fire is the result of having just the right amount of that most important element for complex life, oxygen. There would be no risk of fire if the atmosphere contained no oxy-gen, yet many life forms such as humans would then have to endure severe breathing problems.

Of course, the same point can be made about water—it is responsible for floods and hurricanes, but how could we survive in its absence? "Without water," writes biochemist Michael Denton in *Nature's Destiny*, "life that exists on earth would be impossible." Intuitively, we all know that water is the "liquid of life," and that's why scientists searching for life on other planets often regard the presence of water as a determining factor. But Denton also brings before us obvious—and amazing—properties of water that make possible the existence of life on earth. For example, water is virtu-ally unique among substances in that it is more dense as a liquid than a solid. Because of this property, ice floats on water, insulating the water below from further loss of heat. This simple fact, writes Denton, prevents lakes and oceans from freezing from the "bottom up." If water didn't have this property, and ice were denser than liquid water, each successive layer of ice would sink to the bottom never to thaw again, the result being that the oceans of the world would soon be permanently frozen. But that's not all. "Surface ice also helps to regulate the climate by altering earth's ability to absorb or reflect sunlight," thus helping to maintain the earth's temperature within the range necessary for complex life forms.

The strange abilities and benefits of water go on and on. Water also has a higher specific heat than any liquid except ammonia; this means that water heats up very slowly. Consequently the water in our bodies keeps the body temperature from rising rapidly and precipitously, and likewise the oceans exercise a stabilizing influence on the environment. In fact, evaporation from the oceans takes in heat from tropical regions of the earth; this latent heat is then carried to colder latitudes. There the vapor condenses, once again becoming liquid water. In the process, it discharges its latent heat and warms up the colder regions. Water is a solvent that breaks down and distributes minerals throughout the earth; it does the same for nutrients that it transports to various parts of the body through the bloodstream.

Denton concludes, "The evidence reviewed . . . indicates that water is uniquely and ideally adapted to serve as the fluid medium for life on earth in not just one, or many, but in *every single one* of its known physical and chemical characteristics."[13] Yet this same water is the water of floods, tidal waves, and hurricanes. These, too, have their function within the marvelous ecosystem of nature. Hurricanes, for example, regulate tropical ocean temperatures and circulate elements in a way that is very positive for life in general and humanity in particular.

There is a broader point here, of course. We live on a planet that is extremely rare in its ability to sustain life. Earth is a *biocentric* planet, the only planet that, as far as we know, has life, because it is the only planet we know that has the necessary conditions for life. Other planets, including our next-door neighbors Venus and Mars, don't have those conditions. Mars has dramatic fluctuations of temperature, and large parts of the planet are completely frigid. The south polar cap of Mars is mostly made up of frozen carbon dioxide—dry ice—and the air on Mars is much thinner than it is on the top of Mount Everest. Venus, like Mars, is a dry planet, but unlike Mars, Venus is boiling hot: its surface temperature often reaches nine hundred degrees Fahrenheit. Not only is earth ideally placed in the solar system, but cosmologist Joel Primack notes that our solar system lies in what he calls a "galactic habitable zone." Our solar system does not lie at the center of our galaxy, the Milky Way, but out between two of its spiraling arms. This is a very good thing because, according to Primack, "dangerous radiation is likely to have destroyed or prevented life on planets around stars that happened to lie closer to the center." By contrast, "Out in the galactic suburbs where we live, the nearest supernovas were far enough away from our solar system that their radiation was weak enough for Earth's atmosphere to provide adequate protection."[14]

The point is that life as we know it is dependent on our living on a delicately balanced planet just like ours, located in a solar system positioned pretty much where ours is positioned, and displaying a set of natural processes identical to the ones that we see all around us. These are the processes—including earthquakes and volcanic eruptions—that give us land and water and air and warmth. In the past, it was intellectually respectable to conjecture that these processes were optional or incidental, so that a truly good God could have subtracted them and we could all live happily in an environment without some or most of these processes. Voltaire could get away with that two centuries ago, but today his position is an intellectual embarrassment. Today it is scientifically ignorant to say that we can do without natural processes like earthquakes, destructive and dangerous though they may sometimes be, and yet have our kind of a planet with humans in it. The same natural phenomena that are indispensable to our existence on earth are also responsible for our natural calamities, yes—but these calamities are not gratuitous but rather intrinsic to processes that are fundamentally life affirming.

Why We Get Sick

Now we turn to a second broad source of natural suffering, which is disease. Whereas earthquakes and tsunamis can kill spectacular numbers of people in a single day, disease typically gets us one by one but kills far more systematically and effectively. A few years ago, the writer Joan Didion lost her husband unexpectedly. Didion's account of her suffering, the well-known *The Year of Magical Thinking*, is heartbreaking. And eventually she points the accusing finger at God. "No eye," she concludes, "was on the sparrow."[15]

Like an earthquake, disease appears to be a crime of nature, another "act of God" that cannot be blamed on human action. In his book *Plagues and Peoples*, however, historian William McNeill argues that this is not entirely so. Many diseases and virtually all plagues are spread and exacerbated by human behavior. For instance, the domestication of animals, useful in many respects, also imported a whole range of diseases that were previously confined to four-legged creatures. Wars and migrations, such as the Mongol conquests of large parts of Central Asia and Europe, and also the European discovery of the New World, brought in their wake deadly diseases to which native populations had no immunity. The Native American population, for example, was severely thinned not by genocide but largely by epidemics of malaria and diseases to which the indigenous peoples had no resistance.[16]

Even cancer, at its current levels of magnitude, is related to our modern way of life. In *Why We Get Sick*, Randolph Nesse and George Williams write that the incidence of breast and ovarian cancer in women is connected to the number of children they have. "The more menstrual cycles a woman has," they write, "the more likely she is to get reproductive-system cancer." That's because menstrual cycles cause "wide swings of hormone concentrations," and these cause cellular responses that increase cancer vulnerability. In the past, Nesse and Williams note, women had multiple children and spent much of their adult life lactating; their total menstrual cycles "could not have been much more than 150." A modern woman with one or two children, by contrast, could easily have between 300 and 450 cycles.[17] Other types of cancer occur due to radiation, smoking, diet, artificial chemicals, and other human transformations of the environment. Obviously my point here is not to assign blame, but rather to show that disease and epidemics are the products both of natural conditions and also of human alteration of those conditions.

Still, why would God have allowed Alzheimer's, tuberculosis, leprosy, diphtheria, Parkinson's disease, and cancer? Does disease, too, play a part in the ecosystem of life? Actually, it does, but to see this we have to take a broader perspective. Consider this fact: the earth is teeming with trillions of microbes and bacteria. In fact, our bodies are teeming with billions of bacteria. Your mouth, your ears, even your eyes are filled with invisible living creatures. This seems quite disturbing, and admittedly some of those bacteria cause acute infections. But most of the bacteria that inhabit our earth are quite harmless, and some are quite useful. In the soil, for example, bacteria contribute to the decomposition of dead plants and animals, and thus they help recycle the constituents of life. Even in our bodies, bacteria don't typically cause disease. Some of them are free riders that neither harm nor help us. But most are "good bacteria"—the kind now marketed to us as active cultures and probiotics—that help us digest food, assist in waste elimination, provide vitamins, protect us from harmful germs, and in some cases even delay or prevent cancer.[18]

Normally we focus entirely on the welfare of our own species, and we ask, "What does disease do for us?" This is a legitimate angle of inquiry, but it is somewhat narrow and self-interested. God's angle may well be wider. After all, he did not make us the only creatures in the world. We have to share the earth with countless other creatures, some of them too small for us to see, and all of them in competition with us and with each other to survive and flourish on this planet. Among these rivals are the Anopheles mosquito, the deadly parasite, the opportunistic virus.

These living things are our enemies, but I'm not sure they are God's enemies. We cannot be blamed for asking God to wipe out all these menacing life forms, but in this respect we are like mice, who would like to live in a world without cats, or like fish, who really don't see the point of having seagulls and other predatory birds. God, who made all these creatures, may consider them to have value in the overarching plan of creation. We see this in the thirty-ninth chapter of the book of Job, where God responds to Job's complaints by invoking the welfare of other creatures: the ostrich, the donkey, the mountain goat, the horse, the hawk, the eagle, even the locust. Here God is rejecting the purely anthropocentric view, which says that everything God creates must be directly beneficial to humans. God seems to suggest that though we are the only ones created in his own image, he also has other interests, and it is not too much to suggest that these could include the louse, the termite, and the spider.

Clearly from the perspective of those small creatures, we are the enemy. William McNeill writes that "looked at from the point of view of other organisms, humankind . . . resembles an acute epidemic disease."[19] That's because we do what we can—and we are quite effective—in wiping the pests out. But of course if the termite had human attributes, it wouldn't consider *itself* to be such a pest. If termites could talk, they might even call what they do "progress"! Indeed, though the earth is arranged in such a way as to sustain human life in particular, God's radius of concern may be large enough that it encompasses all the living creatures of the earth, including those that plague and pester humans.

Fighting Back

Granted, God placed us in the world alongside other creatures, but didn't he also make man the sovereign of all the creatures? Didn't God, at least according to the biblical account, put man in charge? Actually, he did, and we can see the evidence of this fact in our possessing a weapon of survival possessed by no other creature: reason. Humans can use reason to tame nature and to combat other creatures that pose threats to our welfare.

The best example of this is the effort to combat disease. Humans were once virtually defenseless against most diseases. There was simply no way to effectively control epidemics. Consequently, human life expectancy was much lower. And we suffered a lot more, even as late as the eighteenth and nineteenth centuries, when people around the world endured such diseases as tuberculosis, typhoid, cholera, malaria, smallpox, and a host of childhood diseases. These were prevalent not only in Asia and Africa but also in Europe: Darwin's family, for example, had virtually all the above-listed ailments, and they took their toll. Even milder natural enemies—like tooth decay, which is caused by bacteria—previously caused humans a great deal of distress.

All of this has dramatically changed in the past 150 years. The application of reason to nature has resulted in important scientific discoveries. Brushing your teeth with fluoride protects the teeth against bacterial infection and decay. Today some of the most lethal diseases of history are not the killers they once were. The discovery of penicillin and antibiotics has dramatically changed the balance of power between humans and disease-causing bacteria. Now humans have a technique for destroying bacteria that doesn't also harm the human host. Admittedly, the bacteria can fight back. Through high rates of reproduction and mutation, bacteria develop natural resistance to the antibiotics that are so lethal to them. Humans must then develop more elaborate and more lethal cocktails of drugs to battle these tougher, more resistant bacteria. The struggle for life goes on.[20] But the fact remains that on the human side, reason is being applied to the battle, and in most cases reason is what it takes to win.

We can use our reason so effectively because we live in a predictable and lawful world. We know why God has made such a world: in order to give scope to humans to exercise their freedom. But we are learning through science that lawful worlds are a package deal. Everything is woven together by a set of elaborate rules and dependencies; yank out a few threads, and the whole ball is likely to come apart. Thus it is simply unreasonable for us to ask of God that he exempt the world from earthquakes, tsunamis, and other natural disasters. We can continue to deplore calamities and wish that the world didn't have them—especially when we witness the devastating effect of a tsunami on a village or when we see it in our own lives with the loss of a loved one to a debilitating disease. But when we consider the alternative of a complete unraveling of the human life as we know it, we can begin to see that humanity as a whole is better off in a world that includes them. Evils they may be, but they are necessary evils in order for us to be here to deplore them.

CHAPTER 8

RED IN TOOTH AND CLAW

Evolution and Animal Pain

The God of the Galapagos is careless, wasteful,
indifferent, almost diabolical. He is certainly not the sort
of God to whom anyone would be inclined to pray.[1]

DAVID HULL, "THE GOD OF THE GALAPAGOS"

THE FEMALE PRAYING MANTIS is a very unromantic creature. This insect has the peculiar habit of feeding on the head of the male praying mantis while the male is mating with her. Obviously this makes courtship particularly challenging for the males! Cannibalism in nature is not limited to the praying mantis; it is also common among shark embryos, who sometimes eat each other while swimming about in their mother's uterus. Biologists also tell us that infanticide is prevalent in several animal species, notably prairie dogs. When lions acquire a new lioness who is nursing cubs from a different mate, the initial task of business is for the new male to kill those cubs. The first eagle chick born into a nest will often kill its younger siblings so as not to have to share food with them. Pelicans sometimes hatch an extra chick, called an insurance chick, just in case the other ones don't make it. If they do, however, the insurance chick is neglected and left to starve. And as Annie Dillard writes in *Pilgrim at Tinker Creek*, "Ants don't even have to catch their prey. They swarm over newly hatched, featherless birds in the nest and eat them tiny bite by bite."[2]

All this sounds very harsh and cruel. We don't have to be scientists—only observers of nature, or of the nature channel—to know that nature can be "red in tooth and claw," as Tennyson once put it. Here we are not just speaking of cannibalism and infanticide, but also about predation. Most animals seem in one way or another to end up in the stomachs of other animals.

Atheists seize upon this grim reality and cite it to show how bloodthirsty the law of nature is. This bloodthirstiness, they insist, is not incidental or random. Rather, it arises from a process of evolution that is a system based on violence and predation. I have noticed that when atheists discuss evolution in opposition to Intelligent Design proponents, they typically sound very positive and enthusiastic about what philosopher Daniel Dennett termed "Darwin's dangerous idea." In private, however, many scientists are ambivalent. It is not that they have doubts about evolution; it's that they are morally revolted by it. Writing a couple of decades ago, biologist George Williams could not contain his disgust: "With what other than condemnation," he wrote, "is a person with any moral sense supposed to respond to a system in which the ultimate purpose in life is to be better than your neighbor at getting genes into future generations, in which those successful genes provide the message that instructs the development of the next generation, in which that message is always 'exploit your environment, including your friends and relatives, so as to maximize our (genes') success'?"[3] And more than a century ago Charles Darwin, who discovered the theory of evolution, noticed that here was a way to question the wisdom of the Creator of nature, if indeed there was a Creator. Darwin once wrote in a letter to J. D. Hooker,

"What a book a devil's chaplain might write on the clumsy, wasteful, blundering, low and horridly cruel works of nature."[4]

To evaluate this apparently horrid cruelty, let's examine more closely what Darwin and Williams are saying. First, they are saying that evolution is the result of chance events—the stresses and challenges produced by the surrounding environment. Darwin didn't even know about genetics; if he did, he would have known about the further randomness of genetic mutations. Between genes and the environment, it seems as if the whole design of living creatures came about through chance. In the words of Jacques Monod, "Chance alone is at the source of every innovation, of all creation in the biosphere." As for man, we are the product of lucky accident. "Our number came up in the Monte Carlo game."[5] Could a loving God allow for the cruel chance of fate?

Second, Darwin and Williams are responding to the fact that evolution is based on vicious competition, not only between species, but often among creatures of the same species. Consider a herd of gazelles being stalked by a cheetah. Who are the gazelles competing with as they seek to elude the cheetah? They are competing against each other. The gazelles who survive don't have to outrun the cheetah; they have only to outrun the slowest gazelle in the herd. When you think about the very bodies of gazelles and cheetahs, you realize that the sleekness and speed of the cheetah are the result of a macabre natural preparation. In effect, the bodies of cheetahs have been shaped to kill gazelles and other antelopes. Richard Dawkins writes, "The teeth, claws, eyes, nose, leg muscles, backbone and brain of a cheetah are all precisely what we should expect if God's purpose in designing cheetahs was to maximize deaths among antelopes."[6]

Of course, gazelles and other antelopes have developed defenses against being eaten—they have, through natural selection, gotten faster over the years, and more adept at spotting predators—but cheetahs, too, have developed weapons to counter these defenses.

It is an evolutionary arms race in which the fittest usually survive, and the weak, the disabled, and the vulnerable are killed and eaten. Eaten! The philosopher Arthur Schopenhauer found this aspect of the process especially appalling. Schopenhauer wasn't just reacting to the idea of "nature red in tooth and claw." He noticed something that the poet Alfred Tennyson missed. Reflecting on the cheetah pursuing the gazelle, he saw that one animal is running for its dinner, while the other is running for its life. What an imbalance of stakes, and what a disproportion of gain and loss. Schopenhauer caustically wrote, "The pleasure in this world, it has been said, outweighs the pain; or, at any rate, there is an even balance between the two. If the reader wishes to see shortly whether this statement is true, let him compare the respective feelings of two animals, one of which is engaged in eating the other."[7]

So atheists find the cruelty of the natural world unacceptable, and here is the great irony. For 150 years, since the publication of Darwin's *Origin of Species*, there has been a great debate in the Christian world about whether evolution supplies an alternative explanation to divine fiat for the design of life—whether evolution precludes the possibility of a creator. Atheists like Richard Dawkins insist that, contrary to the religious notion of God as a divine watchmaker, evolution is the *blind* watchmaker. The genius of evolution, according to Dawkins, is that it makes life *appear* designed, whereas in reality it is adapted to its environment. Atheists contend that chance and natural selection can now explain what previously had to be attributed to God's direct hand. Ironically, some Christians reject the theory of evolution completely because of this line of reasoning—this *atheistic* line of reasoning. Some Christians embrace evolution in part, while others embrace it fully, and still others just don't really understand the discussion at all. But let us be clear that most scientists who are Christians believe in at least the general outlines of the evolutionary theory.

Much of this discussion is so familiar to us as to seem almost tedious by now. My objective here isn't to resolve this discussion about science and faith that has been going on for more than 150 years. But I would be remiss, in a book on theodicy, if I didn't address evolution in our discussion of pain and suffering because atheists use evolution as a battering ram against Christianity. I'm convinced atheists are foolishly charging against the wrong flank—and so, perhaps, are Christians.

What I am suggesting—and this idea has been growing in scientific circles—is that perhaps evolution is not such a strong argument against design after all. Is it not possible that God used the system of evolution to accomplish his design? In fact, it is entirely possible. All that Dawkins and company have shown is that instead of making creatures one by one, God devised a factory or mechanism for making creatures.

Think about this as an engineering problem. It is one thing for an engineer to make a machine that works one way in a very particular set of circumstances; most engineers would tell you that this is quite easy to do. It is a challenge of a different order, however, to create a machine or mechanism that not only replicates itself, but also has an inbuilt monitoring system that realigns and reconfigures the device to changing circumstances, and then passes on those beneficial adjustments to new machines. This is not a perfect analogy—living organisms aren't mere machines—but it's a good description of the magnitude of the design task involved. What Christians might have missed is that a God who makes a life-generating system is hardly a God less impressive than a God who makes each creature separately and distinctly.

What many atheists have missed, however, is that evolution, which provides no argument against the existence of God, does raise powerful questions about God's justice and mercy. In *Darwin's Dangerous Idea*, philosopher Daniel Dennett argues that "Darwin's idea is a universal solvent, capable of cutting right to the heart of everything in sight,"[8] but Dennett entirely misses evolution's implications of theodicy. Here is what Dennett could have said, had he thought of it: We live in a world in which organic design thrives on acute pain. This is not just the "way of the world"; this is the way in which living creatures in the world were literally made. It is a world in which the strong prey on the weak, a world in which survival itself is driven by unceasing predation, and in which nature itself is drenched in blood. What kind of God is this who gave us such a world? This difficulty is recognized by thoughtful Christians; theologian John Hick, for example, terms animal suffering "the most baffling aspect of the problem of evil."[9]

Francisco Ayala, a biologist and former Catholic priest, takes up the challenge and offers a surprising solution. In a recent book, *Darwin's Gift*, Ayala contends that evolution actually solves the problem of natural suffering. Darwin, he writes, has actually given a great gift to theology. How? Consider, Ayala says, some of the inadequacies and infirmities of the human body. The female birth canal is narrow, making childbirth a painful process; our eyes have blind spots; our jaws are often too small, requiring the removal of wisdom teeth. If these are anomalies, then consider the facts that our bones start weakening as we get older, we lose virility and fertility, there is diminished vision and reaction time, and even the brain atrophies. Certainly, all of this seems normal to us, but it is the very norm that we are questioning here. If God is an omnipotent engineer, why would he design such defective and deteriorating creatures?

Ayala's answer is that the defects and deterioration are not the fault of God; they are the fault of evolution. Evolution, he writes, doesn't start from scratch; it works with what is already there. So human limbs are modifications of the limbs of our arboreal ancestors, and in order to evolve a larger brain, *Homo sapiens* had to give up some of the advantages that other primates enjoyed.

A second example that Ayala considers is predation. He gives us a list of horrors that could have come straight from the atheist manual: predators who eat their prey alive, females of many species that devour their babies, cannibalism in the animal kingdom, and so on. If God were directly responsible for all this, Ayala concedes, he would have a lot to answer for. But what was previously attributed to "the Creator's faulty design" can now be attributed to "the clumsy ways of the evolutionary process." Ayala concludes, "Evolution, which at first had seemed to remove the need for God in the world, now has convincingly removed the need to explain the world's imperfections as failed outcomes of God's design."[10]

Ayala's solution, ingenious though it is, doesn't work. At least, it doesn't work in the way that it is presented. The reason was pointed out by William Dembski, a critic of evolution and an advocate of the so-called ID or Intelligent Design movement—though his argument here is a theological one and has nothing to do with the claims of ID. Dembski notes that from a religious believer's point of view, God either designed creatures directly or he designed them through the system of evolution. Either way, God is the designer, and therefore God is responsible for what he makes. An engineer who set up a factory that made defective and dangerous cars could hardly defend himself against criticism and lawsuits by saying, "Hey, it wasn't me. Blame all those defects and accidents on the factory." Dembski gives the example of a mugger. "What difference does it make if a mugger brutalizes someone with his own hands (i.e., uses direct means) or employs a vicious dog on a leash (i.e., uses indirect means) to do the same? The mugger is equally responsible in both cases." By the same reasoning, when it comes to how living creatures are made, "the buck always stops with the Creator."[11]

Yes, I agree that the buck does stop with the Creator. But here we can come to the rescue of Ayala's argument by situating it in a broader context.

The Lion and the Lamb

According to the Bible, predation was not the way things were originally designed—it was not the way life ought to be. There is no
predation depicted in Eden, and the ideal plan of God, as outlined
in Isaiah 11, is for the lion to lie down with the lamb, a picture of
the harmony of nature. The Fall, however, represented a triumph
of selfishness in that it revealed a desire on our part to live our way
rather than God's way. This selfishness, moreover, was reflected not
only in the human interaction with God but also in the way that
humans interacted with each other. Immediately following the eating
of the fruit, the man and the woman began to accuse each other, to
use their newfound independence as a form of power over the other.
So in response to man's choice, God seems to have given man a world
based on selfishness.

For the atheist, all of this may seem a bit far-fetched. This, however, should not be a concern. We are not trying to convince the
atheist that the Fall actually happened, or even that it's true; we are
merely saying that it's possible. Remember, possibility is all that we
need to meet the atheist challenge. What the atheist has been saying
all along is that there is something inconsistent in what the Christians believe, that there is a fundamental contradiction between the
Christian conception of God and, in this case, the bloodbath we
witness in the animal kingdom. What we are doing in response is to
invoke the central Christian doctrine of the Fall to show that there
is no necessary contradiction. We don't expect the atheist to accept
Christian doctrines; if he did, he would no longer be an atheist.
But we do expect him to see that, by the light of those doctrines,
the alleged inconsistency or contradiction within the Christian faith
does not exist.

For the Christian, of course, it matters a great deal whether these
things are true or not. And here's the problem. If the Fall explains

why God may have created an evolutionary world, then why did animals prey on each other for millennia before there were humans on the planet? Once again we turn to William Dembski, who has offered an original way to think about human history and time in order to account for this.

Dembski reminds us of the Christian view that God is outside of time, and so the operations of God in the world are not temporally determined. He asks us to recall what Christians believe about Jesus: does the saving grace of Christ's death only apply to those who lived during and after him, or does it also apply to those who came before? The emphatic Christian answer is that Christ died for the sins of all, those who lived before him and those who lived after. Yet if the effect of Christ's action can work backward as well as forward, Dembski asks, why can't this also be true of the effects of the Fall? God knew that we would fall. Therefore he devised a world from the outset that reflected the impact of that catastrophic human choice.[12] This is the world we live in, a world of self-aggrandizement and predation.

Notice that there is a close correspondence between human nature as depicted in evolution and in Christianity's view of things after the Fall. Both take a "low" view of human nature; both portray man as primarily motivated by selfishness. But more than this, evolution also suggests that life is endlessly creative and innovative, not merely reproducing itself but also generating, through the sweep of time and circumstance, new life forms. Philosopher John Haught says that God's Creation can be viewed not as a single event but as an ongoing process. "The God of evolution," Haught writes, "is an inexhaustible and unsettling source of *new* modes of being."[13]

Haught's argument builds upon one that was made many centuries prior to the evolution question by the church father Augustine. Augustine understood the book of Genesis to be speaking of two "moments" of Creation: an original or primary creation, and an ongoing process of creation. So for Augustine Creation was not a closed, six-day event but rather something that God continually does through the laws of nature.[14] Life is not static; it is embroiled in a process of unceasing novelty and innovation. Yet the novelty and innovation are themselves based on something that came before.

As with the ironic benefit of natural disaster discussed in the previous chapter, there is a beautiful harmony and continuity at work here, despite the predation and violence. Admittedly, the beauty of living creatures is a terrible beauty, purchased as it is with blood. As philosopher Holmes Rolston III puts it, "The cougar's fang has carved the limbs of the fleet-footed deer." Even in the safe confines of a zoo, we can literally see this: the delicate limbs and watchful eye of the fawn are formed out of danger and fraught with vulnerability; yet this is an essential part of its loveliness.

At the same time, all is not predation and violence: we can see in the animal kingdom many examples of serenity, contentment, and joy. See the lioness roll around with her cubs, or the dog lolling in the sun, or the squirrels dancing from tree to tree—nature's severity is unquestionably balanced by nature's bounty and prodigality. Darwin found his own qualms about the harshness of nature giving way to a kind of reverential awe at the beauty and creativity of the whole creative process. "There is grandeur in this view of life, with its several powers, having been originally breathed into a few forms or into one; and that, whilst this planet has gone cycling on according to the fixed law of gravity, from so simple a beginning endless forms most beautiful and most wonderful have been, and are being, evolved."[15]

Taking these various considerations into account, evolution can actually be seen as a unified theory that helps to account for the richness and diversity of life on this planet, with pain seemingly inextricably built into that system. This is a way of reviving Ayala's point that pain is not at all gratuitous but rather instrumentally serves the objective of fostering new life through time. Pain is, in this sense, creative and purposeful. Consider the example of the eagle's sharp eye or its soaring flight; both, scientists believe, have been shaped by evolution in order to enable the eagle to spot and speedily descend upon its prey. So too the lion's imperial roar is no mere sound effect; it is there to ward off rival lions and also to scare away other animals that might seek to make off with the lion's kill. Remarkably the characteristics that we most admire in nature are the product of a process that involves pain, an observation that has been made in many other realms than the scientific one by now. This is not to say that pain is the sole characteristic of animal life—far from it—but still it is true to say that without the pain, there would be none of these characteristics to admire.

Nor would we be around to admire them. Consider one telling example of the beneficial severity of nature, the extinction of the dinosaurs. Atheists routinely cite mass extinctions, of which this is the most famous, as evidence of nature's gratuitous cruelty. Besides the dinosaurs, we no longer have on the earth such remarkable creatures as the woolly mammoth, the mastodon, and the saber-toothed tiger. I "miss" them all, yet I confess that, ever since I was a child, I have been partial to the dinosaurs. My own existence, however—the existence of all mammals—is directly related to the extinction of the dinosaurs. Science estimates that the dinosaurs ruled the earth for 150 million years until they were wiped out sixty-five million years ago, possibly by an asteroid or comet that collided with the earth. "With the dinosaurs gone," Joel Primack and Nancy Ellen Abrams write, "our own mammalian ancestors were able to flourish."[16] What Primack and Abrams are suggesting is that it isn't reasonable to think that we could have a planet that is jointly inhabited by dinosaurs and humans. They had to go in order for us to show up.

The example of dinosaur extinction may lead one to believe that the emergence of complex life is something of a random accident. Biologist Stephen Jay Gould famously suggested that if we were to rewind the tape of life and run it again, we would assuredly not get creatures like us.[17] For a couple of decades this was the conventional wisdom among evolutionary biologists. But now this orthodoxy is being challenged by some of the world's leading scientists, including physicist Freeman Dyson, biologist Christian de Duve, and paleontologist Simon Conway Morris. These scholars point out that evolution shows an obvious progression: from no life to simple forms of life to complex life to rational creatures. Indeed, Dyson points out that this pattern of increasing complexity and order characterizes not just life but the universe itself. Dyson writes, "Before the intricate ordered patterns of life, with trees and butterflies and birds and humans, grew to cover our planet, the earth's surface was a boring unstructured landscape of rock and sand. And before the grand ordered structures of galaxies and stars existed, the universe was a rather uniform and disordered collection of atoms. What we see . . . is . . . the universe growing visibly more ordered . . . as it grows older."[18] That is, the universe did not give way to humans by chance, but by a preordered design.

Conway Morris argues that evolution running on separate tracks has nevertheless often converged on the same type of adaptive solution. He writes that eyes, for instance, have developed independently in multiple species. Even consciousness and mind—defined here as the ability to plan and solve problems—"have all evolved independently from different starting points to strikingly similar destinations." Certain types of birds, for instance, show a level of intelligence comparable to that of apes. All this development, Conway Morris insists, is from simplicity to ever-greater complexity: "What we do see through geological time is the emergence of more complex worlds."[19]

De Duve in his book *Vital Dust* portrays a tree of life "with its progressive rise toward greater complexity." At the root of the tree are the eubacteria and archaebacteria, then primitive eukaryotes and protists, then plants and fungi, then animals, and, at the very top of the tree, humans. De Duve writes about the "arrow of evolution" that proceeds through successive stages, from the "age of chemistry" to the "age of information" to the "age of the single cell" to the "age of multicellular organisms" and finally to the "age of the mind."[20]

These observations about the directionality of evolution lead to a deeper point made by philosopher Michael Ruse in a book examining the compatibility of Darwinism and Christianity. Ruse cites Richard Dawkins to the effect that there is no possibility of adaptive complexity for life without evolution. Natural selection is not optional; it is a requirement for the kind of intricacy and fecundity and diversity that we see among life forms on earth. If this is true, Ruse says that there does not seem to be another lawful way in the universe as we know it ever more deeply to make creatures like anteaters and ostriches and humans. According to Ruse, we know from biology today that, if the laws of nature or the environment were substantially different, then none of the creatures we now encounter would exist. In other words, if God wanted to create anteaters and ostriches and humans, he appears to have supplied precisely the appropriate ingredients and conditions for doing so.

If this argument is right, if there is no other way to create the beings that God wanted to create in the universe we actually inhabit with its own particular laws, then where is the merit in faulting the Creator as atheists do? Of course one might say that there is nothing great about anteaters or ostriches or even humans, that God should have gone with an entirely different palette of creatures. But that is about as nonsensical as saying that we would rather have been made as robots or zombies instead of humans. To opt out of the "bad" aspect of evolution and affirm the abundant complexity of life is akin to wanting earthquakes to be removed: ultimately this amounts to an advocacy of a process that would cause us not to exist at all.

So is it really true that there is no other way for God to have made a universe containing human beings? We'll explore this further in the next chapter. Right now, what we can conclude—and it is significant—is that no scientist or atheist has ever proposed an alternative scheme for doing this. And certainly the burden of proof for those who say that God should have done something other than he did is to show that this alternative option was actually available to God. No such burden has ever been met; no such project has even been attempted. We cannot argue based on fantasy about luxurious life without earthquakes and bedbugs and species predation; we have to argue based on what we actually know. Therefore, we can safely conclude that, based on existing knowledge, in order to produce creatures like us, the pain and violence we witness in the world, as Ruse writes, are "simply an inevitable tariff for achieving the desired end."[21]

The Caterpillar's Plight

But how high is this tariff that nature imposes on life? The philosopher René Descartes confronted the challenge that the magnitude of animal suffering in the world shows God to be cruel and merciless. Descartes offered an audacious reply on behalf of God. Animals, he said, don't hurt at all. According to Descartes, animals are different from people. Animals are a kind of machine; they are, you might say, an organic version of the car or the lawnmower. Now, if you crash a car or kick a lawnmower, it might make an unpleasant sound, but this is not because it feels pain. The sound just means the machine is broken or malfunctioning. So it is, Descartes implies, when an animal shrieks. We think that's a cry of pain, but actually it's just a case of machine malfunction.[22] Most people today, myself included, find this argument pretty appalling. It is the kind of argument that gives theodicy a bad name.

Yet if Descartes was wrong, what can we say about how much animals suffer and feel pain? Today we know a lot more about biology than Descartes did. And we can say that complex mammals like us feel pain the most. Some creatures, a little lower down on the complexity scale, feel pain a little. And many living creatures—perhaps most of them—suffer not at all. How can they? They aren't even conscious, nor do they have a nervous system. The paradox is that the more complex the organism—the more highly developed its consciousness—the more it suffers: that is to say, pain increases up the evolutionary scale.

Consider the humble caterpillar. Richard Dawkins is very concerned about caterpillars. He writes that "if Nature were kind, she would at least make the minor concession of anesthetizing caterpillars before they are eaten alive from within."[23] Dawkins must have been in a careless mood when he wrote this, because as a biologist he should know what his colleagues, who specialize in insects, have written about the subject. The topic is explored in an important review article, "Do Insects Feel Pain?" The authors note that insects do have a nervous system, but it's different from the one that humans have and lacks the nociceptors—the pain receptors—that enable humans to feel pain. True, insects could have alternative mechanisms for experiencing pain, but then they show none of the symptoms that we would expect if they do.

For instance, the authors of the article point out, if you severely injure an insect or rip out its body parts, "our experience has been that insects will continue with normal activities." The authors point to the example of a "locust which continued to feed whilst itself being eaten by a mantis; aphids continuing to feed whilst being eaten by coccinellids; a tsetse fly which flew in to feed although half-dissected; caterpillars which continue to feed whilst tachinid larvae bore into them . . . and male mantids which continue to mate as they are eaten by their partners." Bottom line: "On balance, . . . the evidence . . . of their behavior does not appear to support the occurrence in insects of a pain state, such as occurs in humans." Translation: we should not presume that the insect is responding as we would respond if someone were eating us from the inside or biting our head off.[24]

What about more complex creatures: do goldfish and seagulls and bats suffer? The truth is that we don't know. A couple of decades ago the philosopher Thomas Nagel published an interesting essay, "What Is It Like to Be a Bat?" When I first encountered the essay, my reaction was one of amusement. I thought to myself: look how these philosophers spend their time. I could just envision Nagel sitting around and cogitating about what his life would be like if he were a bat! But as I discovered upon actually reading his essay, Nagel was not asking what it is like for him, or for us, to put ourselves in the place of a bat; rather, he was asking what it is like for a bat to be a bat. Nagel's point is that we can never answer that question because there is no way for us to become bats.

Consequently we can only guess about what animals feel from the inside. Probably it makes sense to say that the less developed the nervous system, the less an animal feels pain. It seems reasonable to say that only higher animals endure pain. Still, this pain is limited because when it is caught by a predator, before the point of death, an animal typically goes into shock. Shock is indeed nature's anesthetic; it prevents the animal from feeling anything. If you watch the nature channel, pay attention to the expression of animals who are in the jaws of their predators. They seem utterly at peace, quite unfazed.

If this seems crazy, consider whether it would be the same if it were you or me. The highly complicated human being also goes into shock at such moments. Describing this familiar phenomenon, neuroscientist V. S. Ramachandran cites the famous example of the explorer David Livingstone, who was attacked by a lion. His arm was badly mauled, yet he felt neither pain nor fear. Livingstone reported that he felt removed from the whole incident, as if he were observing it from some distance away. Ramachandran explains, "During such dire emergencies, the anterior cingulate in the brain, part of the frontal lobes, becomes extremely active. This inhibits or temporarily shuts down the amygdala and other limbic emotional centers, so temporarily suppressing potentially disabling emotions such as anxiety and fear. But at the same time, the anterior cingulate activation generates extreme alertness and vigilance in preparation for any appropriate defensive reaction that might be required."[25] Which is to say that our survival instinct itself reduces the feeling of pain even as it readies us for any possibility of escape.

But there is a difference between the human and the animal response to pain and its attendant triggers. Perhaps one of the worst emotions that breaks down the human body is stress. "Stress," we repeatedly hear the doctors tell us, "is going to kill you." Yet ironically stress protects the lives of animals. "For the vast majority of beasts on this planet," psychologist Robert Sapolsky writes, "stress is about a short-term crisis, after which it's either over with or you're over with." Humans, Sapolsky writes, activate the same psychological responses, but they were not designed to be provoked on a regular basis. "Stress-related disease," Sapolsky argues, "emerges, predominantly, out of the fact that we so often activate a physiological system that has evolved for responding to acute physical emergencies, but we turn it on for months on end, worrying about mortgages, relationships, and promotions."[26] Animals, on the other hand, are much more "sensible" in using stress instinctively to protect their lives, while we use it in a manner that harms our health.

Another difference is that animals, unlike humans, do not seem to be able to anticipate death. This of course greatly reduces animal anxiety. The anticipation of pains and pleasures has the effect of heightening both; in a sense, we feel the sensation before it is actually upon us. For the animal, death is not a constant source of terror; rather, it is something that just happens.

In one of my debates against Bart Ehrman, I remember Ehrman giving as an example of nature's cruelty the case of a cat playfully dangling a mouse before killing it. In Ehrman's portrayal, the cat was a veritable torturer, a kind of Himmler cat. But in reality Ehrman was only displaying a theologian's ignorance of biology. Cats don't torture mice; this is pure anthropomorphism. The cat simply is holding the mouse in a way that we humans think is a "torture position." Moreover, the mouse doesn't feel terror. Here is more anthropomorphism: this is what we would feel if a predator were holding us in this threatening way. Unlike humans, mice actually seem unable to anticipate death. So Ehrman's example, even if it happened as he described, is a misreading of the whole episode.

Getting back to Thomas Nagel, Ehrman seems to be telling us what it would be like for Bart Ehrman to be a mouse, not what it is like for a mouse to be a mouse. Darwin says, "When we reflect on this struggle, we may console ourselves with the full belief that the war of nature is not incessant, that no fear is felt, that death is generally prompt, and that the vigorous, the healthy, and the happy survive and multiply."[27]

Some atheists raise the question of why humans must die at all, and they fault God for not giving creatures a much longer life, perhaps even a life that never ends. We'll discuss death and eternal life more fully in a later chapter, but here it's worth noting an interesting phenomenon: there are living creatures that do not actually die. Amoebas don't die; they just split in half. So one amoeba becomes two, and both continue on their merry way. This is interesting, but even more so is the fact that this constitutes asexual reproduction—and that the only earthly creatures that actually die are those that reproduce sexually. Yet at the same time, sexual reproduction guarantees true individuality. When creatures reproduce sexually, it ensures that their offspring are never exactly like either parent. What this means is that biologists have discovered that a creature's individuality—the quality of being totally unique—is in some way associated with natural processes of death. In other words, whether or not there is a theological reason for death, we must admit that based on natural scientific discoveries, there would be no death if

God simply wanted to make amoebas and other similar creatures. I for one am glad he didn't stop there.

Suffering versus Pain

For us as humans, there is a kind of sober lesson here, and not just about death but also about pain and suffering. We often use the terms *pain* and *suffering* synonymously, but they are not the same. Pain is physical, whereas suffering is mental. Pain is the sensation of hurting, while suffering is the consciousness of pain. Suffering also involves the anticipation of pain, the ability to feel pain even before it comes, as well as the reflective capacity to keep pain going even after the actual sensation of hurt passes. Suffering is often worse than pain. Illness, for instance, causes suffering not merely because of the physical hurt but also because it produces fear and anxiety: worries about finances and career and family, and also about how long this helplessness and dependence on others may last.

While animals feel pain, they do not *suffer*. Suffering in the full meaning of the term seems to be a distinctively human capacity. Now, God could have made a world without suffering if he had made a world without humans. Moreover, God could have avoided pain if he had created only amoebas, viruses, insects, and other lower creatures. It is difficult to imagine any human who would opt for that. Instead, God seems to have taken a different route. By creating complex life forms, God permitted higher forms of awareness, with necessarily more pain and suffering. Consequently we cannot regret the capacity for pain and suffering—we cannot even regret the amount of natural suffering in the world—without regretting the existence of the natural world itself.

Not surprisingly, we like to imagine a natural world like this one, minus pain and suffering. The scientific considerations we have discussed show this to be a child's fantasy, like imagining snow that isn't cold or sweets that never spoil—or, as we've seen, life without earthquakes and volcanoes. Equally unsurprising is the fact that we don't like pain. Pain hurts! But this is how it should be, because the purpose of pain is to teach us some important lessons. Pain is in fact nature's most efficacious instructor. Few people who have placed their hands on hot stoves or almost drowned have forgotten the experience and the lesson to be drawn from it. Even when our bodies are in pain from a wound, it is a message to us to stop and rest and let the wound heal: without the pain, we might continue with our activity and worsen or take longer to heal. The symptoms of illness, such as fever and headache, are likewise part of nature's health manual, and their message to us is slow down and take care of ourselves.

Consider the disease of leprosy: lepers don't feel pain, and this is very bad for them. That's because a person who doesn't feel pain can put his hand on a stove and just leave it there. Such a person can lose a finger without knowing it. Paul Brand, a physician who works with lepers, has written a book titled *Pain: The Gift Nobody Wants*. Brand notes that the truncated limbs of lepers are not the product of the leprosy itself; rather, they are the result of the lepers not being able to feel pain. "I now regard pain as one of the most remarkable design features of the human body," Brand writes, "and if I could choose one gift for my leprosy patients, it would be the gift of pain."[28] Brand's point is that we who experience pain don't know how valuable it is for us. Many of Brand's patients view the rest of us with envy; they wish they had the capacity to hurt more, because that would enable them to live safer, more protected lives.

Leprosy patients aren't the only ones who can appreciate the gift of pain. There are also people who suffer from congenital painlessness—they are unable to feel pain. Some patients who have diabetes and other nerve disorders are also in a similar condition. And then there is pain asymbolia, a strange condition in which people respond to pain stimuli not with grimaces or screams but with amusement and laughter. All such people may be deemed fortunate on account of their immunity to pain, but in fact they are very unfortunate. In a book on illness, Randolph Nesse and George Williams remark that "people who cannot feel pain are nearly all dead by age thirty."[29]

None of this is to try and convince anyone to enjoy pain, but rather to show that we can appreciate the role that pain plays in conserving our life and health. We have learned that pain is a fact of life, for humans as well as for animals, but not necessarily a gratuitous one. Rather, pain and suffering are built into the fabric of nature's laws. They contribute to the way in which nature creates novelty and beauty and us. The pain of animals is real, at least for the higher animals, and yet it is not the same kind of suffering that we endure as humans. Our pain is greater, and yet at the same time it is a reflection of our richer and more complex human capacities. Moreover, our pain is often useful to us, even when—indeed largely because—we don't like it. Nature may sometimes be red in tooth and claw, just as Tennyson suggested, but if we thought about it, we wouldn't, and couldn't, have it any other way. With regard to what we can discern by reason about the only world we can really know, pain and suffering are inextricably bound up with the good.

CHAPTER 9

A FINE-TUNED UNIVERSE

The Anthropic Principle

The more I examine the universe and study the details of
its architecture, the more evidence I find that the universe
in some sense must have known that we were coming.[1]
FREEMAN DYSON, *Disturbing the Universe*

ATHEISTS SEEM TO THINK that a better universe should be an easy thing
to build, especially if you are God. "There is no reason why better
laws of nature governing the existing objects are not possible. . . .
Surely if God is all-powerful, he could have made a better universe
in the first place, or one with better laws of nature governing it, so
that the operation of its laws did not produce calamities and pain."[2]
In the last two chapters, we have raised problems with this thesis by
looking at some specific things: earthquakes, tsunamis, disease, and
predation. We have seen why Earth needs to have special characteristics in order to sustain life. Truly we live on a biocentric planet, a
lucky planet, a life-sustaining planet, or, as we Christians might put
it, a providential planet. The evils and suffering that we endure here
on Earth are the necessary price for us as free and rational creatures
to inhabit this marvelous abode.

This argument, unassailable on its own terms, is, however, open to a serious objection, advanced by physicist Victor Stenger. Stenger argues that "since the universe contains hundreds of billions if not trillions of planets, then it would seem that the chance of finding one someplace with the right conditions for our kind of life would be pretty good." This for Stenger is hardly providential; it is merely a case of playing the odds. "We just happen to live on one suitable planet, having evolved to survive under its specific conditions."[3]

Of course we could still ask, "But why us? And why here?" Yet the answers are utterly obvious. It had to be us, and it had to be here. There is no one else around to raise the questions. In other words, we are the product of what scientists call a "selection effect." If tens of billions of stars, through some combination of forces, produce a few lucky outposts of conscious life, then only in those outposts will there be creatures who can marvel at their good fortune. Indeed, from the atheist point of view, the universe as a whole remains a testament to God's aimless architecture. "If God created the universe as a special place for humanity," Stenger writes, "he seems to have wasted an awfully large amount of space where humanity will never make an appearance." An atheist website sarcastically adds, "Only a Designer would have had the infinite wisdom to create vacant worlds that circle the Sun along with the earth; and also create immense discs of matter, and planets, that have been detected circling other stars, i.e., countless acres of presumably uninhabited and barren territory."[4]

At first glance, this atheist rebuttal seems to leave our theodicy untouched. After all, who cares if God built lots and lots of extra space? So what if God is an "overbuilder"? But what the atheist is really saying is that the way the universe is structured, with trillions of acres of empty real estate, shows that there is no solicitous architect responsible for constructing it. Moreover, even if there is a God, clearly he doesn't have a special concern for humanity. He did not make the world with us in mind. He may not have made us at all;

perhaps, through the luck of the draw, we just happened to show up on a lucky planet in a pointless universe. Perhaps our suffering can be explained as a consequence, and a necessary one, of the forces that brought us here. But God deserves no credit for those forces. If he is not to blame for our suffering, then neither does he deserve praise for our existence.

This chapter will be devoted to answering this argument. I will show that the Lucky Planet refutation is based on a fallacy. Yes, we do live on a lucky planet. In this respect there is a "selection effect." But modern science shows that the whole universe has to be as large as it is, and as old as it is, and to have the specific characteristics that it does, in order for us to be here. Regarding the universe, physicist John Barrow writes in *The Constants of Nature*, "Many of its most striking features—its vast size and huge age, the loneliness and darkness of space—are all necessary conditions for there to be intelligent observers like ourselves."[5] Incredible though it may seem, we now know that billions of years, and billions of stars, are all required for there to be just one lonely outpost of life on one single planet. We don't just inhabit a lucky planet; we inhabit a lucky universe. This is the Anthropic Principle, the principle of the fine-tuned universe. For several chapters now we have been pointing toward it; now we can finally get into it.

How You Got Here

Does it take a whole universe to make a human being? Yes, it does. If this seems preposterous, consider all the circumstances that it took to make you. If your parents hadn't come together when they did, contributing precisely that particular sperm and egg, you would not exist. Moreover, if your grandparents hadn't met and married, you wouldn't be here. In fact, if a single one of your ancestors had been childless, your existence would be impossible. Perhaps one of those ancestors migrated to America from England—if the Anglicans had not persecuted dissenting Protestants, this emigration would not have happened. In sum, literally millions of events and thousands of people were involved as necessary actors in your current existence on earth. "No big deal," you might say. "If things had happened differently, I might not exist, but someone else would." This is exactly my point, and it applies not just to you but to human beings in general. If the universe had been constructed differently, some other types of creatures might inhabit it, or possibly no creatures at all, but we can be sure that humans would not be around to interact with them.

Not only does it take a whole universe to make a human being; it takes one that is billions of years old, just like the one we live in now. Let's examine why this is so. Our bodies are made up of chemical elements, such as carbon, iron, and oxygen. Altogether the human body has around twenty-five elements. So where did these elements come from? Actually there was no carbon, iron, or oxygen in the early universe. When the universe was first formed, it contained mainly hydrogen and helium. Most of the other elements were formed later, either in deep interiors of stars or in exploding supernovas that ended the lives of massive stars.

"Medium-sized stars more massive than our sun," writes cosmologist Joel Primack, "produced the medium-weight atoms like carbon and nitrogen that make up more than 20 percent of the weight of your body." The carbon in particular "mostly came from planetary nebulas," which are gas clouds exhaled by so-called red giant stars. Dying stars or supernovas are responsible for blasting these elements within stars into space where they could form new stars, planets, and people. We are made of material ejected into the galaxy by the violent death throes of earlier stars, some of which exploded before the solar system formed nearly five billion years ago, and others that exploded only a few million years ago. "Stardust is thus part of our genealogy," concludes Primack. "Our bodies literally hold the entire history of the universe."[6]

That's how elements like oxygen were formed, but how did oxygen become available for us to breathe? For roughly half of the earth's history, the atmosphere had no oxygen but was full of noxious gases like carbon dioxide, methane, and ammonia. There are certain life forms, including plants and very simple creatures called extremophiles, that can survive in such an environment. But not you or me. Oxygen at its current level appeared much later through the process of photosynthesis, in which the energy of the sun converts carbon dioxide into organic compounds. Through photosynthesis, water is split into its components hydrogen and oxygen; hydrogen combines with carbon dioxide to form carbohydrates, and oxygen is released into the atmosphere as a by-product. Oxygen, however, doesn't last long because it is highly reactive and easily combines with other elements in a process called oxidation. Fortunately, we have plants to come to the rescue. Humans have enough oxygen to breathe because plants produce it faster than it is lost to the oxidation of iron and other minerals.

Since oxygen came late in the earth's history, we humans came late as well. We are among the complex creatures in the world that not only require oxygen to breathe but are also conscious. Consciousness is something we share with dogs and elephants, yet there are many other creatures that survive and reproduce and get along in the world without it. For us, of course, consciousness is the necessary but not sufficient prerequisite for free will. We cannot be free, rational creatures without also being conscious. And while no one understands exactly how consciousness arises in humans, what we do know is that it arises through the medium of highly complex brains.

Preconditions for Evolution

The human brain is an organ of almost stupefying complexity. No other creature has a brain whose size even remotely approaches that of the human, when measured in proportion to the size of the accompanying body. Brain size increases as creatures become more complex, and in this sense, humans can be viewed as the pinnacle of evolution. And since evolution shows a gradual pattern of development from very simple organisms like bacteria to more complex organisms like sea turtles and giraffes, and eventually humans, the universe and the earth both had to be billions of years old to give this process time to produce complex, conscious organisms like us. There is a critical point here. Atheists often invoke evolution as a master explanation for life, but evolution only explains the development of creatures that survive and reproduce in the world—it doesn't account for why we humans can also understand the world. "The ultimate measure of evolutionary 'value,'" writes Daniel Dennett, "is *fitness*—the capacity to replicate more successfully than the competition does."[7] None of our survival or mating skills—including our courtship skills, or the capacity to elude the wolves and the bears—requires us to be able to figure out the rotation of the planets or the behavior of stars in distant galaxies. Even the much heralded "selection effect" that I alluded to earlier in this chapter only accounts for the existence of creatures who can observe the world; it does not account for creatures who can also comprehend the world. Observation and understanding are two separate things. We might have been here, with eyes to see, and yet know nothing of how the universe began or how it functions. Yet in fact we do.

So there is a deep puzzle here, elegantly expressed by physicist Paul Davies: "Scientists themselves normally take it for granted that we live in a rational, ordered cosmos subject to precise laws that can be uncovered by human reasoning. Yet why this should be so remains a tantalizing mystery. Why should human beings have the ability to discover and understand the principles on which the universe runs?" Davies adds, "The existence of mind in some organism on some planet in the universe is surely a fact of fundamental significance. . . . Somehow the universe has engineered not just its own awareness, but also its own *comprehension*. Mindless, blundering atoms have conspired to make not just life, not just mind, but *understanding*. . . . This can be no trivial detail, no minor product of mindless, purposeless forces. We are truly meant to be here."[8]

Remarkably, this whole debate about the unique conditions in the universe that are required to produce life and specifically human life is only a few decades old. In 1973, the physicist Brandon Carter produced a seminal paper at a symposium honoring Copernicus's five-hundredth birthday. Most of the talk at the symposium was about how Copernicus had demonstrated that we humans do not occupy a privileged status in creation, nor does our planet have a privileged status in the universe. Carter amazed the audience by arguing the opposite. "Although our situation is not necessarily central," he said, "it is inevitably privileged to some extent." Integral to Carter's argument was not only the structure of the universe but also its location, by which Carter meant location in time as well as in space. For us to be here observing and comprehending the universe, Carter said, it has to be structured exactly the way that it is, and be as ancient as it is, and have us located pretty much precisely where we are. It was Carter who coined the term *Anthropic Principle* to describe this remarkable phenomenon of a universe fine-tuned for us, and the subject has been a hot issue in science ever since.

Since Carter's paper, there has been an impressive body of research concerning the Anthropic Principle. The central question, for this research as well as for Carter, is how the universe is constructed in such a way as to permit or even ensure the appearance of conscious, rational observers who can understand that universe. Let's begin by noting that the universe operates according to a whole set of numerical values. In particular, the universe has four known forces: the force of gravity, the electromagnetic force, the strong nuclear force, and the weak force. The universe also has numerous constants. These are the fixed values that describe the important relationships between things.

Now, all these laws and constants have very precise values; there are very specific numbers attached to each one of them. Yet physicist John Barrow writes that "we have never explained the numerical value of any of the constants of Nature. . . . The reason for their values remains a deeply hidden secret." What Barrow means is that there is no theory that generates these values, that shows why they have to be what they are. "So far, the only way we can know their values is by measuring them."[9]

Consider one of these constants of nature: the ratio of the mass of the proton to the electron. The proton is roughly 1,832 times more massive than the electron. As Barrow suggests, no one knows why this is so. But let's ask a different question: What if this ratio were different? What if the proton were seven thousand times more massive than the electron, or just two hundred times more massive? What would change if this were the case, if, in other words, the constants of nature were other than they are?

Physicist Paul Davies frames the question by way of an analogy. He imagines God sitting at a desk, at which are arranged some thirty different dials. Each dial is set precisely. If we enter the room, Davies says, and manipulate the dials—moving them even a very tiny bit— we would soon find that "the universe would be a very inhospitable place."[10] In other words, the dials have to be set exactly where they are. Otherwise, we would have no universe hospitable for life, and consequently no humans in that universe.

So what are the odds of these dials being randomly set to these "correct" values? John Barrow and Frank Tipler write in *The Anthropic Cosmological Principle*, "The present universe possesses features which are of infinitesimal probability amongst the entire range of possibilities." Astrophysicist Michael Turner puts it more vividly. "The precision," he writes, "is as if one could throw a dart across the entire universe and hit a bull's-eye one millimeter in diameter on the other side."[11]

First let's look at the force we all know about, the force of gravity. Shortly after the Big Bang, gravity pulled the atoms in the universe together into what eventually became stars and galaxies. This pull, however, had to be of a very precise strength. A stronger pull would have drawn all the atoms of the universe together into a single ball—the Big Bang would have ended in a Big Crunch. On the other hand, if gravity were even slightly weaker, so slightly weaker that your own body weight would only be reduced by a few grams, then the atoms in the universe would never have been drawn into stars and galaxies.

No stars means no sun, and no sun means no humans alive on planet earth. The force of gravity (in case you don't recall your introductory classes in science) is governed by the inverse square law, also discovered by Isaac Newton. The law says that the gravitational attraction between two objects varies directly in proportion to their mass and inversely in proportion to the square of the distance between them. So what if the inverse square law could be changed a little bit? Astronomer Carl Sagan writes, "It turns out that virtually any deviation from an exact inverse square law produces planetary orbits that are, in one way or another, unstable. An inverse cube law, for example . . . means that the planets would rapidly spiral into the Sun and be destroyed."[12]

In his book *A Brief History of Time*, physicist Stephen Hawking writes that the initial conditions for the universe—its density and its rate of expansion—would have to be very finely tuned for the formation of stars and planets and creatures like us. If the overall density of the universe were changed by even 0.0000000000001 percent, no stars or galaxies could have formed. Hawking adds, "If the rate of expansion one second after the big bang had been smaller by even one part in a hundred thousand million million, the universe would have recollapsed before it ever reached its present size."

Likewise, Hawking says, the other forces and constants are very precisely fine-tuned. "The remarkable fact is that the values of these numbers seem to have been very finely adjusted to make possible the development of life." Change the electric charge of the electron just a bit, he says, and "stars either would have been unable to burn hydrogen and helium, or else they would not have exploded." No stellar explosions, no planets; no planets, no us. Referring specifically to the Big Bang, Hawking concludes, "It would be very difficult to explain why the universe should have begun in just this way, except as the act of a God who intended to create beings like us."[13]

Six Providential Numbers

Perhaps the most comprehensive popular exposition of the Anthropic Principle is in astronomer Martin Rees's book *Just Six Numbers*. In this book Rees focuses on six crucial numbers. He does not hesitate to call these numbers "providential." They are, he says, the "recipe for a universe." None of the numbers, he writes, can be predicted from the values of the others. Moreover, "if any one of them were to be 'untuned,' there would be no stars and no life."

Let's look at a few of these providential numbers. One of the numbers is N, and its value is 1,000,000,000,000,000,000,000, 000,000,000,000,000. A big number. N measures the strength of the electrical forces binding atoms, divided by the force of the gravity between them. "If N had a few less zeros," Rees writes, "only a short-lived miniature universe could exist: no creatures could grow larger than insects, and there would be no time for biological evolution." Another is E, a number that specifies how strongly atomic nuclei hold together. E's numeric value describes the way stars form all the other elements of the periodic table out of hydrogen. Its value is 0.007. "If E were 0.006 or 0.008," Rees writes, "we could not exist." The origins of all cosmic structures, including stars and galaxies, can be traced back to the big bang. The structure of the universe depends on the number Q, which represents the ratio of two fundamental energies. Its value is around 0.00001. "If Q were even smaller, the universe would be inert and structureless; if Q were much larger, it would be a violent place, in which no stars or solar systems could survive, dominated by vast black holes."[14]

We could go on like this, but the point has been made. Electrons are fine-tuned, gravity is fine tuned, and the rate of expansion of the universe is fine-tuned. Astronomer Carl Sagan sums up the result: "If the laws of Nature and the physical constants—such as the speed of light, the electrical charge of the electron, the Newtonian gravitational constant, or Planck's quantum mechanical constant—had been different, the course of events leading to the origin of humans would never have transpired. . . . Different laws, no humans."[15]

There is a subtle point to be made in this context. Humans are in a position to understand the universe not just because we have conscious minds, but also because of our specific position in space and time. This is why, in his initial 1973 paper, Brandon Carter placed such a high emphasis on "location." We are, it happens, positioned in a galaxy that is a very good vantage point from which to observe the rest of creation. Michael Denton writes in *Nature's Destiny*, "Ironically our relatively peripheral position on the spiral arm of a rather ordinary galaxy is indeed rather fortunate. If we had been stationed in a more central position—say near the galactic hub—it is likely that our knowledge of the universe, of other galaxies, for example, might not have been as extensive. Perhaps in such a position the light from surrounding stars could well have blocked our view of intergalactic space. Perhaps astronomy and cosmology as we know these subjects would never have developed."[16]

Moreover, we are midsized creatures built, as cosmologist Joel Primack points out, "midway between the size of a living cell and the size of the Earth." Primack notes that "this turns out to be the only size that conscious beings like us could be." In addition, it turns out to be a very good size for us to perceive both very small things and very big things.[17]

In addition, we are living at a time when the data of the universe is available for human observation. Consider this: the universe is rapidly expanding, and so remote galaxies that we can now see will eventually have moved so far away from us that they will become unobservable. Even the evidence for the origins of the universe will eventually disappear, not because it will cease to exist, but because it will no longer be accessible to human observation. We live, Primack writes, in a "special window of time that can only happen during a relatively brief epoch in the entire history of the universe: late enough that intelligent beings have evolved who have instruments to observe the distant galaxies, but not so late that the galaxies have begun to disappear."[18] Thus to the coincidences that have shaped our existence we have to add another, and perhaps the most wonderful of all. Somehow the fine-tuning that produced a universe with complex living creatures has also produced the conditions for some of those creatures to observe and comprehend the universe.

Some scientists who are not religious believers are nevertheless deeply impressed. "It is hard to resist the impression," Paul Davies writes, "that the present structure of the universe, apparently so sensitive to minor alterations in the numbers, has been rather carefully thought out." He adds, "The seemingly miraculous concurrence of numerical values that nature has assigned to her fundamental constants must remain the most compelling evidence for an element of cosmic design." The astrophysicist Fred Hoyle, who used the Anthropic Principle to predict one of the previously unknown properties of carbon, bluntly states, "I do not believe that any scientist who examined the evidence would fail to draw the inference that the laws of nuclear physics have been deliberately designed with regard to the consequences they produce inside the stars. . . . A commonsense interpretation of the facts suggests that a super-intellect has monkeyed with physics, as well as with chemistry and biology, and that there are no blind forces worth speaking about in nature."

Astronomer Robert Jastrow called the Anthropic Principle "the most theistic result ever to come out of science."[19]

This is a bitter pill for the atheists! And, truth be told, it is hard medicine even for many scientists. In his book *The Cosmic Landscape*, physicist Leonard Susskind calls the Anthropic Principle "a huge embarrassment to physicists." Physicist Murray Gell-Mann says the idea of fine-tuning is "so ridiculous as to merit no further discussion."[20] This is not simply atheist bile. Many scientists are still deeply attached to the so-called Copernican view that human beings are peripheral to the overall scheme of creation. Moreover, many scientists want secular explanations for physical events. Now the fine-tuned universe is a problem because it raises the issue of a supernatural fine-tuner. As Susskind puts it, it provides "the false comfort of a creationist myth." Moreover, the Anthropic Principle undermines the Copernican view by showing that humans do matter, and that while Earth may seem like an ordinary, unimportant planet, in fact it is not ordinary or unimportant, because it is the only known outpost of life and mind. No wonder that the Anthropic Principle is giving fits to so many atheists, and also scientists like Gell-Mann.

A Selection Effect?

Instead of condemning it, atheists like Richard Dawkins and physicist Steven Weinberg seek to dismiss the Anthropic Principle by saying it is no big deal. Dawkins and Weinberg attempt to explain away the fine-tuned universe by invoking—you guessed it—the selection effect. "You don't have to invoke a benevolent designer to explain why we are one of the parts of the universe where life is possible," Weinberg writes. "In all the other parts of the universe there is no one to raise the question." Fine-tuning, Dawkins adds, "doesn't have to mean that the universe was deliberately made in order that we should exist. It need mean only that we are here, and we could not be in a universe that lacked the capability of producing us."[21]

The difficulty with Dawkins's argument is exposed by philosopher John Leslie. Leslie asks the question, Suppose a massive terrorist bomb exploded a few feet away from you. Given the extremely low odds of survival, wouldn't you be amazed to find yourself still alive? How impressed would you be with Dawkins's contention that there was nothing to warrant surprise? Obviously you had to have survived, because if you hadn't, you wouldn't be here to discuss the subject. Leslie's point is that your survival under the circumstances remains highly improbable and in need of explanation.[22]

Not only is fine-tuning invulnerable to such sophistry; it is also, as Dawkins probably knows, invulnerable to Darwinian assault. Evolution merely explains how life form A gave rise to life form B. Evolution doesn't account for why cells have the properties they do, including the property of self-replication. Evolution doesn't account for why the earth is old, or for why it contains dry land. Evolution doesn't explain why the universe contains the chemical elements that it does. Evolution doesn't account for why gravity is as strong as it is. In fact, all those things are necessary for evolution to operate in the first place. If those conditions weren't just right, there couldn't be evolution! Michael Denton states a fact whose obviousness does not reduce its significance: "The many vital mutual adaptations in the constituents of life were given by physics long before any living thing existed and long before natural selection could have begun to operate." Physicist John Wheeler puts it even more succinctly: "It is not only that man is adapted to the universe. The universe is adapted to man."[23]

Victor Stenger hates the fine-tuned universe, and he has devoted a good deal of his writing to attempts to debunk it. Most of Stenger's arguments are clumsy, such as his Lucky Planet thesis cited earlier in this chapter. One of his arguments, however, has some merit and is worth examining. Stenger acknowledges that the universe is finely tuned for carbon-based life, such as we find in humans and other animals. Yet it's quite possible, he suggests, for there to be other types of life in the universe. Perhaps there is silicon-based life, or something else that is so strange we cannot even look for it. "We can only speculate what form life might take on another planet, with different conditions."[24]

Yet even Stenger doesn't bother to speculate, probably because his speculations are likely to come out empty. Scientists know that carbon is ideally suited for life because of its ability to spontaneously form a large variety of compounds. Carbon compounds are perfectly balanced in that they are neither too stable nor too unstable. If they were too stable, they would not act and react in the chemical processes that biological growth and metabolism require; if they were too unstable, then they would routinely break down or never form in the first place. "This is not to say that other forms of life are impossible," John Barrow and Frank Tipler write, "just that these other forms could not evolve to advanced levels of organization by means of natural selection." While silicon-based life may fuel the imagination of science fiction writers, in fact "silicon could not replace carbon in any biosphere."[25]

But even if Barrow and Tippler are wrong, even if there may be other types of living creatures somewhere, none of this is relevant to my argument. Let's be clear on what has been said up to this point. My argument is not that human life is the only form of life in the universe; we have to admit that this is unknown. Rather, what I am saying is that the universe must be the way it is in order to foster human beings. That's a different claim, and that's the one that matters to this argument. I am not trying to prove that God made only us and no other kinds of intelligent creatures. I am trying to prove that, if God wanted to make us, he constructed the universe in the necessary way to get that result. Whether these same laws of nature allow the existence of other, perhaps silicon-based, creatures or whether God also chose to make other creatures in the Andromeda

Galaxy—none of this makes any difference to our theodicy. We are, after all, advancing a theodicy for human beings who suffer; we are not primarily concerned about the fate of possible extraterrestrials.

Physicists Alejandro Jenkins and Gilad Perez also detest the concept of the fine-tuned universe, and in a recent issue of *Scientific American* they attempt their own refutation. The fallacy of the fine-tuning argument, they say, is that scientists typically examine the consequences for life if a single parameter, say the gravitational force, is changed or tweaked. "But there is no reason why one should tweak only one parameter at a time." Consequently, Jenkins and Perez attempt to juggle the forces of nature to see if they can still come up with solutions that permit life. And they contend that they have. There are other universes, they say, that might do with a stronger or weaker gravitational force as long as other forces are also adjusted to compensate for this change. But then the authors blow their inquiry by admitting that "one quality still seems to be fine-tuned to an extraordinary degree: the cosmological constant, which represents the amount of energy embodied in empty space." This is a biggie: "A deviation in even the one-hundredth decimal place would lead to a universe without any significant structure."[26] So Jenkins and Perez need to go back to the drawing board.

The Many Universes Solution

Perhaps the most intelligent critic of the fine-tuned universe is physicist Stephen Hawking, and in his recent book, *The Grand Design*, Hawking joins other scientists in finding a different "solution" to the Anthropic problem. Hawking contends that the fine-tuned universe can be accounted for without having to resort to God. Hawking's explanation works if there is not a single universe but multiple universes. Hawking posits trillions of universes—actually an infinity of universes—all combined into what may be called a multiverse. "The multiverse concept," writes Hawking, along with coauthor Leonard

Mlodinow, "can explain the fine-tuning of physical law without the need for a benevolent creator who made the universe for our benefit."[27]

The idea of other universes is not a new one; earlier in this book, we saw that Leibniz argued for the possibility of other worlds—worlds that God did not create. Moreover, the contemporary concept of multiple universes comes in different versions. There is Hawking's version: a multiverse subdivided into innumerable "local" universes. Other physicists have advanced the idea of innumerable worlds, competing with each other in a strange imitation of Darwinian natural selection, with some worlds surviving and other disappearing. Then there is Carl Sagan's version, which draws heavily from a theory arising out of quantum physics: "If at every micro-instant of time the universe splits into alternate universes in which things go differently, and that if there is . . . an enormously, tremendously large, perhaps infinitely large, array of other universes with other laws of nature and other constants, then our existence is not really that remarkable."[28]

Wow, Dorothy, we are definitely not in Kansas anymore. This is the rarified atmosphere of modern physics and cosmology, where even bizarre ideas like these are avidly discussed. And granted, there is logical consistency to what Hawking and Sagan are saying; such suggestions are within the mainstream of contemporary science. Even so, how plausible are such claims? Let's explore the argument more closely by way of an analogy. Imagine if you enter thirty state lotteries—one contest representing each of the constants or "dials" of the universe. Incredibly, you win all the lotteries. The odds of winning a single one are infinitesimal. And if someone were to win thirty in a row, then you would know that there is a plot. Someone has "fixed" the lotteries. This is utterly obvious. Now imagine that you are being prosecuted for participating in this fraud. You call on Hawking and Sagan as expert witnesses. They grant to the jury that your thirty-win streak looks impossible. But what if, they suggest, there are millions of universes and each of them has state lotteries? True, in a single universe the probability of so many wins in a row may seem preposterous. But in an infinity of universes, even extremely unlikely events occur sometime. And so, ladies and gentlemen, we have "explained" the anomaly. The multiverse concept has accounted for how you won thirty state lotteries in a row. Do you see a jury going for this? I don't.

Of course the multiverse argument would seem less implausible if there were empirical evidence for the existence of universes other than our own. Advocates of multiple universes, such as Hawking and Mlodinow, agree that there isn't. Most scientists seem to hold that we will never have empirical evidence for other universes. That is because if there are universes other than our own, they are likely to have laws that are different from the laws that govern our universe. Consequently those universes would be inaccessible to us; we would have no way of finding out about them. A multiverse enthusiast must hold that they exist largely on the basis of faith.

Despite Hawking's impressive pedigree, many leading scientists remain dissuaded by multiverse since the concept seeks to account for the peculiarities of one universe by positing trillions of universes, Davies calls it "a case of excess baggage carried to the extreme." Another physicist, Lee Smolin, remarks of the multiverse: "The problem with this is that it makes it possible to explain almost anything. . . . To argue this way is not to reason, it is simply to give up looking for a rational explanation."[29] As for me, I find the whole debate over the multiverse quite amusing. In order to abolish one invisible God, Hawking and his pals have to conjure up an infinity of invisible universes. At the same time, I am intrigued by the multiverse and recognize that it is a concept that is taken seriously by physicists and astronomers. So I am going to take it seriously as well.

Incidentally, even if it were true, the multiverse "solution" may not really solve the fine-tuning problem completely. Why? Because some physicists now suggest that even the conditions that would generate multiple universes have to be fine-tuned. Moreover, the universes that contained any form of life would have to be specifically fine-tuned for that form of life.[30] These caveats may seem trivial, but they are significant for two reasons. First, they suggest that the fine-tuning problem has not really been solved. All that multiverse theorists have done, in fact, is pushed it onto a larger, unacknowledged framework that produces other universes. Religious believers who are advocates of "design" can continue to say that a fine-tuned multiverse points to a supernatural fine-tuner.

But this is not the implication that interests me. Rather, I want to focus on a second implication of fine-tuning in the multiverse, one that is especially relevant to the issue of theodicy. If there are multiple universes, then physicists tell us that the vast, vast majority of them would be devoid of life. Only in a very few and far-between cases might there be universes that have living creatures, and in even fewer might there be universes that have conscious, rational creatures. Let us postulate, for the purposes of argument, that there are such universes and such creatures; leave aside the issue of what they are made of and how they function. Here is the key point: in those rare universes, there would also be lawful physical constraints. For instance, physicists insist that the Second Law of Thermodynamics, which is a law of order and disorder, a law that says that things inevitably break down, would apply throughout the multiverse. So all universes would contain decay and dissolution—in other words, death.

Moreover, life in any other universe, just like life in this world, would be subject to a whole set of prerequisites and preconditions; without those conditions, it could not exist. Certainly in other universes, or other pockets of the multiverse, there might not be earthquakes or tsunamis or malaria, but there would be other restrictions and limitations that would cause suffering—assuming of course that there were conscious creatures capable of experiencing suffering. Moreover, if those creatures were rational and free, as we are, then they would also be capable of moral evil, and this means they would be capable of hurting each other. Here is the bottom line on all scientifically feasible concepts of the multiverse: there is likely to be a good deal of evil and suffering in any universe that operates according to laws and has in it creatures with free will. Far from undermining our theodicy, multiple universes actually help us to make our case even more comprehensively.

Let's come back down to earth—or perhaps I should say, let's return to the only universe we actually know about: our own. I acknowledge that there is an ongoing debate about whether fine-tuning points to a divine creator. That remains controversial, as we have seen. What is not controversial in science, however, is the idea that if we are going to have a lawful universe that produces human beings like us, then it would have to be designed in precisely this way. In other words, there is only one recipe that lawfully produces planets and platypuses and people. Consequently it is reasonable to suppose that if God wanted to make creatures like you and me, there was, as far as we can tell, only one formula available to him. And he used it.

Our universe is a very big place, a very old place, and an occasionally violent and dangerous place. We survive precariously in it. Still, it was constructed according to a design that was required for our existence. No other design, to the best of our knowledge, could have produced the same result. It follows that if there is a God, he wanted this universe with beings like us living in it. He didn't make any kind of universe; he made a universe that would foster creatures who could recognize not only the design of the universe but who could contemplate, and perhaps enter into a relationship with, their Creator.

The Spandrels of Nature

Natural suffering is part of this universe, so is this suffering something that God must have intended for man and other creatures? Not necessarily. Just because something is part of the architectural framework doesn't mean that it was intended by the architect. This is a crucial point: just as man's use of free will can produce results that were not part of God's plan or purpose, so the necessary structure of the universe can result in miseries that were also not intended by God. Perhaps natural suffering is incidental baggage, a kind of uninvited traveler. We can understand this admittedly odd notion of suffering hitching a ride on God's plan by considering an analogy supplied in another context by two prominent scientists, Stephen Jay Gould and Richard Lewontin. The two wrote an essay with the intriguing title, "The Spandrels of San Marco and the Panglossian Paradigm." In this essay the authors introduce the architectural concept of spandrels to the scientific discussion.

Spandrels are the triangular spaces formed by the intersection of rounded arches. And in the San Marco Cathedral in Venice, where we see a beautiful dome mounted on rounded arches, there are many beautiful spandrels, each with an elaborate design fitted to its space. "The design is so elaborate, harmonious, and purposeful," the authors write, "that we are tempted to view it as the starting point of any analysis, as the cause in some sense of the surrounding architecture. But this would invert the proper path of analysis." In reality, the authors say, the architects wanted to place a dome upon rounded arches, and when you do that, you necessarily get spandrels. Spandrels are a by-product of the design, but they are not necessarily an intended part of the architectural blueprint.[31]

I cite this example because I think that much of the natural suffering in the universe can be regarded as a spandrel. No, pain is not a spandrel. We saw in the previous chapter that pain is needed as a physiological alarm system to protect the body against serious harm. Suffering, however, can outstrip pain. In such cases, suffering can be viewed as an epiphenomenal by-product of the way in which the universe is constructed. Certainly the Architect knew it would be there, but in order to build the universe in this way, God is constrained in somewhat the same way as the architects of San

Marco. Those architects wanted to place a dome on rounded arches, and in the process they got spandrels. This, by the way, is not the result of the architects having limited power or resources; even if they were omnipotent, they would still get spandrels. Why? Because spandrels are a necessary outcome of geometry: by the very nature of a straight line and a half circle, if you rest a line or beam on two half-circles (or arches), you get a spandrel space, consisting of two back-to-back right triangles, each with a circle's arc for its hypotenuse. Similarly, even an omnipotent God who wants to make creatures like us may have no choice but to design a universe that contains a certain amount of natural suffering. I'm not suggesting for a moment that suffering is beautiful, in the manner of the decorated spandrels in San Marco. But it may be that suffering is unavoidable, just one of those spandrels of nature that is required by the overall scheme of the divine Architect.

Whether we regard suffering as divinely intended or not, the main point is that it is not a dispensable part of the universe. Rather, the suffering is a necessary ingredient to the recipe; were there no suffering, there would be no laws of this sort, and consequently, no creatures like us. It is time for a restatement of what should now be our understanding of God's objectives: he allowed natural suffering in the form of earthquakes, disease, and predation because they are part of the formula for achieving a natural good; namely, conscious, intelligent, and free humans. Moreover, the moral evil perpetrated by those humans is the direct outcome of God having made free creatures with the capacity for moral evil and moral good. Certainly the moral evil is avoidable, but it is only avoidable by the humans who are doing it. It is not avoidable by God, at least not unless he wants to take away human freedom. And of course moral evil, like earthquakes and cancer, adds to the toll of human suffering.

We can see from this understanding of God's purposes and God's actions that human suffering is not gratuitous but necessary, not only from God's point of view but also from ours. We are talking about suffering in the world, our world, not some imaginary, impossible world of science fiction or atheist daydreaming. Nor are we talking about the world of Eden, or the perfect new creation promised to believers in Christ. I will say more about heaven later, but so far we have been talking about the world as it is, the world as we understand it on the basis of reason alone. If this universe is worth it, if our particular type of life in this particular universe is worth it, then the suffering must also be worth it, because it is part of the whole. Suffering will continue to cause grief, as it always has, but perhaps this grief can now be accompanied by understanding, an understanding that if we are to exist at all, then this is the best—which is to say the only—way things can be.

PART 5

The Character of God

CHAPTER 10

CREATE OR NOT

Does God Hate Amputees?

You can also look upon our life as an episode unprofitably
disturbing the blessed calm of nothingness.[1]
ARTHUR SCHOPENHAUER, "ON THE
SUFFERING OF THE WORLD"

UP TO THIS POINT, we have attempted to show how evil and suffering
are inextricably bound with the structure of creation, and the reason
God made it that way. But we still haven't examined the underlying
question: Should God have created at all? God obviously didn't have
to create. He is recognized by believers as self-sufficient, so creation
didn't fulfill some burning need. God created because he wanted to,
not because he had to. So perhaps God should have abstained.

The issue of whether God should have left well enough alone is
taken up by the philosopher Arthur Schopenhauer. Now, I never
read Schopenhauer except when I am in a very good mood. If I start
out feeling good, Schopenhauer can bring me down to normal; were
I to take him up in a dejected frame of mind, I don't know what
state he would leave me in. Schopenhauer is the great philosopher

of pessimism. He isn't just a pessimist; lots of people are pessimists. Indeed the world seems roughly evenly divided into optimists and pessimists, those who see the glass half-full and those who see it half-empty. Schopenhauer, however, invests an enormous amount of thought and intelligence into his pessimism. He tells us why we should recognize that life is not worth living.

When we are young, Schopenhauer says, we look upon life with excitement and eagerness. We are "like children sitting before the curtain in a theatre, in happy and tense anticipation." Then Schopenhauer adds, "Luckily we do not know what really will appear." So the positive anticipation is unwarranted, and indeed it turns out to be short lived. Soon we discover what life is actually like. Then, says Schopenhauer, we realize that children are simply deluded, "sentenced not to death but to life," although they have "not yet discovered what their punishment will consist of." When we reach middle age, Schopenhauer says, the honest person will have to admit that, on the balance, life is a disappointment, even a bit of a betrayal. Schopenhauer writes that, if two men who were friends in childhood meet a generation later, their main feeling, stirred up by their recollections, will be one of "total disappointment with the whole of life. . . . This feeling will dominate so decidedly over every other that they will not even think it necessary to speak of it but will silently assume it as the basis of their conversation."

Deflating stuff. Schopenhauer shows us the relevance of his pessimism to our inquiry when he writes that, contrary to Leibniz, we live in the "worst of all possible worlds." Indeed, life in the world feels like inhabiting "a penitentiary, a sort of penal colony." If God actually created the world, Schopenhauer concludes, then he has made a dreadful mistake. "It would have been so much better not to have made it at all."[2] Nonexistence rather than existence: what an idea! Still, it's worth asking, if the world is a package deal, if free will for man means the choice to do good or evil, and if natural suffering comes built into the infrastructure of nature and of evolution, well, then is the whole thing worth it? Did God do us a favor by creating us, or would he have done us a greater favor not to have created us in the first place?

To answer this question, it might help to try an exercise in reflecting on your life. Make a list of the really bad things that have happened to you. Don't focus on the things that are your fault, though; enumerate all the unfair and terrible injustices you have suffered, either at the hands of others or through unavoidable calamity. Don't leave anything out; go ahead and show us all your scars. Do this for the past year, and then do it for your whole life. Now make a second list, and here I'd like you to put down all the really good things that have happened to you. Again, let's not focus on the rewards of your own efforts, on the successes you feel you have merited. Rather, enumerate, as far back as you can remember, all the sublime and wonderful and hilarious experiences that you've had. I did this recently, and I found that my "good" list vastly outweighed my "bad" list. In fact, it was no contest. And I suspect that for the vast majority of people, positive experiences will be common and bad experiences relatively rare. The point here is that by the irrefutable test of experience, life for most of us is a very good thing, and thus our overall response to it is not regret but gratitude.

Experiences, however, are personal and anecdotal. Can Schopenhauer's eloquent pessimism be refuted for the species as a whole? I believe it can by considering the collective judgment of the human race. Here we don't examine what people do; we focus on what they don't do. Consider this: the human race now has the power to obliterate itself. Through a series of nuclear explosions strategically deployed, we can wipe out the whole species. Yet no one, as far as I know, has even proposed this. Were someone to do so, he would immediately be considered a deranged lunatic. Yet this attitude is instructive: it means that all sensible humans consider life to be a net positive, such that the very idea of bringing it to a voluntary end is not even worth discussing. So obviously the whole thing is worth it, and obviously God did us a favor by creating us.

The same attitude holds in the vast, vast majority of individual minds. Alluding to the philosopher Hobbes's famous quotation, Susan Neiman raises an interesting question: "If life is solitary, poor, nasty, and brutish, who can complain if it's short?" Yet Neiman adds, "But complain we do, without stint or measure."[3]

Old people feel keenly the hardship of life, yet very few of them take their own lives. Much more common is the sight of folks who seem to have nothing to live for clinging on to life as if it were their most precious possession, as indeed it is. This perspective may seem distorted, but I don't think so. On the contrary, it is suffering that distorts perspective, at least for those who are not habituated to it. Schopenhauer himself gives the example of a person who is serenely happy and in perfect health until he suffers a single annoyance, such as a blemish on the face or an itch on the back. Schopenhauer notes that this single annoyance will occupy the person's full attention and all thoughts of happiness or contentment will be banished until the problem is addressed.[4] Older people, however, have a wider angle of vision. Beset with problems that don't go away, they tend to take in life as a whole. When they do, they realize that their hardships are counterbalanced by their quotidian pleasures. Moreover, their lives are enriched by their storehouses of memory. Memory has the peculiar facility of converting past pains into cherished recollections.

Leibniz writes in *Theodicy*, "Had we not the knowledge of the life to come, I believe there would be few persons who, being at the point of death, were not content to take up life again, on condition of passing through the same amount of good and evil, provided always that it were not the same kind: one would be content with variety, without requiring a better condition than that wherein one had been."[5] The same point is made in a different way by Rousseau, responding to Voltaire's gloomy meditations in the aftermath of the Lisbon earthquake. We all face times of hardship in life, Rousseau said, but we have to judge our lives as a whole. "In the ordinary course of events," Rousseau wrote, "no matter what evils are scattered through our lives, life is not, all in all, a bad thing to be given." Then he added, "Now if it is better for us to live than not to live, then that's enough to justify our existence."[6]

An Advocate for Amputees

While this may settle the case for humans in general, it doesn't do so for individuals who suffer extreme hardship, and those persons will be the focus of the rest of this chapter. Recently I was accosted at a debate by an angry atheist who shouted at me, during the question and answer session, "Mr. D'Souza, answer me if you can. What does God have against amputees?" At first I did not respond, not knowing what the man was saying. He explained, "God is supposed to have done miracles, and some people say he still does them. So why doesn't God heal amputees?" The man wore an expression of gleeful triumph on his face. Earnestly I studied him, looking for his missing arm or leg. But he was perfectly normal, a normal fellow with an evident passion for divinely neglected amputees! Subsequently I discovered that atheists have a special website devoted to amputees. It's called whydoesgodhateamputees.com. The founder of the site, one Marshall Brain, urges a global prayer campaign to petition God to restore the limbs of the world's amputees. "Even with millions of people praying," Brain confidently assures us, "nothing will happen." After all, "there is no documented case of an amputated leg being restored spontaneously."[7] From this, Brain derives his sober conclusion. You heard it before: God hates amputees.

Hate is a pretty strong word. Before we go along with it, let's ask a few pertinent questions. An amputee may lack an arm or a leg, perhaps both arms or both legs, but he or she still typically has the rest of his body and faculties. If a missing limb is evidence that God hates this person, is a beating heart and a well-functioning pancreas evidence that God loves him? In other words, if evil and suffering constitute evidence against God, shouldn't goodness and blessings count as evidence for him? The atheist seems to think that all the amputee's benefits and pleasures are fully deserved, while all his troubles and pains are God's fault.

"I cannot focus on God's blessings," the amputee may say, "because all my attention is occupied by my deformity." We'll come back to this, but for now, let's give this person the benefit of the doubt. Let's assume that his deformity has him so distraught that no blessings are evident in that person's life. Still, cases of amputees are rare, so we'd be dealing with an atypical situation. Even in the Islamic world, where the Koran prescribes that thieves have their hands or legs cut off, there is a remarkable paucity of one-legged and one-armed people walking around! In any case, my broader point is that the very example of amputees proves that when we indict God in this way, we are doing so on the basis of the exception, not the norm. Even if we broaden our inquiry to cover deformed people in general, the fact remains that such cases are relatively uncommon. Our emphasis on abnormal situations shows that in normal cases, the balance seems decisively on the side of life being worth whatever price is paid in hardship and suffering.

In his work *Pensées*, Pascal enlarges our perspective by asking, "Who is miserable for only having one mouth? And who would not be miserable for only having one eye? Perhaps we have never considered the idea of being distressed at not having three eyes, but without any at all we are inconsolable."[8] Pascal's point is that if the norm for humans was for each person to have only one hand, probably no one would be disturbed about not having two hands. The amputee's complaint is not about how little he has, but about how little he has compared to everyone else. This raises a legitimate issue of God's distributive justice, but notice that it does not imply that on the whole the amputee's life is not worth living. Studies of people who suffer serious disability and have chronic pain show that 14 percent have contemplated suicide and 8 percent have attempted it.[9] Eight percent may seem like a lot—it is a lot compared with a suicide rate in the United States of 0.01 percent—but I am still struck by the fact that 92 percent of people in this condition have never tried to take their lives, and 86 percent haven't even considered it. The disabled and chronically ill may be disadvantaged compared to everyone else, but they recognize they are better off compared to not existing. Facing Alzheimer's disease, Ronald Reagan was once asked on his birthday how he felt about turning seventy-nine. "Pretty good," he said, "considering the alternative."

What God Owes His Creatures

Yet Reagan wasn't severely disabled, as amputees are. So let's honestly pursue the issue of God's justice and ask, has God wronged amputees, in comparison with the rest of us, so that we can legitimately say that God hates amputees? Let's begin our inquiry by asking what right creatures have to live. Can we assert a "right to life" against God? Recently I came across some interesting data on life expectancy in *Scientific American*. I discovered there that chimpanzees and horses can expect to live around sixty years, cats and bats around thirty to thirty-five years, mountain lions and jackrabbits around fifteen years, mice around four years, dragonflies around four months, and mayflies just one day.[10] So is God being unfair to cats by giving them a shorter life than chimpanzees? Do mice have a raw deal by getting less than half the life span of mountain lions? And does the poor mayfly have the strongest case of all, being confined to a life expectancy of a single day? If the answer to these questions is no, then on natural grounds, we have no cause for complaint.

As for believers, the Bible insists that creatures have no such claims on their creator. Paul writes in Romans 9:20-21, "Should the thing that was created say to the one who created it, 'Why have you made me like this?' When a potter makes jars out of clay, doesn't he have a right to use the same lump of clay to make one jar for decoration and another to throw garbage into?" This is clearly a rhetorical question; obviously the potter can do what he wants with the clay. Job, too, understands that despite his protests he doesn't have any real case against God. In Job 1:21, he says, "I came naked from my mother's womb, and I will be naked when I leave. The LORD gave me what I had, and the LORD has taken it away. Praise the name of the LORD!" Even Abraham utters not a word of protest when God asks him to sacrifice his son Isaac. Why? Because Abraham understands that God stands in an analogous, indeed in a higher, position over Abraham than Abraham stands over Isaac. God gave Abraham the boy, and God has every right to ask for him back.

The question of what God owes his creatures is taken up in an important essay by the philosopher Robert Merrihew Adams. Adams asks, "Must God create the best?" In other words, let's say that God can create a world in which everyone has normal health and there are no amputees. Or he can create a world in which most people have all their limbs but some are amputees. Adams asks, does God have a moral obligation to create the first world and not the second? To this question, Adams answers with a resounding no. Why? Because uncreated or potential beings have no rights against their would-be creator. The only legitimate question for a created being to ask is, Am I better off than I would have been if I didn't exist? If the answer is yes, then for that creature the issue is settled. God has not wronged that person or abrogated his rights.[11]

Notice we are not considering the reasons why God may have decided to go with a second-best creation, or a creation that imposes special hardships on some creatures. Rather, we are saying that even if God had no reasons, even if it was simply his will, still the creature with the hardship has no legitimate grievance against God. What has any creature done for God to impose on God the obligation to give that creature even a single hour of life? God's gift of life is clearly his to give, and whatever he gives is better than the creature would have had otherwise. God in his plentitude has every right to create a multitude of beings, each in its time, each endowed with different attributes, each having its own given span of existence.

Moreover, within each species, God likewise is fully justified in giving some more strength, speed, and even duration of life than others. Just because some other people have more, what cause do we have for complaint? After all, still others have even less than we do. Moreover, we have done nothing to earn any of it. With what ingratitude do we spurn what is, after all, a free gift? Merely because the giver has been more generous with someone else? Interestingly, atheists never seem to complain that God has given anyone more than he deserves, even though God has in fact given every single creature more than it deserves.

Adams takes the point even further when he asks, if we consider our own existence on balance to be a good thing, then how can we regret the circumstances, however harsh and painful, that have brought it about? Consider the Irish American family that is today living a full and hearty life in America. We can listen patiently to this family's account of all the hardship and suffering that was endured by ancestors in the old country. From the potato famine to the exploitation of the peasants to indentured servitude, it's a long and lamentable narrative. Maybe there was even an amputee featured somewhere in the family tree, and let's say that the poor man's arms had to be cut off because proper medical care wasn't available at the time. Despite all this, the Irish family telling the story is in a strange position. They are recounting evils and hardships, and perhaps raising complaints to high heaven, but these same evils and hardships are for the most part necessary conditions of this family's current existence. No evils and hardships, and we wouldn't be hearing the story, because there would be no family sitting around the dining table in America telling it. Adams argues that it makes no sense to complain about the very circumstances that are responsible for our existence. If on balance we cherish our life, then we are affirming all the factors—including all the horrific events of the past—that have brought about that life.[12]

I made some of these points in my reply to the atheist champion of amputees. I doubt I convinced him, but at least the fellow faded back into the crowd. But my debate opponent, the philosopher Peter Singer, came roaring back with an impassioned objection. God, Singer said, is a bad parent. Imagine a parent who broke his child's legs and then defended himself by saying, "I gave this child life, so this is my prerogative." Even though the parent did give life to the child, Singer insisted, we would consider such a parent to be quite a monster!

Singer's analogy, however, doesn't really work. First, parents don't actually give life to their children. Parents have sex, and their children show up. Sure, parents are responsible for raising and looking after their children. Parents are the natural guardians of their children, and they do have the right to direct their children's activities until they are adults. These rights, however, are limited. Parents don't literally own their children, and so they are not allowed to maim or kill them, on pain of prosecution. God, however, is in a different position vis-à-vis the creatures that he makes. If God created a person without a leg, there is no violation of obligation or justice, and it makes no sense whatsoever to call God a monster for doing what he has every right to do. God even has the right to recall the benefits he has given. Theologian Richard Swinburne writes, "A benefactor has the right to take back . . . some of the benefits that he gives to someone, so long as he remains on balance a benefactor."[13] Swinburne's point is that, if God allows a person to lose a leg, say in an accident, the deprived person should in fact still be thanking God for his other leg, and his arms, and everything else that he has graciously been given.

This emphatic assertion of God's absolute rights may seem a little insensitive to the feelings of amputees and people suffering serious disability. So far, we haven't consulted any of these people about how they really feel. Even the atheist who confronted me at the Peter Singer debate wasn't an amputee himself. And undoubtedly he would be outraged if I were to ask him how much amputees actually suffer. Surely he would have said that a seriously disabled person's life is extremely hard and awful and miserable, an unbearable life! We all feel this way. But research now shows that our perception is an illusion. Often when we embark on a passionate defense of others, we are not thinking of their actual situation but about how we would feel if we were in that situation. Consequently we misjudge how the people who are disabled actually feel about themselves. There is now an impressive body of research that proves this.

How Paraplegics Really Feel

In his book *The Happiness Hypothesis*, Jonathan Haidt writes, "If I gave you ten seconds to name the very best and very worst things that could ever happen to you, you might well come up with these: winning a 20-million-dollar lottery jackpot and becoming paralyzed from the neck down." Winning the lottery, you might think, would solve all your practical problems, give you unimagined freedom, and bring you enduring satisfaction. Being paralyzed, you can be sure, would force you to jettison your aspirations, give up on sex, and become reliant on other people. Even death may seem preferable to such a state! Haidt writes that we might feel this way about how things would turn out for us, but in both cases we'd be wrong.[14]

Haidt cites a series of studies of people whose fortunes have dramatically changed. One fascinating study—called the Brickman study because of its lead author, Philip Brickman—focused on lottery winners and accident victims. The authors interviewed the lottery winners soon after they had won, and they were predictably ecstatic. Equally predictably, the accident victims were plunged into depression and despondency. Then the Brickman team did follow-up interviews with their subjects several months later. Here is where the study gets really interesting. Brickman's researchers found that, in a relatively short time, the level of happiness of the lottery winners had gone sharply down. In some cases it was still higher than before the lottery, but in most cases it was close to that original level. Equally remarkable, the accident victims who were subsequently interviewed were no longer depressed and despondent. Some of them were marginally less happy than they were before the accident, but many of them had returned to their "normal" level of happiness, and a few even claimed to be happier than they had ever previously been.[15]

What's going on here? The lottery winner begins with whoops and cheers, then he quits that boring job, buys new clothes, and goes on vacation. But soon the novelty fades, the new comforts are now taken for granted, and new problems arise. Wealth now draws opportunistic strangers and long-lost relatives; family members may begin to squabble about issues of money and inheritance; taxation and litigation have now become hassles to deal with. Not only does the lottery winner feel harassed, but no one seems to understand; everyone says, "What are you whining about? You won the lottery!"

At the other extreme, the person who has become an amputee or quadriplegic reacts with horror and sobbing, thinking that his life is finished. But like the lottery winner, he soon adapts to his new situation. Suddenly small things that he previously took for granted, like getting dressed or having brunch, can now seem like accomplishments and bring acute pleasure. Generally, the person slowly improves his situation—not his actual disability but his way of coping with it—and since there is nowhere to go but upward, he finds that his general level of happiness keeps increasing. After adjusting to the physical and emotional jolts, the former victim begins to feel almost the normal sense of happiness that he did before, and now everyone is cheering him on; people say, "Look at So-and-So. He's so brave and cheerful, and he's in a wheelchair!"

The Brickman study was done in 1978, but since then there have been numerous studies that support and even strengthen its conclusions.[16] In his book *The Pursuit of Happiness*, psychologist David Myers writes, "People who become blind or paralyzed will, after a period of adjustment, typically recover a near-normal level of day-to-day happiness." To prove his point, Myers cites a Michigan study of car accident victims who suffered paralyzing spinal-cord injuries. Three weeks later, he writes, "happiness was again the prevailing emotion." Myers also invokes a University of Illinois study showing that there is no difference in the level of happiness between able-bodied students and disabled students. "To within one percentage point, disabled students described their emotions identically."[17]

The principle involved here is what psychologists call hedonic adaptation. It means that our happiness is marvelously adaptive; it adjusts itself to whatever situation we are in. Psychologist Dan Gilbert writes in *Stumbling on Happiness* that humans have a psychological immune system that protects the mind against misery in much the same way that our physical immune system safeguards the body against illness. Gilbert notes that, since most people don't know this, they arrive at completely wrong judgments about how disability is actually experienced. Gilbert observes that "when sighted people imagine being blind, they seem to forget that blindness is not a full-time job. Blind people can't see, but they do most of the things that sighted people do—they go on picnics, pay their taxes, listen to music, get stuck in traffic—and thus they are just as happy as sighted people are."[18]

This research is a remarkable confirmation of the truth of what the Stoics said two thousand years ago. The Stoics were known as the people who didn't show emotion. The Stoics believed that both good news and bad news were to be received calmly, almost as if they hadn't happened. And now we know that the Stoic attitude is what happens anyway in the long term. In the short term, of course, we go into an emotional frenzy, and that's natural enough, but it is also a sign that we lack long-term perspective.

That was the problem with the atheist who indignantly asked me about God's hatred for amputees: he lacked long-term perspective, and equally important, he lacked the amputee's perspective. While atheists seem inconsolable about the plight of amputees, and use their disability to score a point against God, the reaction of the amputees themselves is often quite different. Many amputees show levels of resilience that command our admiration; some even respond with resilient humor. Asked how his life was different with a prosthetic limb, Patrick Marziale, who lost a leg during the Iraq war, responded, "The only difference is if a dog bites my ankle, it ain't going to hurt me." Moreover, many amputees find that their disability strengthens rather than weakens their faith. Perhaps the most famous example is Bethany Hamilton, who lost an arm to a shark while surfing; her story was made into the film *Soul Surfer*. "I truly believe that faith is a big part of what did get me through it," she says of her disability. "It's a tremendous relief to be able to put your trust in God."[19]

The Purpose of Miracles

So far we have shown that even the plight that seems horrible to observers isn't as horrible when viewed through the experience of the person himself. Still, why put amputees and other such people through pain at all? "God is supposed to be able to perform miracles," writes the atheist philosopher Walter Sinnott-Armstrong. If God intervened regularly in the Bible, adds Bart Ehrman, why has he gone silent on us now? Couldn't he intervene "more of the time? . . . Or indeed, all of the time?" And Christopher Hitchens notes with his usual irony that "if Jesus could heal a blind person he happened to meet, then why not heal blindness?"[20]

This is not the place to debate whether God can do miracles, or whether miracles contravene the laws of science. In my earlier book *What's So Great About Christianity* I discuss both of these issues at length. Here let me just say that if there is a God, obviously he can do miracles. What is a miracle, after all, but a rare event that human experience has not encountered before? The poet and ecclesiastic John Donne once wrote, "There is nothing that God hath established in a constant cause of nature, and which therefore is done every day, but would seem a miracle, and exercise our admiration, if it were done but once."[21] Here's what Donne is getting at: we see the sun rise every day, so it is routine for us, a kind of law of nature. But what if the sun never rose? Then the sun's rising on a single day would be a marvel, indeed a miracle. Consequently it is no big deal for God to perform occasionally the marvels that he performs regularly through nature's laws.

Yet if miracles are no big deal for God, why doesn't he do more of them? Since miracles are discretionary acts of God, we can't give a full answer to this question. But we can formulate a partial answer by looking at the kinds of miracles that the Bible does describe. Let's take up Hitchens's example—why doesn't Jesus heal blindness?—by looking at Christ's miracles as described in the New Testament. In Luke 5:17-26 and Mark 2:1-11, we read about a paralyzed man who was brought to Jesus on a sleeping mat. Jesus said to him, "Your sins are forgiven." The Pharisees accuse Jesus of blasphemy, since only God can forgive sins. Jesus then says, "I will prove to you that the Son of Man has the authority on earth to forgive sins." Then he turns to the paralyzed man and says, "Stand up, pick up your mat, and go home!" In this case, the purpose of the miracle is to confirm Christ's power to forgive sins. In John 5:14 this same story is given a new postscript. Jesus later found the same man in the Temple and told him, "Now you are well; so stop sinning." So we can attribute a second purpose to the miracle, to give the man a sign to turn his life around.

In John 9 we read about Christ healing a blind man. The disciples asked him why he did this. "This happened," Christ says, "so the power of God could be seen in him."[22] The whole incident is laced with gentle comedy. The Pharisees come upon the man who has been healed, and their main objection is that Christ had the audacity to heal the fellow—to do "work"—on the Sabbath. The Pharisees also interrogate the man and his family, insisting that he is a sinner and that he had never been blind. The man, however, says he doesn't know about these great matters; all he knows is that he has been healed. Still, the Pharisees cast him out. Jesus hears about it and finds the man. He talks to him not about healing but about believing in the Son of God. "Who is he?" the man asks, and Jesus replies, "You have seen him and he is speaking to you!" And the man says, "Lord, I believe!" Jesus responds, "I entered this world to render judgment—to give sight to the blind and to show those who think they see that they are blind."[23]

The term *miracle* literally means "a sign," and miracles are just that: spiritual signs. They are not cases of Jesus playing doctor, or Jesus trying to heal the body for its own sake. Leibniz puts it a different way. "I hold," he writes, "that when God works miracles, he does not do it in order to supply the wants of nature, but those of grace."[24] Consequently, if we don't see miracles today, or miracles of the type that are common in the Bible, the reason is most likely connected to the spiritual condition of the world. Maybe God doesn't see the need to give us more signs; maybe God believes that we have had enough signs.

This should not be taken as a claim that miracles never occur today. I believe that they do. What we don't see today, however, are unambiguous miracles, miracles that would command universal assent as displaying the handiwork of God. Even in the New Testament, on many occasions Christ performed a miracle and then said, "Tell no one." Apparently the miracle was for that particular person's spiritual edification; it was not to create a spectacle or make a demonstration to the whole community. A residue of mystery surrounds miracles, now as in the past, and perhaps this is how God wants it, in order to preserve his hiddenness. To reaffirm Pascal's point, as given in an earlier chapter, when God does act in the world today, perhaps he supplies enough evidence for believers to be affirmed in their faith, and yet not enough to convince those who are not seeking God in the first place. There is even sufficient ambiguity to give the scoffers room for their scorn.

Should we pray, then, for healings and miracles when we or our loved ones get sick or face tragedy? Yes, of course we should. The God of the Bible is not a detached, deistic God. He wants to hear from us. At the same time, we should be careful that our prayers are not a way of telling God what he should do. They should not be offered in the spirit of "Hey, God, I know that you have a plan, but I have a better plan." Rather, prayer should convey our intentions while at the same time praising God's perfect will. The true prayer always takes its cue from Christ. Christ was not afraid to say in the garden, "Please take this cup of suffering away from me." At the same time, he ended his prayer, "Yet I want your will to be done, not mine."[25]

We began this chapter by asking the question, Should God have created at all? We cannot give a full answer to this question, because we don't know why he created, except perhaps to express his creativity and also to have creatures that could relate to him. What we can address, however, is whether from our point of view God should have created. In other words, are we glad that he made us and that we have life to enjoy, despite hardship and occasional disability? The emphatic answer—given by amputees and the rest of us—is yes. It seems that thanks, rather than curses, are due to whoever is responsible for us being here.

CHAPTER 11

RAGE OF YAHWEH

Crimes of the Old Testament God

In those towns that the LORD your God is giving you as a special possession, destroy every living thing. You must completely destroy the Hittites, Amorites, Canaanites, Perizzites, Hivites, and Jebusites, just as the LORD your God has commanded you.

DEUTERONOMY 20:16-17

SO FAR, WE HAVE focused on the evil and suffering that God fails to prevent, and we have considered the reasons for why he does not prevent them. In this chapter, however, we take up a much more serious allegation. This is the charge that God himself is the perpetrator of evil, violence, and suffering. Atheist David Lewis calls this "divine evil."[1] What Lewis means is that God in Scripture is called good but at the same time his actions are depicted as bad. God is described as doing things that we would be roundly condemned as wicked and malevolent for doing. Incredibly, we find these descriptions of divine evil not in atheist literature but in the books of the Old Testament.

Reflecting on the Hebrew Bible, Robert Ingersoll writes, "The portrait is substantially that of a man—if one can imagine a man charged and overcharged with evil impulses far beyond the human limit; a personage whom no one, perhaps, would desire to associate with now that Nero and Caligula are dead. In the Old Testament, his acts expose his vindictive, unjust, ungenerous, pitiless and vengeful nature constantly. It is perhaps the most damning biography that exists in print anywhere." Along the same lines, Sam Harris writes in *The End of Faith*, "The Creator who purports to be beyond human judgment is consistently ruled by human passions—jealousy, wrath, suspicion, and the lust to dominate. The God of Abraham is a ridiculous fellow—capricious, petulant and cruel. . . . He is not only unworthy of the immensity of creation; he is unworthy even of man."[2]

Atheists are not the first ones to notice, but they do take special relish in enumerating the crimes of the Old Testament God. Biologist E. O. Wilson writes, "Over a hundred cities were consumed by fire and death, beginning with Joshua's campaign against Jericho."[3] Philosopher Michel Onfray in *Atheist Manifesto* notes that "the vocabulary of the rest of Deuteronomy includes: smite, perish, destroy, burn, dispossess, and other terms straight out of the repertory of total war." Here, Onfray concludes, many centuries before Islam and more than two millennia before Hitler, is the call to "the first genocide."[4]

These atheists seem to have a lot of biblical evidence for their accusations. In Psalm 137:8-9 we read, "O Babylon, you will be destroyed. Happy is the one who pays you back for what you have done to us. Happy is the one who takes your babies and smashes them against the rocks!" In the book of Numbers, God orders Moses to smite the Midianites. Here is what happens: "They attacked Midian as the LORD had commanded Moses, and they killed all the men. . . . Then the Israelite army captured the Midianite women and children and seized their cattle and flocks and all their wealth as plunder. They burned all the towns and villages where the Midianites had lived. After they had gathered the plunder and captives, both people and animals, they brought them all to Moses and Eleazar the priest." This seems bad enough, but what follows is worse: "Moses was furious with all the generals and captains who had returned from the battle. 'Why have you let all the women live?' he demanded. . . . 'Kill all the boys and all the women who have had intercourse with a man. Only the young girls who are virgins may live; you may keep them for yourselves.'[5]

Along the same lines, in the book of Joshua, we read about Joshua's assault on the cities of Jericho and Ai. God himself informs Joshua that "Jericho and everything in it must be completely destroyed." Joshua obeys. "The walls of Jericho collapsed, and the Israelites charged straight into the town and captured it. They completely destroyed everything in it with their swords—men and women, young and old, cattle, sheep, goats, and donkeys." Ai meets with a similar fate. Except for the king, who was taken captive, "not a single person survived or escaped." The Israelites, however, were not contented with killing the male combatants. "When the Israelite army finished chasing and killing all the men of Ai in the open fields, they went back and finished off everyone inside. So the entire population of Ai, including men and women, was wiped out that day."[6] All this is terrifying stuff. Novelist Gore Vidal calls it Bronze Age morality, and whether or not we agree with this characterization, it seems a morality utterly unsuited to our way of thinking. Indeed, its closest practitioners today would seem to be the followers of Osama bin Laden.

Perhaps the classic case of divine evil is the famous story of God ordering Abraham to sacrifice his son Isaac. Jews call this story the "binding of Isaac." What makes the story especially appalling is that Abraham is not an enemy of God; he is a righteous man. If this is how God treats his friends, imagine how he treats his enemies! Of course in the end God stays Abraham's hand; the whole thing was a test. Still, as atheist Christopher Hitchens writes, the point of the story is to "honor Abraham's willingness to make a human sacrifice of his son." But what can one say about a man who is willing to kill his son on someone else's command, even if that someone else is God?

"Abraham appears not as a man of faith," Martin Gardner writes, "but as a man of insane fanaticism. He would have done better to have supposed that he was listening to the voice of Satan."[7] The voice of Satan! This raises the obvious question, Can one really love and worship a sovereign who issues such commands? The answer would appear to be no. Of course one can give moderating interpretations to the binding of Isaac, but Hitchens concludes, "There is no softening the plain meaning of this frightful story."[8]

In *The God Delusion* Richard Dawkins mentions Abraham and Isaac, but then he takes up a story that he considers far worse. This is the story in Judges 11 where the military leader Jephthah makes a bargain with God. Jephthah says that, if God will guarantee him a victory over the Ammonites, Jephthah will sacrifice as a burnt offering "whatever comes out of my house to meet me when I return." Jephthah does rout the Ammonites, and when he returns home, he is greeted at the door of his house by his only daughter. While Jephthah feels bad about this, nevertheless for him a promise is a promise. So he gives his daughter a respite to go into the mountains for two months, and when she returns, he burns her! "God," Dawkins wryly notes, "did not see fit to intervene on this occasion."[9]

The indictment doesn't end there. Atheist Elizabeth Anderson raises an assortment of other issues, all of which give a very unflattering portrait of the biblical God. This God creates humans and then repents of having created them. But if God is omniscient, Anderson asks, didn't he know from the outset that humans were going to turn out that way? God hardens the heart of Pharaoh, and perhaps this serves his plan for the liberation of the Israelites, but in Anderson's view shouldn't Pharaoh have the chance to use his own free will instead of being manipulated by God in this way? God also issues a whole set of prohibitions, and most of them are violated on pain of death. Death to adulterers, death to homosexuals, death even to disobedient children! Finally, Anderson raises the troubling matter of explicit biblical sanction for slavery, an institution that has perhaps imposed more suffering on humanity than any other.[10]

How can we respond to this indictment? A few years ago, I was in a three-way debate called "Christian God? Jewish God? Or No God?" The debate was held in a synagogue in Orange County, California. The atheist position was represented by Hitchens, the Jewish position by radio host Dennis Prager, and the Christian position by me. During the debate, Hitchens recited several Old Testament passages referring to wiping out the Canaanites and the Midianites. Then he asked me, "What do you say about all this, Dinesh?" I responded, "Christopher, you have scored an effective strike against the rabbi." Then I turned the microphone over to the man representing the Jewish position, i.e., the Old Testament. "Dennis?" Sure, I was engaging in some debate strategy here and shifting the onus from me to Prager. I wasn't, however, just being evasive. Christians have a very special way of reading the Old Testament, making it much less vulnerable to this sort of attack. I'll come back to this. First, however, I want to take the Old Testament critique of God on its own terms and ask what a devout Jew might say in defense of Yahweh. Prager made two points that are worth considering.

How Jephthah Got Carried Away

First, Prager said that many of the crimes attributed to God were neither done nor approved by God. We can see Prager's point by reexamining the Jephthah story that has Richard Dawkins so exercised. Some Jewish commentators don't even think Jephthah actually sacrificed his daughter. Pondering the Hebrew understanding of the word *offering*, Gerald Schroeder writes, "Jephthah's daughter was consecrated not for death, but for a life dedicated to God."[11] But even if Jephthah did kill his daughter in fulfillment of a macabre promise, there is no indication that God asked Jephthah to make his promise. It was entirely Jephthah's idea. Nowhere in the Bible is there any suggestion that God granted Jephthah the victory in response to his offer to sacrifice his daughter. All we read is that Jephthah prevails. God emphatically does not cash in on Jephthah's promise and say, "Okay, Jephthah, now it's time to pay up." In fact, while human sacrifice was common in the ancient world, it receives no support in the Bible, as we will see later in our examination of the story of Abraham and Isaac. The bottom line here is that Jephthah makes his own vow and decides, in some manner, to carry it out. Dawkins, of course, knows this because he has read the story. So what's his point? If it is that biblical characters are often deeply flawed, Dawkins is merely repeating what Jews and Christians have long affirmed. Notice that in his indictment of God, based on this story, the best Dawkins can do is to charge God with failing to *prevent* Jephthah from carrying out his promise. But since Jephthah has free will, it's hard to see why God should do that. Even granting Dawkins his point that God should have stepped in, still the primary fault for this unjust murder lies with Jephthah, not with God.

A careful reading of the Old Testament shows that many—although not all—of the evils attributed to God are actually the result of human characters doing things for their own purposes. The rape of Tamar (2 Samuel 13), for instance, is clearly a violation of God's law. The rape is carried out by one of David's sons, and the incident is portrayed as a clear case of David not being able to keep his son under control. Lot gives his daughters to be ravished in a truly weird episode described in Genesis 19. The episode's weirdness is heightened because Lot is generally depicted as a sensible and righteous man. Even so, the Bible says nothing about the morality or immorality of Lot's action in this case. We may (and I do) find this silence puzzling, but by itself it is not culpable. The rape of the two daughters is prevented by angels who strike the would-be assailants blind, and Lot and his family make their escape. While there is some moral ambiguity in this Lot episode in Genesis, we don't find this in the book of Judges. There the Bible describes several massacres, but these are not ordered or even condoned by God; the whole point of these sections is that men are doing what is right in their own eyes. Many times atheists presume that because the Israelites are God's chosen people, what they do reflects what God intends or directs. In fact, the Old Testament is a story of both the fidelity and the infidelity of the Israelites. The fact that the Israelites think they are justified in taking severe action against their enemies, or even that they say they are doing God's bidding, doesn't mean that they are always right or that they are actually carrying out God's will.

A related point about the writers of the Old Testament is that they sometimes tend to exaggerate. But this is not the shocking statement it may appear on the surface. My point is not that the Bible isn't always truthful, but that not every Bible passage was meant to be taken literally. When the Bible says that the rivers and trees clap their hands, I assume we can all agree that this is intended metaphorically.[12] Casual readers and theological scholars agree that the Bible uses various literary devices to make its point: simile, metaphor, parable, and yes, exaggeration—in literature, an intentional technique called "hyperbole." It is widely used today, but we also find it in early literature such as that of Homer, Aeneas, and Shakespeare. One reason we might miss it in the Bible is that we think the Bible is written in a purely "realistic" mode, akin to the writing of Flaubert in the nineteenth century or a documentary filmed in the twentieth. But realism is itself a literary technique, and while the Bible uses this technique, it also uses others to communicate its message. This widely understood principle of literary style in the Bible brings us to Prager's second defense against the charge of an immoral God.

Joshua in Jericho

Consider the famous story of Joshua's assault on Jericho. What precisely occurred at Jericho has been a matter of debate among biblical archaeologists and theologians. If we read the story at face value, we get the impression that Joshua led a huge Israelite army against a great city; Rahab alone among the citizens believed in God and was saved from the assault; Jericho's large army resisted Joshua's advance until the walls collapsed; and a great city was routed. Biblical archaeologists have argued for nearly a century whether the destruction of Jericho occurred this way since the archaeological evidence points to the walls of Jericho being destroyed several centuries before the Israelites entered the land of Canaan.

The agnostic Bible scholar Bart Ehrman is familiar with this debate; he writes, "There is no archaeological evidence . . . to support the claim of the complete destruction of Jericho in the thirteenth century BCE." Yet Ehrman deplores what he terms "a divinely appointed bloodbath" in Jericho—how can there be a divinely appointed bloodbath if there was no bloodbath in the first place? Ehrman's explanation is that in condemning the bloodbath he is not even concerned with the facts, but only about the biblical narrative. "What I am interested in here is how the Deuteronomistic historian himself thought about these events."[13] Yet Ehrman does not consider why, if things happened one way, the writer of Deuteronomy chose to portray them in a different way.

Assuming the contested archaeological evidence around the Jericho site isn't reinterpreted in the future by another archaeological discovery, let's try to answer this question for Ehrman. Depending on which biblical archaeologist you consult, they will tell you that Jericho was a small settlement, probably defended by a fort manned by a few hundred or a few thousand warriors. It's possible the "wall" referred to in Scripture may have been a belt of houses that formed a ring around the settlement. There were most likely few civilians involved in the battle, and perhaps Rahab and her family are singled out because as innkeepers they represent the few noncombatants in an otherwise armed camp. The Israelites, led by Joshua, were probably a small force themselves. While they were successful, their victory was in itself a modest and insignificant one. Why, then, does the Bible make such a big deal about Joshua's invasion of Jericho?

In an important article, Richard Hess argues that, because "this battle was the first in which Joshua was the leader," here the Bible wants to dramatize Joshua's effectiveness as a leader and to show that he is a worthy successor to Moses. It seems that literary hyperbole is being applied to a historical situation in order to make a theological point. The point is that God is with Joshua, and the outcome of the battle will be determined by God himself.[14]

For some secular readers, and even some contemporary Christians, this may seem like a strange way to read the Bible. But in fact I am reading the Bible in the traditional way that it has been read for centuries by Jews and Christians. For most of that long period of the Bible's readership, the accusation that God is a murderer and a genocidal maniac didn't even occur to them. Why? There are two reasons. The first is that they understood that the Bible is not written in the form of a philosophical treatise but rather in the form of a story. What this means for our purpose is that the Bible anthropomorphizes God: it portrays God as a human being. Obviously we know that God is not a human being. Indeed, we know from the attributes of God—his omnipotence, his omniscience, and so on—that he cannot be anything close to a human being. He is not even superhuman, which, after all, is a term only for human qualities writ large. Reason tells us that though we alone of God's creatures are made in his image, God is utterly different from us—he is, we might say, in a different category altogether—and this means that we have to read the stories in the Bible as telling us something above and beyond their obvious and literal meaning.

I am suggesting that philosophical reason be used to interpret the anthropomorphic references in the Bible—precisely the way that believers have read the Old Testament for more than two millennia.

We should be willing to consider historical evidence and also, naturally, the rest of the Bible, to shed light on confusing passages. Let's examine the one expressing God's apparent regret over humanity, Genesis 6:5-6, which reads, "The LORD observed the extent of human wickedness on the earth. . . . So the LORD was sorry he had ever made them and put them on the earth." Philosophically speaking, this makes no sense at all. In the first place, an omniscient God would have known that humans were going to sin and succumb to wickedness, so he could not have said, essentially, "Oops, I had high hopes for man, but this has turned out to be a big mistake." Second, this reaction would be out of character; elsewhere the Bible says God "never changes or casts a shifting shadow."[15]

It seems equally preposterous to suggest that God hardened Pharaoh's heart, even though the Bible says that God did this on many separate occasions.[16] But then did God make Pharaoh do something that Pharaoh didn't want to do, or wouldn't otherwise have done? This would be an abrogation of free will and a divine compulsion to sin. There is nothing in the rest of the Bible or in the broader Judeo-Christian understanding that suggests that God operates in this manner. It is much more consistent with God's character to read this passage as meaning that God did not interfere when Pharaoh harshly rejected the demands and pleas of the Israelites. God "hardened" Pharaoh's heart in the same way that a lovely dessert on the table "beckoned" to me—the point being that we are dealing here with metaphor. The real meaning of the passage is that Pharaoh decided, and God acquiesced in Pharaoh's decision. As biblical scholars often say, we have to distinguish between the permissive will of God and his directive will; in other words, between what God allows and what he himself does.

Theologians have long understood that we should read other "hard sayings" in the Bible through the same interpretive framework of our overall understanding of God. For example, Jews and

Christians recognize God as a spirit and not a material being. One result of this idea is the recognition that God must not have feelings in the way that we do.

Does God Have Feelings?

Now this topic is a difficult and controversial one: many contemporary scholars, including Richard Swinburne, Alvin Plantinga, and Nicholas Wolterstorff, insist that God does have feelings. After all, Christian and non-Christian historical tradition assigns all sorts of feelings to God, not least of which is anger. But we must consider that the mainstream tradition of Christianity, going back to the Reformation, the Middle Ages, and the church fathers, actually affirmed the opposite. The great Catholic thinker Thomas Aquinas and the great Reformation leader John Calvin had their disagreements, but they were united in considering God to have the attribute of "impassability." That is, they saw God as being eternally unchangeable and not subject to the vicissitudes of emotion.

There is a theological reason to understand God in this way. Feelings are not something that we do; they are something that we have. Notice that in feelings we are not in control; feelings are things that happen to us. Now God, the great Creator, cannot be passively subject to things that are outside his control. He cannot be "consumed" with rage or "overtaken" by regret. His perfection, in other words, requires that he remain, as it were, "above" the outside influence of emotions—at least emotions as we experience them. Calvin, in support of this view, remarks on a passage in Genesis that describes God as vexed and wrathful. "Certainly God is not sorrowful or sad," Calvin writes, "but remains forever in his celestial and happy repose." God is only described this way, according to Calvin, to convey "God's hatred and detestation of sin."[17] As for me, I agree with Aquinas and Calvin on this and side with them and the mainstream tradition on the issue of whether God has feelings.

Let's look at the implications of this potentially jarring idea. Does it mean that God does not love us? Certainly not; the Bible is abundantly clear on the points of God's deep regard for humans, his inclination to show us compassion and mercy, and sometimes his disappointment in us. But it does mean that God cannot "grieve" or express "love" in the human sense, and that he cannot "hate" or "regret" in the human sense. While this understanding of God as "impassable" or without emotion developed theologically, it also makes sense from a scientific point of view. We know from science that emotions, at least as we experience them, require physical and neurobiological mechanisms. Without a physical brain and nerves, there is no way to have feelings. So God doesn't have feelings in the manner that we do.

This may seem unsettling, but it needn't be. Consider that God is not callous because of being unfeeling, any more than the ocean is callous because it doesn't have feelings. When we call the ocean "angry," we mean that it is heaving and swirling and that it would be dangerous for us to go out in it; so, too, when we attribute emotions to God, we are projecting our own emotions onto him. But these are our feelings, not his. God doesn't feel emotions—because he doesn't feel anything. And obviously a being that doesn't have feelings can't "repent" of anything.

When the Bible ascribes feelings to God, therefore, it refers not to how God actually feels but rather to how we would feel if we were in that situation. God's "love" and "compassion" can be understood by us as what we would feel in a close and intimate relationship. God's "jealousy" can be comprehended by us as something akin to how we would react if our spouses gave their allegiances to others. God's response to sin, including his "regret" for having made man, can be understood by us as what we would feel if we were confronted by beings that chose to rebel against their Maker.

So does this mean that Christians worship an unloving God?

How can we approach him in our prayers, how can we trust him with our hearts in our times of suffering? Again, let us look to the rest of Scripture to apply this understanding. The classic consolation so often quoted from Psalm 23, for example, still holds: "The LORD is my shepherd; I have all that I need. He lets me rest in green meadows; he leads me beside peaceful streams. He renews my strength. . . . Even when I walk through the darkest valley, I will not be afraid, for you are close beside me. Your rod and your staff protect and comfort me. . . . Surely your goodness and unfailing love will pursue me all the days of my life, and I will live in the house of the LORD forever." Nothing I have said above should be understood as in any way inconsistent with this scriptural reassurance.

Bronze Age Morality

A second point that Jews and Christians have long understood is that the actions and teachings of the Bible are an accommodation to the level that man has reached at a given time. In Calvin's words, God through the Bible "accommodates himself to our capacity."[18] In practice, this means that God recognizes that cultures are at different stages of development, and he deals with each group as it is, seeking always, albeit sometimes gradually, to raise it up higher. Certainly some of the ancient cultures of the Old Testament were in pretty bad shape, not only economically but also morally. Gore Vidal deplores the Bronze Age precepts of the Old Testament, but he seems to forget that many of these precepts were given to Bronze Age people. Even in the Bronze Age, however, there is change and there is progress, and we can see this progress registered in the books of the Old Testament. By the time we are in the Christian era, of course, society is quite different, and therefore there is a dramatic contrast in tone and moral language between the Old Testament and the New Testament.

A single example can be found in the book of Genesis. Early in the book we see God destroying the world through a flood and saving only Noah and his family. Noah is the one righteous man left on earth, and God saves him and his family. This is a very stern principle: let the city perish and save only the good guy. But in a similar situation later in Genesis, we see Abraham bargaining with God, urging him to save a city on account of a few righteous individuals. There is some haggling over this, but basically God relents. He spares the city because there remains a handful of good people in it. So God has changed his modus operandi: this time he does not wipe out the city and spare only the righteous. This time, on account of the righteous, he spares everyone. Later still, because of the righteousness of Moses bargaining on behalf of his people, God relents and agrees not to destroy the entire nation of Israel.[19] I don't think this is a case of God "going soft"—himself changing—but rather recognizing that conditions have changed. Perhaps man, who at one time understood only the language of force, is now more responsive to subtler languages: prophetic urgings, legal covenants, and so on. In this light, many examples of God's actions that appear to be harsh or fickle on the surface are seen to be much more understandable when placed in their historical milieu, that is, in the actual context of real people living in particular circumstances.

The Bible's acquiescence in slavery is another clear example of accommodation to the low level of human practice at the time. Let's recall that all of humanity was, for centuries, at this low level. Slavery was practiced in every known culture, and it was not even controversial.[20] So what does the Bible do with slavery? First, it recognizes that slavery has become an ingrained human institution, and it offers some teachings for how to ameliorate its evil effects. Masters, for instance, are told to be kind to their slaves, and slaves to be obedient to their masters. Does this constitute approval of slavery? By no means. If I urge the Chinese to obey their laws and also urge the Chinese government to be considerate of its citizens, am I through such counsel approving of Chinese totalitarianism? Not at all. I am simply taking the world as it is and trying to move it in the right direction—like taking a very warped board and slowly, carefully bending it back toward straightness rather than breaking it by trying to make it fully straight in one quick motion.

Now the biblical approach to slavery can be faulted for its gradualism, except for one notable fact: historically it is the Christians and no other group that mobilized to end slavery. There is no example of an antislavery movement outside of Christianity. It was the Christians, and only the Christians, who opposed slavery in principle, and they did so for an unmistakably Christian reason. They reasoned that if all men are created equal in the eyes of God—a central tenet of Christianity—then no man has the right to rule another man without his consent.[21] This became the core principle of the antislavery movement, which ultimately triumphed over the institutionalization of human greed and human bondage.

So accommodation is a key idea in understanding the Bible, and yet it is easily open to misinterpretation. By accommodation, I do not mean that the Bible should be understood as going along with the morality of the moment. By that logic, if men were barbarians, then the Bible would have to endorse a barbarian code of ethics. Not so. My point, rather, is that the Bible recognizes that progress takes time to be realized, and that there are periods in history when harsh people have to be dealt with in a harsh way.

This point was bluntly made by Dennis Prager in my three-way debate with him and Christopher Hitchens. When I turned over the microphone to Prager and urged him to address the seeming atrocities against the Canaanites and the Midianities, Prager basically responded, "What atrocities?" Prager insisted that these people deserved everything they got. I confess I found his answer shocking, and I'm sure many in the audience also felt this way. Upon reflection, however, Prager's answer is not so outrageous; there is a kind of logic to it.

Imagine one of the small tribes of native Indians who were confronted by the depredations of the Aztec Empire. The Aztecs were notoriously bloodthirsty, and it would make no sense to send them emissaries to try and talk sense into them. Probably the only way to respond would be to attack and destroy the Aztec warriors; otherwise, they would attack and destroy you. A more recent example is Hitler's Germany. Again, we know from history that attempts to appease and persuade the Nazis proved worse than useless. They actually proved counterproductive, because the Nazis pretended to go along while building up their military strength. It would have been better to rout the Germans before they became so strong. Evil that is not dealt with severely from the beginning tends to metastasize. Ultimately more force is needed to root it out, as turned out to be the case in World War II.

Today we speak of the Canaanites and the Midianites, but we have virtually no conception of who these people were; they are just names to us. Consequently, we tend to assume that these were fairly decent, peace-loving folk who just happened to be the rivals of the Israelites, and so these poor nations were arbitrarily and mercilessly slaughtered. But in fact, these were barbaric cultures that resembled the Aztecs and the Nazis in their thirst for blood. Human sacrifice, for example, was widely practiced by the Canaanite nations. When this is understood, God's judgment of the Canaanites is reasonable. According to the book of Genesis, God had allowed the Canaanites hundreds of years to repent of their unspeakable evils. Just as the Allies were morally compelled to end the wicked horrors of Nazism and Japanese imperialism, so God was using the Israelites to stop the evil rampant among the Canaanites.

Horrors are perpetrated even by the "good guys" under such circumstances. The bombing of Dresden was a horror, and so was the dropping of the atomic bombs. Even so, they were a lesser horror than allowing the Axis powers to triumph. By the same token, the Israelites undoubtedly committed excesses in dealing with their enemies, but it is still good that they triumphed over them. Israelite excesses proved to be the lesser evil than granting victory to the Canaanite nations.

Prager takes the destructive passages in the Old Testament at face value, but there is another way to interpret them. Considering the psalm I cited in an earlier chapter, which calls upon God to take revenge upon Babylon and dash the infants against the rocks, theologians observe that there is a tradition in the Hebrew Scriptures of what are called "imprecatory" prayers. These are prayers that lash out against oppression and injustice and call upon God for righteous revenge. And did God in fact dash the infants against the rocks? Theologian Walter Kaiser insists that he did not. First of all, *infant* is a misleading term. "The Hebrew word does not specify age, for it may mean a very young or a grown child." Rocks? "One thing Babylon was devoid of was rocks or rocky cliffs against which anything could be dashed." I admit I find this odd: even if Babylon didn't have boulders, surely there were stones there that could be used to inflict harm. Still, I get Kaiser's central point. When the psalmist speaks of dashing infants against the rocks, he is speaking figuratively and metaphorically."[22]

Along the same lines, Paul Copan says that, biblical rhetoric to the contrary, there is evidence in the text itself that the Canaanite nations were not, in fact, destroyed. Copan isn't disturbed by all the talk of wiping out the women, the young, and the old; he finds this "merely stock ancient Near Eastern language that could be used even if women and young and old weren't living there." Moreover, Copan observes that shortly after biblical passages that speak of wiping out the Canaanites, the Canaanites reappear. Same with the Amalekites. The text leads you to believe that they have been entirely destroyed by Saul, and yet they turn up again during the reign of King Hezekiah a couple of centuries later. Copan also insists that when God tells the

Israelites that they should take for themselves the virgins among the Canaanite nations, he means that these women should be taken not as concubines but as wives.[23]

So far we have examined the Old Testament on its own terms. I have been trying to show that God is not the monster that he is made out to be. So has the case been made, and should the defense rest? By no means. The defense has yet to produce its star witness, none other than Jesus Christ. My point is not that as Christians we believe that Jesus Christ is God and therefore Jesus' words and actions in the New Testament somehow cancel out Yahweh's words and actions in the Old Testament. That would not only be nonsense; it would also be rank heresy. Rather, my point is that, for Christians, Jesus Christ is the interpretive key to the Old Testament. The Old Testament must be read, in a sense, in the light of Christ or through the perspective of Christ. "Directly or indirectly," John Stott writes, "Jesus Christ is the grand theme of the Old Testament."[24]

New Testament, New Understanding

There is a classic saying in Christianity that "the New Testament is in the Old Testament concealed; the Old Testament is in the New Testament revealed." Invoking this thinking, the literary scholar Northrop Frye writes, "The New Testament . . . claims to be . . . the key to the Old Testament, the explanation of what the Old Testament really means." While the Old Testament focuses on law, Frye notes that "for Christianity the Old Testament was primarily a book of prophecy, foretelling the future event of the Incarnation and thereby pointing to the transcendence of the law."[25]

We can see the significance of this if we consider a famous passage in Isaiah. "But he was pierced for our rebellion, crushed for our sins. He was beaten so we could be whole. He was whipped so we could be healed." This is a reference to the suffering servant, one who is, in Isaiah's words, "oppressed and treated harshly, yet he never said a word. He was led like a lamb to the slaughter."[26] For Christians, it is virtually impossible to read such passages without thinking of Christ. The Christian view is that Isaiah forecasts the passion of the Messiah. But Jews read the same verses for centuries without anyone suggesting that they pointed to a future Messiah. For Jews, the passage is about Israel; Israel is the suffering servant. Here I am not trying to say which interpretation, the Jewish or the Christian, is correct. Rather, I want to show that these differences of interpretation are important for our examination of evil and suffering. In fact, they offer Christians a mode of argument that is not available to Jews.

What mode of argument is that? For Christians, the tribal God of the Old Testament gives way to the universal sovereign of the New Testament. Again, we see this progression to universality—that is, availability for all peoples to choose—in the Hebrew Bible itself, but it is consummated in the New Testament. Both the tribal God and the universal God are present in the former, but only the universal God is featured in the latter. In the Christian understanding, Jews remain the "chosen people" but not in the sense that they alone are marked for salvation. Rather, salvation is open to everyone, and everyone who accepts Christ's gift of salvation is "chosen" in the New Covenant.

What about the harsh laws of the Old Testament? They are completely gone in the new. Contrast the way that the Old Testament treats adultery, for instance, with the way that Jesus treats the woman taken in adultery, or the woman at the well who has had five husbands. Jesus is, even by the most modern standards, extremely gentle with these offenders. Nowhere does he suggest that adultery is not an offense: in this respect, the New Testament maintains continuity with the Old. But the whole tone of the divine response is different. Thus when atheists cite lengthy passages of ancient Jewish law, Christians have only to respond with a nod of agreement. Rarely have Christians taken such passages as applying to them or to anyone today. The Old Testament is not merely interpreted through the lens of the New; it has also, in important ways, been superseded by the New.

As a consequence of the Christian understanding, events in the Old Testament that are understood one way by the Jewish faith are understood in a completely different way by the Christian faith. We can see the difference in how we comprehend the story of Abraham and Isaac. For Jews, this is basically a story of Abraham's fidelity. The binding of Isaac is simply a test, and Abraham passes the test. This is one way of defending God. One might say that, while ancient cultures were drenched in blood, God deserves credit for staying Abraham's hand. Human sacrifice was common in ancient religion, but here the God of Abraham is differentiating himself and saying that he is not a deity that requires such sacrifice. Christians, of course, agree with all this, but the Christian defense of God goes much further.

Let's look at what happens when Abraham and Isaac are walking up the mountain. Abraham has told Isaac that they are going to perform a sacrifice. But Isaac is puzzled. He asks his father, "Where is the sheep for the burnt offering?" And Abraham answers, "God will provide."[27] Now for Christians, this is highly significant. Many times in the New Testament, Jesus is described as the Lamb of God. For example, the Gospel of John refers to "the Lamb of God who takes away the sin of the world!"[28] Consequently in Christianity the story of Abraham and Isaac presages a massive role reversal. Instead of man sacrificing blood to appease the anger of God, God will sacrifice his own son in order to atone for the sins of men.

So in the Jewish understanding of the story, God is not so bad because he is only testing Abraham, even if his test seems excessive and perhaps even sadistic. In the Christian view, however, God is beyond reproach, because he is willing to sacrifice himself for Abraham, for Isaac, and for all. Christians don't ask mournfully, "What kind of a God could ask a father to sacrifice his own son?"

Rather Christians say, gratefully, "What kind of a God would sacrifice his own son for the redemption of sinful human beings!" This, then, for Christians is the real meaning of the story of the binding of Isaac.

I confess, having come this far, that there are some passages in the Old Testament that continue to bother me. I wish they weren't in there. But just because I don't understand why they are included, or what they really mean, doesn't prove that the God of the Bible is a terrible monster. On the contrary, the consistent overall portrait of God, both in the Old Testament and in the New, is that of a sovereign who is righteous as well as loving, severe and yet merciful, a hater of sin and also a victor on our behalf over it. It remains to be seen if such a God deserves our full allegiance, but he certainly does not deserve our crude contempt.

CHAPTER 12

ABANDON ALL HOPE

Heaven, Hell, and Divine Justice

Abandon all hope, ye who enter here.[1]
DANTE, *The Divine Comedy*

SO FAR WE HAVE been considering evil and suffering in terms of an earthly scheme: we have considered moral evil and natural suffering and explained both as the unavoidable consequence of a lawful world inhabited by free, conscious creatures like us. Still, the world as it is does not ultimately satisfy any reasonable conception of justice. We say that "what goes around, comes around," but we know it isn't always true. Sometimes the wicked guy ends up on top; sometimes the good guy comes to grief. Consequently there is unpunished evil, the result of bad actions, and there is undeserved suffering, imposed on the victims of those actions. If God left things at that, he would still have a lot to answer for.

Christians, however, believe that God didn't leave it at that. He also created heaven and hell. At first glance, this extraterrestrial scheme seems to solve the problem of unmerited suffering and unpunished evil. But as Christians know, and as atheists are delighted to point out, it does so at the price of raising another, even more serious, problem. This has been called the problem of hell. Hell is of course the greatest evil of all, the realm of the greatest conceivable suffering. Consequently, hell poses perhaps the deepest difficulty for Christian theodicy. Far from resolving the theodicy problem, hell seems to make it even worse.

The sufferings of hell are portrayed in the Bible in stark and garish terms: there is unquenchable fire, wailing and gnashing of teeth, unremitting pain and misery. Not only is hell the realm of ultimate evil, but the suffering described in it is also eternal. Revelation 20:10 says that the inhabitants of hell "will be tormented day and night forever and ever." Moreover, Christ says in Matthew 22:14 that "many are called, but few are chosen"—disturbing words on two counts. First, they seem to suggest that the vast majority of humanity is headed for hell: heaven is the narrow gate and hell is the wide gate. Second and equally troubling, the word *chosen* implies that God chooses people for heaven and consequently God decides not to save others who end up in hell. Why would God create humans if most of them are, by his arbitrary election, predestined to a future of eternal torment?

"The damnation of one man," writes David Hume, "is an infinitely greater evil in the universe than the subversion of a thousand millions of kingdoms." Arguing that finite sins should merit finite punishment, Hume terms hell unjust because "punishment . . . should bear some proportion to the offense."[2] It's hard to disagree with Hume's basic principle that human crimes, however outrageous, do not deserve unending grief. Sure, we humans put criminals in the penitentiary. But as the name suggests, the penitentiary is the place of repentance. At least in most countries, prisons exist to offer the guilty the hope, if not the probability, of rehabilitation. In human society, the worst criminals are given the death penalty, the ultimate human punishment, which itself has many critics. Yet God—who is said to be a God of love—does far worse than this. For him the death penalty is not enough; he is only content, it seems, when a substantial portion of his beloved creation is hurled into hell for all eternity.

Philosopher Bertrand Russell asserts, "I do not myself feel that any person who is really profoundly humane can believe in everlasting punishment."[3] Hell, claimed atheist Robert Ingersoll, "makes man an eternal victim and God an eternal fiend."[4] Calling hell a classic case of "divine injustice," David Lewis charges God with placing numerous temptations before us and keeping his own presence far from obvious, then punishing us for succumbing to those temptations and refusing to acknowledge his far-from-obvious presence.[5] Martin Gardner was a theist who on account of the Christian teaching of hell refused to call himself a Christian. Hell, he says, is "the supreme disgrace of Christendom." Gardner adds, "If Jesus did indeed teach such a damnable doctrine, it is the strongest possible reason for not believing him to have been God."[6] And Christopher Hitchens blamed Christ not only for teaching about hell but for single-handedly inventing the idea. In his standard speech, Hitchens lambasted the God of the Old Testament, portraying him as a tribal dictator; then he sarcastically turned to "gentle Jesus meek and mild." Jesus, insisted Hitchens, is the greatest villain of all. While the Old Testament God wipes people out, annihilation is the worst he does; Jesus, on the other hand, devises and promulgates the idea of eternal damnation. Jesus proclaims hell as the just and fitting recompense for people who do not worship him, including tens of millions who have never even heard of him.

So compelling are these objections to hell that even some Christians go along with them. Theologian John Hick terms the very idea of hell "morally intolerable." How can we say that a loving God created hell? Hick says we can't. Therefore there is no hell; everyone ultimately gets to heaven.[7] A similar position of universal salvation is adopted by the Christian philosopher Marilyn McCord Adams.[8] Most recently pastor Rob Bell caused something of a sensation—even landing on the cover of *Time*—when he embraced this position in his book *Love Wins*.

Somewhat disingenuously, Bell implies that universal salvation has been a legitimate Christian position throughout the centuries. Bell speaks of a "long tradition" in which "an untold number of serious disciples . . . across hundreds of years" have proclaimed universal salvation.[9] But this is nonsense; in reality, only a tiny minority of Christians have taught the universalism that Bell's musings most closely resemble. Still, it's significant that some have felt the need to take a stance so clearly opposed to what the Bible repeatedly teaches. It shows that even some committed believers have found it virtually impossible to simultaneously affirm hell and divine goodness. Other Christians, including the pastor John Stott, have rejected the idea of eternal suffering in favor of divine annihilation. Stott interpreted the biblical passages on hell to say that it constitutes ultimate destruction: the wicked are completely destroyed, but they don't suffer forever.[10] Again, we see a strenuous effort to rescue theodicy from the apparently insurmountable problem of hell. While he embraced the traditional doctrine of hell, even C. S. Lewis recoiled from it. "There is no doctrine which I would more willingly remove from Christianity than this, if it lay in my power."[11]

Heavenly Recompense

In this chapter I intend to show that hell is actually a good idea and one that is fully compatible—indeed fully required—by the goodness of God. But first I want to say something about heaven. It's interesting that those who rail at the injustice of hell do not also rail about the injustice of heaven. For if it is wrong to penalize people, however bad, with eternal punishment, isn't it equally wrong to reward people, however good, with eternal joy? Shouldn't rewards, no less than punishments, be proportioned to merit? Atheists seem to think that, wonderful people that they are, they are fully deserving of perpetual happiness, while the very thought that God might assign them to the other place fills them with unutterable loathing against God. We'll come back to this issue of just deserts; here, however, I contend that heaven provides a powerful reply to the atheist claim that there is gratuitous evil and suffering in the world. The Christian answer is that this world is not the only world, and it's quite possible that the wrongs of this world will be fully corrected in the next. Heaven, for this reason, is a powerful vindication of Christian theodicy.

But hold on! David Hume raises the obvious objection: how do we actually know there is a heaven? Hume insists that it is unreasonable to address the problem of evil by positing a realm of eternal happiness. "To establish one hypothesis upon another is building entirely in the air," he writes. To invoke heaven, he adds, is to introduce "arbitrary suppositions" for which there is no clear proof.[12] Now Hume might have a point if Christians had, in response to the problem of evil, added heaven to their theological scheme in the fourth century or even in the modern era. This would make heaven look highly dubious, a cheap theological fix. But in reality heaven was there from the outset; heaven was a part of the original Christian scheme. So it is Hume who is being unreasonable here. If this seems like mere semantics, let's recall the general problem that we set out to resolve in this book: the atheist's claim that there is a contradiction between divine goodness and earthly evil and suffering. Christians simply have to show that, when their full picture of God is taken into account, there is no contradiction. Christians don't have to prove that heaven exists any more than they have to prove that God exists. The atheist is saying, "Given what you believe, we can show that you are being contradictory." The Christian needs to counter, "Given what we believe, there is actually no contradiction." So all that Christians need to show is that there is no necessary inconsistency between their theology and the prevalence of evil and suffering in the world. It is entirely legitimate, in this context, to introduce heaven as a solution to the problem.

Having been cleared for use in solving the theodicy problem, then, how does heaven solve it? Think of it this way. There is a great deal of evil and suffering in this world. Much of it seems unjustified and without purpose or compensation. But if there is an afterlife, then it's quite plausible that all of this will be corrected and vindicated in that realm. Certainly if this life is a mere second in the vast expanse of eternity, it seems shortsighted in the extreme to complain about hardships that turn out to be very short lived in comparison. Heaven introduces a new perspective, *sub specie aeternitatis*. As real and painful as it is down here, evil and suffering on earth appear insignificant and ephemeral when viewed from the high perch of eternity. Even more than this, heaven provides cosmic recompense. Consider the child whose life is tragically truncated due to cancer, or the just man who remains lonely, neglected, and destitute in prison. If there were no heaven—if terrestrial justice were the only justice to be had—then we would have to conclude that the world is, as we so often grumble, basically unfair. Even Job's recompense, the restoration of his fortune and a new family, is not really adequate; he has still lost his original family, and he cannot have them back. We all know that there is uncorrected evil and unmerited suffering in this world, and if God doesn't address this issue, then that is a powerful indictment of his goodness and justice.

But heaven vindicates God's goodness and justice, because heaven is the place where the victims come out on top, where the righteous and the godly enjoy eternal bliss. Revelation 21:1-4 promises a "new heaven and a new earth" and "no more sea" (KJV). Theologian N. T. Wright puzzles over that little detail. Why, he asks, should the new creation exclude the beautiful ocean? We love the sea, he notes, because "we can observe its enormous power and restless energy from a safe distance." But in reality the sea is very dangerous, the source of seaquakes and drowning. The new creation won't have the sea, Wright suggests, because there will be no more natural suffering. Heaven will be a realm where, the Bible promises, God "will wipe every tear from their eyes, and there will be no more death or sorrow or crying or pain. All these things are gone forever."[13]

Now that's something to look forward to. And the hope of heaven is certainly relevant to our problem of theodicy. What if all the deprived and wronged creatures on earth receive their due compensation in the form of eternal bliss? What if Job, in addition to the revival of his earthly fortunes, enjoys eternal reunion with the God that he has been seeking all his life? No reasonable person can say that eternal joy is not enough compensation for what we have suffered. Finite suffering is a small price to pay for infinite happiness.

In the biblical parable of the rich man and Lazarus, the rich man is devoted to earthly joys. Lazarus, a poor man, enjoys none of them. But in the eternal afterlife, their roles are reversed. Lazarus is in heaven, while the rich man is in the other place. "Now he is here being comforted, and you are in anguish."[14] This is what is meant by the famous biblical phrase: the last shall be first. Heaven is the venue of cosmic justice. This is where the faithful servants of the Lord who came in last receive their due prize and reward. Moreover, we read in Scripture that God will create a new earth that doesn't have the deficiencies of the old one. "We know that all creation has been groaning as in the pains of childbirth right up to the present time," Paul writes in Romans 8:22. So creation itself has to be redeemed and transformed.

So what will heaven be like? Setting aside medieval depictions of harps and cherubs, some of which don't even look very appealing today, no one really knows. When it comes to heaven, even the Bible is remarkably reticent on the details. Some, including John Wesley, speculate that even the animals will have a new life on this new earth. Others insist that the new earth is reserved for God's favored species, man. Augustine assures us that the celestial paradise is even lovelier than the terrestrial paradise into which Adam and Eve were first deposited—and thus the effects of the Fall will be reversed. What we do learn from Scripture is that, while in the laws of this world, pain and suffering are inescapably woven into the fabric, in the new heavens and new earth, we will be back in God's immediate presence, and there even our bodies will have been transformed in some way yet unimaginable.

Still, what about hell? Contrary to atheist accusations, Jesus Christ did not invent the concept of hell. We can read about hell in the later books of the Old Testament, so we know that hell was an accepted idea in Judaism before Christ. Even so, he does repeatedly talk about hell; arguably, he refers to it more than anyone else in the Bible. Hell is mentioned around a dozen times in Scripture, five of which are in Jesus' Sermon on the Mount. So can we reconcile hell with the belief that Christ is such a compassionate, loving figure? Is hell compatible with God's love? Right away we have to acknowledge that God, in both the person of the Father and the person of the Son, is indeed loving and compassionate, but that these are not his only attributes. If Christ were nothing but compassionate, and if God the Father were nothing but love, then the atheist would be right. There is no way that a merely compassionate Christ, and a merely loving God, would talk and act like this.

But God is not merely love; he is also holiness and truth and justice. And the same can be said of Christ, who is, after all, the Son of God and shares in these divine attributes. Consequently we have found a major flaw in the atheist argument. The atheist has located an incompatibility between eternal suffering and God's goodness and love, but the atheist is assuming that these are God's only attributes. On the other hand, when we fill out the Christian view, when we recognize that God is also holiness and truth and justice, then the incompatibility becomes less obvious. Moreover, Christians believe that God's attributes are inseparable; God can no more stop being just than he could stop being benevolent or all-powerful. Consequently, the loving God may withhold salvation from some because it is incompatible with his holiness or with justice or with truth; none of this would prove that God was unloving, only that his love is circumscribed by his other divine attributes that also have to be satisfied.

Why Jesus Had to Suffer

With Jesus, however, we have a specific difficulty. Christian writers on theodicy habitually "solve" the problem of evil and suffering by saying that Christ himself suffered with us and for us. Christ took on the evils of the world, and through his suffering he redeemed us. In his book *Defending God*, James Crenshaw writes, "The biblical God . . . understands human suffering firsthand, through his own experience. God himself suffers."[15] Theologian John Haught writes that "the agony of living beings is not undergone in isolation from the divine eternity." He asks us to reflect upon "the picture of an incarnate God who suffers along with creation." This cosuffering, he contends, leads to the "remarkable religious insight that divine influence characteristically manifests itself in ways that do not correspond to conventional views of power."[16] The same themes can be found in Jürgen Moltmann's *The Crucified God*, where Moltmann informs us that we can be consoled in our suffering knowing that Jesus himself suffered "at God's hands."[17]

Yet upon examination, I don't find these ideas very reassuring. If Jesus suffered at God's hands, and God was willing to impose the death penalty on his own innocent son, what hope do I have of escaping divine wrath? Besides, how does it help matters to know that Christ suffers with us? How does this palliate our suffering?

Imagine if I had a pain in my chest, and I went to a doctor who had the knowledge and the medicine to get rid of my pain. Yet the doctor informs me that he isn't going to relieve my pain, but he wants me to know that he has an even greater pain in *his* chest. Perhaps he is even willing to inflict pain on himself, or in any case to endure it, for my sake. He will not remove my suffering, but he will suffer with me. My attitude would be, "Thanks for nothing, doc. What you are doing may be well meaning, but it doesn't really help my situation."

We need an explanation of what Christ's suffering does for us. How exactly does Christ take on the evils and sins of the world? What redemption does he offer us? And why doesn't he offer it to everyone? Can it really be true that non-Christians are automatically headed for hell, and that some are actually selected by God for redemption while others are consigned to damnation? These are the questions that will occupy us for the rest of this chapter.

Let's begin by looking closely at what happened to Christ during his passion and death. First, we notice that he is reluctant to die. The Passion, for him, is a painful ordeal. In this, Christ is most unlike Socrates, who seems to go cheerfully and willingly to his death. The film *The Passion of the Christ* portrays Christ's pain in lurid fashion. There is great emphasis on the beatings and the blood. Now, the Crucifixion certainly would have been painful, and it certainly would have involved some blood. Oddly, though, the Bible says very little about Christ's physical pain. And if Christ's sacrifice is measured purely in terms of physical pain, it would have to be said that there are many humans who suffered more than he did; some of Christ's own disciples were subjected to physical tortures that he never endured. I believe that Christ's passion should be understood in a different way.

More than the physical pain, it involved the humiliation of God: God having to take on finite human attributes. Christ did this in order to fully experience the world, with its delights and horrors, from the limited human perspective. While this is a glorious project, from our point of view, it must be viewed quite differently from God's point of view. From God's perspective, this would be akin to asking a human to become a centipede; we might be willing to do it, but it would involve some lowering of the self-image.

In addition, Christ's suffering involves alienation from God. He is incarnate in a fallen world, and his life is ended experiencing the horrifying absence of God. Christ keenly feels this alienation; he cries out, echoing Psalm 22, "My God, my God, why have you forsaken me?"[18] Christians can hardly miss the significance of this. Christ himself, in the midst of his suffering, seems to be asking the central question of theodicy. Christ, who is himself divine, is radically separated from God. The son is radically cut off from the father. Most likely, this separation is endured both by God the Father and by Christ the Son. The son suffers the Passion and the Crucifixion, and the father suffers the death and loss of his son. Yet while Christ endures the agony of being forsaken by God, and while he pleads with the father to spare him that agony, his prayer to God ends with submission. In effect, Christ says to God, "While I would rather have it my way, I submit to you and agree to do things your way."

This is the precise opposite of what Adam and Eve said to God in the Garden of Eden. Adam and Eve sinned by disobeying God's command, by deciding to do things their way even though they existed in a state of exceeding happiness, devoid of suffering. Christ reverses the effect of human sin by acquiescing in the will and plan of God even though he must do it in a state of exceeding misery, drenched in the full suffering intrinsic to the fallen world. This is why Christ is referred to as the new Adam. Paul writes in Romans 5:18, "Adam's one sin brings condemnation for everyone, but Christ's one act of righteousness brings a right relationship with God." It takes us beyond our original state of happiness, to a happiness beyond our reckoning in heaven, giving us far more than we'd lost.

A Fortunate Fall?

In Christianity, the Fall is a tragic event, and yet Christians through the centuries have often used the phrase "the fortunate fall." O felix culpa! What can this possibly mean? How can it be "fortunate" for humans to revolt against God and go their own way? A friend of mine, the philosopher Benjamin Wiker, cringes at the expression, to which he retorts, "O Horrenda Culpa." And Wiker rightly points to the consequences of man's rebellion and disobedience: the expulsion from Eden, the alienation between man and God. Wiker cannot get over the fact that human redemption required nothing less than the assassination of God; in other words, an extremely heavy cost.

Still, we must count the gain even more. If man hadn't fallen, then Jesus would not have come down to earth. Surely this has some bearing on how we view the Fall. In an important essay, philosopher Alvin Plantinga asks us to imagine two possible worlds. In one, there are free creatures who do not fall, who do what is right, who follow God's will. In the other, God creates the very same creatures, but they do fall, they reject God's will, and they go their own way. God, in his graciousness, sends a Savior who takes on the sins of that second world so that those wayward creatures are reconciled to God. Now which, Plantinga asks, is the better of those two worlds? He answers: the second one. Why? Plantinga points to "the unthinkably great good of divine incarnation and atonement."[19] As I suggested earlier, without the Fall we wouldn't have Christ. But we can add to Plantinga's case here. I do so by relying on a point that J. Gresham Machen makes in his book *God Transcendent*.[20] In the first world, there is always the possibility of a fall. The creatures there may not have sinned yet, but they could sin at some point in the future. And then they would be cut off from God. "Innocence is indeed a glorious thing," writes Kant. "On the other hand, it is very sad that it cannot well maintain itself, and is easily seduced."[21] In the second world, the creatures are no longer innocent. They have sinned and continue to sin, and they are liable for the penalty of that sin. Christ, however, has fully paid the price for sin, not only for the sins that preceded him but also for the sins to be committed after him. So the inhabitants of the second world are in an incomparably better position because all their wrongs have already been righted.

We can draw two important lessons from this. First, we see God's providence working at both the higher and the lower level. The lower level is the Anthropic Principle, the fine-tuned universe. This shows God designing the only type of universe that would enable free, conscious human beings. Yet when humans rejected God, and inflicted evil and harm on one another, God sent his Son into the world to address and solve that problem. So the lower providence of the fine-tuned universe is integrated into the higher providence of Christ's incarnation. We have here a precious insight into the mind of God.

Second, we also see in the Incarnation God's ability to bring good out of evil. In Augustine's terse summary, "[God] judged it better to bring good out of evil, than not to permit any evil to exist."[22] It's important to recognize that God didn't cause the evil so that he could produce good. This would be like saying God produced an injury just so that he could offer the bandage. No, man caused the injury through his unwise and disastrous rejection of God; but God found a way to turn that evil into good—by entering the fallen world, a world in which there are thorns in the garden, and the thorns are taken by God as a crown.

The story of the Fall and the Atonement is a powerful vindication of Christian theodicy. It shows that while a partial examination of God's plan seems to show evident defects, the plan on the whole removes those defects. In fact, the plan on the whole proves to be better than a plan that didn't have those defects in the first place. Again, we don't have to prove any of this to the satisfaction of the atheist. We are not trying to show that the Christian outlook is irrefutable; we are trying to show that it is consistent, that there is no contradiction between God's perfection and the evil and suffering in the world.

So what do we have to *do* to be saved from our sins? The Christian answer is nothing, because Christ has already done it; he has performed the atonement in our place. Why him instead of us? Because there is no way that we could pay. We are in debt, but our accounts are empty. Think of it this way. How would you go about atoning for your sins? You cannot answer, "From now on I am going to go with God's plan instead of my plan." Even if you could do this, it would hardly be atonement, since this is what you should have been doing in the first place. So Christians believe that God had to himself pay the price for man's sin, because his holiness and justice demand it, and because we are not in a position to pay it. Salvation is made available to us—to all mankind—as a free gift.

All we have to do is to receive it. Notice that here, as in the Garden of Eden, what God is asking man to do is embarrassingly easy. There we could eat of every tree, but God said, just don't eat from this particular one. Here we are given the free gift of eternal life, if only we are willing to accept it. And we are going to accept and appreciate the gift only if we recognize that we need it. In other words, a humble and repentant heart is the proper way to receive the gift. The repentance means that we are sorry for our sins: we regret choosing our way over God's way. Repentance doesn't signify that we won't sin anymore; we may (and in fact often will) continue to go our way. But repentance shows that we know which way is better. We want to go with God's plan, even if we slip up on occasion and carry out our own plan.

We see here the great Christian redefinition of what it means to be good. Being good no longer means performing good acts and rejecting evil acts. That's good, but it isn't good enough. Acknowledging our sinfulness—our departure from God's way—is the most important thing. It is the only thing that can heal the original fault from which all our other faults flow. In this respect we are like Socrates, for whom wisdom mainly consisted of knowing how little he really knew. For Christians, goodness consists mainly of knowing how bad we really are, and how little we really know about our own true good and our own evil intentions and actions. And repentance is not something we do; it is an interior condition, an attitude. Repentance is more a state of being than a state of doing.

Yet repentance, no less than anything we do, has to be something that we choose. And we know from experience that there are some who will not choose it. They don't care whether the gift is free or not; they don't want it, and they in fact refuse it. These are the people who go to hell. They go to hell not because they are sinners, but because they are unrepentant sinners—a crucial distinction. They are sinners who have been offered a way out, but they refuse to take it. The door is open, but they insist on staying inside their prison cells.

Why do they stay inside? For the same reason that Adam and Eve sinned in the first place. They stay inside because they remain convinced that their way is better than God's way. They want to stick with their path rather than travel on God's. They would rather have a world on their own terms, of their own devising, even if they are devising their own misery. They don't care that God's path offers them relief from travail and suffering; in the words of one of Milton's devils, they "prefer hard liberty to the easy yoke of servile pomp."[23] From God's point of view, they remain prideful, ungrateful, and recalcitrant; from their own point of view, they are pioneers of reason, self-sufficiency, and adventure. So God, who respects their freedom, lets them do what they want. And in eternity, there is a name for this condition of ultimate separation from God: hell.

God isn't flinging anyone into hell; we choose hell by rejecting God. God is goodness and truth and beauty; by rejecting him, we reject all those good things. And what we get in hell is ugliness and horror and deprivation, not because we actually seek them, but because they are what is left when God is absent. Here on earth we have a mixture of good and evil, of pleasure and pain. That's because earth is a middle kingdom, suspended between heaven and hell. Earth is, on account of the Fall, in a state of rebellion against God, yet earth still reflects the imprint of God's beneficent creation. But what would earth be like if we subtracted from it all of God's influence, which is to say, if we subtracted all the beauty and the goodness and the happiness? Well, we would have hell on earth. And so we can get, through this mental subtraction, a very good idea of what the real hell is like.

This is what the author of Revelation is pointing toward when he uses a phantasmagoria of fiery images to describe the condition of those living apart from God. Over the centuries, Christians have debated whether hell involves literal flames. I believe, as Calvin and other theologians have, that such a discussion misses the main point of these Scripture passages—namely, we must take hell seriously. The Bible warns us in the strictest terms that it's not a place we want to be in. And this dire warning isn't intended merely to scare us; it is intended for our protection.

While God doesn't want anyone to go to hell, given the world God chose to create, he really has no choice in the matter. This is not merely because God is holy and good and cannot endure unrepentant sin; it is also because for God to save people from hell, he has to give them the gift of himself. "It is by grace you have been saved, through faith—and this is not from yourselves, it is the gift of God."[24] Notice that the Bible doesn't say salvation is the gift *from* God; it is the gift *of* God. God himself is the gift. Yet this is not a gift that God desires to force on anyone. Having created us free, he must respect our freedom to reject him if we so choose. Of course, we have already rejected him—this is the meaning of the Fall—and so God has, through Christ, offered us a way back. But we can reject that solution also, a kind of second slap in the face to God. To reject God and Jesus Christ is to reject heaven. The remarkable thing is that we don't have to make any kind of great decision to reject God in these ways. While repentance reflects a desire to turn back to God, the road to hell simply means continuing to go the way we are going, on our own self-constructed path.

Destined for Damnation?

The decision to go to hell is a free choice, and it is our choice. For this reason I cannot go along with an extreme form of Calvinism, which holds that we have no choice in the matter. According to this view, our salvation or damnation is predestined: God decided even before Creation who goes to heaven and who goes to hell. Yes, we act, but our action itself is determined by God's prior decision to give or withhold grace. So ultimately God saves whom he chooses and damns whom he chooses. This Calvinist view is drawn from some supporting passages in Scripture; it is also inferred from a very strong understanding of divine omnipotence. In other words, God is completely in charge, and therefore he must be in charge of who is in heaven and who is not.

Now these Calvinists are quick to defend the justice of God. They emphasize that all humans deserve damnation on account of sin; therefore it is not unjust for God to let humans suffer the consequences of their sin, while mercifully exempting a few. It is God's grace to give, and he has every right to give it to the ones he prefers. As John Feinberg puts it, "If God doesn't give grace to some, there is no obligation that he has failed to meet."[25]

Still, I find this concept of God extending grace to some while keeping it from others to be unworthy of God. It is an idea not lacking in justice, perhaps, but certainly lacking in benevolence. It would be easy to fear such a God, but not so easy to love him. Moreover, it follows from this view that Jesus didn't die for all mankind, only for those who were chosen in advance for salvation. I find this deeply shocking, and no theodicy, it seems to me, is possible that takes so hard a line on divine predestination. I find it amusing that people who advance this view always list themselves among the elect; never does someone count himself among those that God has marked out for hell.

Moreover, this unyielding view of salvation is one that also appears to be based on a highly selective reading of the Bible, explaining away the plain meaning of numerous passages that stress that Christ's atonement and saving grace are intended for all people. In 1 Peter 1:17 we read that "the heavenly Father to whom you pray has no favorites." Romans 5:18 speaks of salvation offered "for everyone." 1 Timothy 2:3-4 says that "God . . . wants everyone to be saved and to understand the truth." And the most famous passage in the Bible, John 3:16, says that "God loved the world so much that he gave his one and only Son, so that *everyone* who believes in him will not perish but have eternal life" (emphasis added).

Theologians wrangle over how to interpret these texts, but my contention is that the plain, commonsense meaning of Scripture appears to indicate that God is inviting everyone to believe in him. Whether we choose to believe or not is another matter, but there is no indication here that God has denied some the opportunity to accept the free gift. On the contrary, the point seems to be that God has given to every person the grace, which is to say the ability, to decide either way.

Paul writes in Romans 2:15 that even the pagans—those who have not heard of the Christian God—have no excuse to turn away from God, because God's law is implanted in every human heart. From Paul we get the idea that even pagans have, through the moral law, the imprint of the divine. So do individual Hindus in India and Confucians in China, who haven't heard of Christ, automatically go to hell because they don't become Christians? The honest answer to that question is that God only knows—but we should be content to leave the matter to God's justice and mercy. Let him sort out whether people who have been offered a gift but don't know about it should be given or denied the benefits of it.

I agree with C. S. Lewis on this point in his *Mere Christianity*: "We do know that no man can be saved except through Christ; we do not know that only those who know Him can be saved through Him."[26] Dante expresses a similar view in the *Divine Comedy*. Dante describes how when we reach the upper rings of heaven, we get an entirely different perspective on salvation from the one we have on earth. God doesn't use the same scales that we do; his perfect and transcendent justice cannot be reduced to human formulas. Dante isn't saying that pagans can or cannot go to heaven; he is saying that our knowledge of such high things is very imperfect. For Christians, as for everyone else, better to confess ignorance and to attend to one's own spiritual condition, responding to what is clear in Scripture, than to feign omniscience about such mysteries that God has hidden from us.

Heaven is a great expression of God's generosity toward us, and he made it an easy place to get to: we must only place our faith in him. Hell, too, is a tribute to God's generosity. How? By being a testament to God's commitment to human freedom: we have the opportunity to go there if we so choose. Right up to the end, God permits us to go our way instead of his way. Of course, we have to go there without him, since if God accompanied us to hell, it would no longer be hell. Moreover, since happiness and virtue are attributes of God, and there is neither happiness nor virtue entirely apart from God, there is great evil and misery in hell. Through a free act of the will to place our faith in God, however, we can avoid this misery and enjoy all of God's blessings in heaven. Through the sacrifice of Jesus, God has cleared the path; the decision whether we will receive this priceless gift that has been offered to us is now ours.

PART 6

Conclusion

CHAPTER 13

NOT FORSAKEN

Delivering Us from Evil

Here on earth you will have many trials and sorrows.
But take heart, because I have overcome the world.

JESUS CHRIST, JOHN 16:33

THIS BOOK HAS THREE purposes. First, to answer the atheist argument that evil and suffering in the world somehow contradict the idea of a God who is both omnipotent and good. Second, to convince both unbelievers and believers that there is reason and purpose for evil and suffering, that even these bad things have their place in God's great providence. Third, to specifically address Christians who are suffering. Thinking through the subject as we have doesn't make suffering go away—I am trying to explain suffering, not explain it away—but I hope to offer a way to cope better with that suffering. This is possible if we understand why we go through suffering and what we can do to make it easier to endure. The challenge is especially acute in addressing those who experience horrendous suffering. Consider the rape victim, or the survivor of some massacre or holocaust, or the parent of a child who has been abducted or tortured. What can we, at the end of our inquiry, say to such a person?

I'll begin with the atheist. If you are an atheist, this book offers you something that you probably didn't want: a refutation. Many atheists think that there is a basic contradiction between the existence of an omnipotent, benevolent God and the design of the world—a design that includes so much evil and suffering. To remove this contradiction, the Christian has to show that there is a possible explanation for why God designed the world in this way, despite the evil and suffering. This is a way understandable through reason. Through the Anthropic Principle—the principle of the fine-tuned universe—we have that possible explanation; in fact, we have much more. The Anthropic Principle offers not just a possible answer to the problem of suffering; it offers a plausible and convincing one. Drawing on the best understanding of modern science, we can say that God designed the world in this way because, given what he wanted to create, there was no other way.

Let's briefly review the implications of this idea. The universe is fine-tuned like a musical instrument. The violin, for example, has to be built in a particular manner, and tuned in a particular manner, in order to produce a particular kind of sound. Similarly, the universe must have the particular laws and features that it does in order to produce a particular kind of free and intelligent observer, a creature whose freedom and intelligence entail moral choice. Given this fact, whatever the universe contains—from distant galaxies to smoldering comets, from earthquakes and tsunamis to predation and disease, from saints to sinners, Mother Teresa to Hitler, and everything in between—is all part of the necessary infrastructure to produce creatures like us.

Certainly, we can object to this or that feature of the universe, as we can object that a well-made violin is too heavy or unwieldy or has too many strings. But the objection has little force if we want a violin that makes a certain desired type of sound. Similarly, it is futile to protest against the order of nature as it exists when it is that same order that results in our very existence. And here, as we have seen, I am not speaking merely of existence in itself but of a certain kind of existence, one that culminates in our being the kind of creature that has moral choice, the capacity to suffer as a free and intelligent being who can reflect deeply on that suffering and even protest it. If God were to take our protest all the way to its end and "fix" the problem, either by taking away natural calamities or by getting rid of free will and free choice, that end would be a world in which we as conscious, rational creatures would not exist. At best, we would exist as lower animals with no moral culpability and no deep suffering, like the dog or the gazelle that has no ability to frame or feel the question, "Why is this happening to me?" For God to remove our complaint in this way is to remove the possibility of a complainer! If on balance we regard our lives as valuable, and if on balance we regard the human race as worth having, then we are conceding the wisdom and value of God's architecture. Finally we have a theodicy that offers a very good reason for why God made the world as he did. This theodicy doesn't downplay the thistles and thorns, or pretend they aren't sharp or troublesome; but it does show that in this world, they are the necessary components in the overall providential framework.

For a couple of decades now, Christians have invoked the fine-tuned universe as proof that the universe has a fine-tuner. Atheists concede the Anthropic Principle, but they insist that fine-tuning can be accounted for by the possibility of multiple universes or the multiverse. I have my own views on this, and have written about it elsewhere; here, however, I don't have to take sides in this quarrel. The novel approach of this book is to take the debate to a new level by showing the implications of the fine-tuning argument for theodicy. The Anthropic Principle accounts not only for natural suffering but also for moral evil. Think about it this way: you can't get human beings with free will without getting evil moral choices, just as you cannot get free human beings without earthquakes, tsunamis, predation, and disease. The fine-tuned universe explains natural calamities that cause suffering, but it also explains the evolution of consciousness, human free will, and intelligence. These capacities that can be used for evil as well as good are also part of the Anthropic scheme.

It's worth reflecting on this for a moment. Our ability to ponder and admire the natural order of things, and to make real moral choices within that order, is built upon and built into that order from the beginning. In fact, we are in some sense the culmination of the whole scheme. Remarkably, the appearance of the kind of mind that can ask about the justice of the Lisbon earthquake is built upon a creation blueprint that includes earthquakes. The moral capacity to tend to earthquake victims in compassion, or to turn away from them in bitterness or indifference, also depends on earthquakes, and just the right amount of oxygen in the atmosphere, and just the right mass and size and distance from the sun to the earth, and just the right position in the right kind of galaxy, and so on back to those astoundingly elaborate and exact conditions of the Big Bang itself. From the beginning, the universe was biocentric, which is to say delicately tuned for the eventual emergence of complex living creatures and, even more, for conscious and free creatures, namely us. It is as if the universe were devised in such a way as to "see ahead," carefully setting down the foundational prerequisites that make possible our existence in it.

So the Anthropic Principle does for providence what the Big Bang did for Creation: it provides scientific corroboration or explanation for God's ongoing creative and sustaining action in the world. Even more than the Big Bang, the fine-tuned universe puts modern atheism completely on the defensive. How? Christians have long believed not only that God made the world, but that he exercises providential supervision over the world. He didn't just get things started; he designed them with great care so that the details would come out just right and culminate in conscious, rational, free biological beings. Now with the fine-tuned universe, we see ever more clearly on the natural level how providential supervision has been exercised. The ancient claims of Scripture are thrillingly confirmed and even elaborated by modern science. Christians have long held, through faith, that God had this kind of jurisdiction; now we perceive, through reason, how he may be using it. So this book offers the atheist something unexpected and probably unsought: a convincing answer to the problem of evil and suffering.

Christians, unlike atheists, aren't looking for refutations. They are looking for answers. Christians want to know how to relate to a God who designed the world in this way—a world that obviously includes plenty of both evil and suffering. Can the Christian find reassurance in the Anthropic argument I am advancing here? I believe the answer is yes. My friend Bruce Schooley, who has been fighting a very aggressive form of cancer, says that it is consoling for him to realize that even the trauma he has gone through, with its outcome still uncertain, becomes more understandable and endurable when he sees that God made the universe in a way that results in people like Bruce—that is to say, humans with consciousness and freedom. God loved Bruce so much that he designed a whole world that would not only give Bruce life but would also give him the capacity to appreciate life and all of God's creation. Not merely Bruce's existence but his reason, his moral faculties, and his ability to choose are all products of God's fine-tuned universe. And so if that universe includes cancer, then so be it; Bruce is still going to use his free choice to praise God and thank him, not for the cancer, but for the providential gift of human life that remains very much worth having and worth clinging to even when it is battered by irredentist cancer cells.

So the Anthropic Principle offers something valuable both to the atheist and to the believer. But understanding suffering is one thing, and coping with it is quite another. At this point, it's worth pushing the inquiry further and asking the question, Does atheism or Christianity offer a better way of coping with suffering? Let's see what the atheists have to offer a suffering person in the way of accounting for the purpose of their suffering. Richard Dawkins says, "The universe we observe has precisely the properties we should expect if there is, at bottom, no design, no purpose, no evil and no good, nothing but blind, pitiless indifference." Jacques Monod says, "The ancient covenant is in pieces; man knows at least that he is alone in the universe's unfeeling immensity, out of which he emerged only by chance." Steven Weinberg says, "The more the universe seems comprehensible, the more it also seems pointless." And Bertrand Russell contributes, "Only on the firm foundation of unyielding despair, can the soul's habitation henceforth be safely built."[1] So if as a suffering person, you are looking for despair, you know where to find it.

The Consolation of Faith

Christianity, by contrast, at least offers some consolation, if only the consolation of faith. It is simply an empirical fact that religious believers who pray will often feel a sense of comfort in their trials. We don't need data on this point; it is shown by the fact that believers routinely pray when they encounter difficulty. Obviously they wouldn't keep doing that if they received nothing, not even a sense of solace or calm, as a result of these prayers. Even if the believer receives nothing, it's still on par with what the atheist, who is not praying, receives. So religion comes out ahead if only by offering the believer at least the hope of a divine ear that is listening to the anguished human pleas. Atheism, as we have seen, cannot offer anything comparable, and may even leave the sufferer feeling worse.

The example of death allows us to contrast very vividly what atheism offers versus what Christianity offers. We all face, as humans, a certain anxiety about death. Death produces in all people who reflect upon it a quiet terror, because death means annihilation—a complete end to this life and its associations—and the concept of losing everything is a terrifying one. So now let's ask the question, Which approach, atheism or belief in God, offers the dying man greater relief from this anxiety and terror? The obvious answer is religion: belief in God. Religion offers the hope of life after death, and even if this is only a hope, it is vastly better than what atheism offers. As psychologist William James put it, the issue here is not whether this hope is real or not. In truth, we won't know the answer to that until we are on the other side of the curtain. The real issue is that we all have to deal with death and, in James's words, "Religion thus makes easy and felicitous what in any case is necessary; and if it be the only agency that can accomplish this result, its vital importance as a human faculty stands vindicated beyond dispute."[2]

The atheist Karl Marx understood very well that God provides consolation in times of suffering, famously calling religion the "opium of the people." Even though Marx meant this as a criticism, his diagnosis contains the acknowledgment that religion relieves distress and suffering. For Marx, the cure is a false one because it relies too heavily on the expectation of another world that will remedy the ills of this world. Marx wanted people to be atheists so that they would squarely face, and resist, the suffering of this world: "The abolition of religion as the illusory happiness of the people is required for their real happiness."[3]

We can safely set aside Marx's ultimate goal of a revolutionary Communist society. Today we can all agree not only that this is impossible, but that, if it were possible, it would be a nightmare, a virtual hell on earth. Why? Ironically it is because Marx wanted a political program to get rid of evil and suffering. His "solution" was one that is implied in some of the atheist critiques of God. Marx believed that if you had a revolutionary Communist society which got rid of hierarchy and inequality and bad human choices, the result would be utopia. The great enemy of all Communist societies wasn't poverty or inequality; it was human free will. And the Communist answer was political tyranny, forced collectivization, and centralized control of all the major decisions of life. The actual result we know, and the world has rejected the Marxist nightmare, even though it endures in North Korea and one or two other wretched outposts. Ironically the regimes that tried to completely eliminate evil and suffering became, and some of them continue to be, the most god-forsaken outposts on the planet.

Here I want to go beyond the failure of Marxism and question Marx's underlying assumption about Christianity. Marx assumed that atheists are more likely than Christians to want to eradicate the evil and suffering of this world, and here I think he couldn't be more wrong. Christians, no less than atheists, are repelled by evil and moved by suffering, and they share with atheists the human motivation to reduce and ameliorate these things. But what Marx missed is that Christians are even more likely than atheists to actually work against evil and suffering. That's because Christianity supplies an additional motive to eradicate suffering that is not present in atheism. Moreover, the Christian way of doing this is entirely different from the Marxist way of tyranny and violence—heaping evil upon evil.

Consider the famous scene in *The Brothers Karamazov* in which the two brothers Ivan and Alyosha discuss the horrors of the world. Ivan, the atheist, invokes these to declare his moral independence from God. He wants nothing to do with God, and he even corners his younger brother, the devout Alyosha, into a seemingly blasphemous concession. Alyosha concedes that he cannot go along with a divine plan that includes a single case of gratuitous suffering. Yet it is this same Alyosha who actually commiserates with those who are suffering. He shares their stories and their pain, and he does what he can to improve their situation. Meanwhile, Ivan marinates in his atheist resentment. As Kenneth Surin writes, "Ivan professes to be on the side of the victims, but it is Alyosha who enacts this solidarity."[4] Atheist resentment seems not to produce very much charity, possibly because atheists see so little hope in humanly addressing all the evil and suffering in the world. Inveighing against it is so much easier than doing something about it.

Christians can certainly be guilty of inaction, but they are more likely to do something about injustice and suffering than atheists are, and it's worth asking why. Why does Christianity, truly embraced, produce charity rather than resentment or despair? Why does it produce rational, moral agents capable of seeing the magnitude of evil and suffering in the world, who recognize that we cannot, this side of paradise, eliminate those things, and who nevertheless work as much as they can to remedy and ameliorate them? We can answer this question by looking at what once happened to Mother Teresa on the streets of Calcutta. A group of Indians walked by and saw that she was hugging a leper. "I wouldn't do that," one of them commented, "for all the money in the world." To which Mother Teresa replied, "Neither would I. I am doing it for the love of Christ."

The point here is that even an evolved primate may feel compassion, but this does not necessarily translate into a desire to place the removal of suffering at the center of one's life. In fact, there are good Darwinian reasons to focus on our own survival and flourishing, and this of course is how most people live their lives. In his book *Darwin's Cathedral*, biologist David Sloan Wilson writes that, from an evolutionary point of view, we are not strongly motivated to serve our flawed fellow men. Christianity, he argues, provides a transcendent justification for overcoming this natural reluctance. "Loving and serving a perfect God," he writes, "is vastly more motivating than loving and serving one's imperfect neighbor."[5] And this was in fact Mother Teresa's motivation. She wanted, as she once put it, to do "something beautiful for God." Her answer to the question, Where is God when it hurts? was a simple and direct one. God is right here, in each one of us. We are the eyes and ears and hands of God in the world. So we do good for God's sake, even as we recognize that it can only marginally reduce the hurt and suffering in the world.

None of this is to suggest that atheists can't work assiduously to relieve pain and suffering; many can, and do. Nor do I wish to imply that atheists do not have any resources for coping with evil and suffering. Atheists, like believers, can work to bring good out of suffering. It is critically important to realize that suffering by itself is not good. Nowhere in this book do I suggest that suffering is a net plus, or even that it has a purpose unto itself. The merit comes entirely in what we do about suffering. Handled correctly, suffering can lead to some good results. First, suffering provides opportunity for compassion and help. Think about it: if there were no suffering, there would be no need for compassion, or solidarity, or charity. So suffering is a call to virtue; it offers us an opportunity to become better people through our response to it. Second, suffering is a call to wisdom, giving us a chance to learn from our mistakes. Happiness is an incompetent instructor; much of the knowledge we get in life comes from hardship and folly. Experience, in this sense, gives us wisdom, although at a considerable price.

Moreover, suffering has a spiritual benefit: it can provide us with an inducement to draw closer to God. Atheists probably don't regard this as a benefit at all, and yet suffering also draws many atheists closer to God. Many conversion experiences begin with some sort of reversal or catastrophe: when the person has nowhere to go, he looks to God as a kind of last resort. Recall the parable of the Prodigal Son: would that wasteful sybarite have come back to his father had his provisions not run out? C. S. Lewis notes that it is very gracious of God to respond when we turn to him only in desperation and need; even so, Lewis says, God will take us any way he can get us. God doesn't mind if we call on him when we are down and out, so long as we call on him in the end. Lewis terms this a "divine humility."[6]

So there are many ways to turn evil and suffering into good, although none of these outcomes is guaranteed. Sometimes calamity has the opposite effect: some people respond by becoming more bitter and mean and blaming the world and God for their problems, even problems that are largely of their own making. Others invoke suffering to reject God, not merely to turn away from him but to become his sworn enemy; their atheism becomes a way of spitting in God's face. My experience is that traumatic events tend to force people to go one way or the other. Either they become better and holier, or they become nastier and more blasphemous. Even here, there is free will.

Horrendous Suffering

Thus far, we have been talking about evil and suffering, but we haven't been focusing on horrendous suffering. How then can an atheist or even a secular person deal with horrendous suffering? Here there are generally two approaches. The first is Stoicism, the doctrine of the stiff upper lip, a calm endurance of life as it comes. Stoicism is vindicated in the psychological studies cited in an earlier chapter, which show that good news doesn't bring as much happiness as we anticipate, and bad news doesn't last as long as we fear it will. Life typically returns to its equilibrium. Consequently, there is much to recommend in the uncomplaining philosophy of the Stoics. Indeed Stoicism has much in common with Eastern religions that locate suffering not in the world but in the mind. These religions say that by controlling the mind through meditation and self-examination, you can control and regulate your suffering. Pain is inevitable, but suffering is optional. For all its apparent coldness, Stoicism can provide a healthy balance to our moist-eyed culture; holding it in is often a better option than letting it all hang out. In many ways, it accords with the anthropic view, accepting suffering as part of a larger, good order.

A second approach I want to consider is the Nietzschean one. We find in the philosopher Nietzsche a remarkable contrast to the tone of most atheists today. First of all, Nietzsche is outraged that these atheists "have got rid of the Christian God, and now feel obliged to cling all the more firmly to Christian morality." In other words, it is Christianity that gave us the virtue of compassion and concern for the poor underdog, and now the atheists are taking up those Christian ideas against Christianity itself. Nietzsche regards this not only as a Pyrrhic victory but as intellectually dishonest. "When one gives up Christian belief, one thereby deprives oneself of the right to Christian morality." Most atheists seem completely oblivious to this point.

Nietzsche would have found today's atheists to be wimps and whiners, what he terms "slanderers of life." His advice to them: stop sniveling about suffering. Nothing worthwhile, Nietzsche writes, is achieved without suffering. He admired the Greeks of the Homeric Age because he said they found a way to turn misery into something great and noble. Nietzsche praises not only the willingness to endure suffering—"What doesn't kill us," he famously writes, "makes us stronger"—but he also cherishes "the will to inflict great suffering." The greatest of empires, for instance, were "soaked in blood thoroughly and for a long time."

For Nietzsche, life should be affirmed. We should revel in life, even in its great hardship, tragedy, destruction, and cruelty. Cruelty for Nietzsche is not a vice; pity is. Cruelty, after all, is natural; the lion doesn't have to learn what to do with the stag. Nietzsche berates soft people for making a virtue out of weakness, one that they call pity. Once again, Nietzsche blames Christianity for fostering the emotion of pity. "Pity," Nietzsche writes, "is considered a virtue only among decadents." Such people, he concludes, are responsible for "the regression of mankind."[7]

There is something audacious and bracing about Nietzsche's writing. And in a way different from the Stoics, he is also embracing the anthropic view: that suffering is essential and not accidental, and that to attempt to remove rather than use it is both futile and dehumanizing. Yet Nietzsche's approach seems ultimately quite blustering and hollow. Neither the Stoics nor Nietzsche seems to have a real answer to horrendous suffering. When a man has to watch his wife being raped and then see her body sawed into little pieces, it is simply obscene to say to him, "Endure this calmly, because your emotions will eventually return to normal," or "Embrace this suffering, because what doesn't kill you will make you stronger." Some people never get over suffering of this sort, and it breaks them rather than making them stronger.

So finally we turn to the Christian solution to the problem of evil and suffering. Christianity offers the only way to make some sense of even horrendous suffering. Simply put, this is possible when we offer our suffering to Christ. In practice, of course, it is not so simple, so let's look at what this means. First the skeptic or even the Christian might ask why Christ would want us to suffer for him. This brings us to an important distinction. Christ does not in fact ask us to suffer *for him*; he is the one who suffered for us, and his suffering atonement for our sins is presented to us as a free gift, ours for the asking. So this is not the reason why we offer up our suffering to Christ. Christ does, however, explicitly ask believers to suffer *with him*: "take up your cross daily, and follow me."[8] Jesus asks us to follow him and warns us with the phrase "your cross" that such obedience will involve suffering. Thus, we believers can offer our suffering up to God because it is one of the best ways that we can respond to what Christ has done for us. Obedience is the way that we can truly show our love for him, and our obedience will necessarily involve some suffering. In fact, this suffering is the true measure of our love.

To see why I say this, let's focus for a minute on what suffering means to us. Let's say that I get a phone call and learn that a distant relative has just died in a car accident. Am I upset? Certainly I am—to a degree. I didn't know the person very well. At the same time, I am sorry to hear the news. But, to be frank, it isn't going to ruin my day, and in a few hours, I may no longer think of it at all. Now contrast this with my reaction if I found out that my only child, Danielle, had just died in an accident. This would overturn my day, my week, my year, my life! Why? Because of how much I love my daughter. The point I am making is that we suffer for the loss of others in exact proportion to how much we care about them. The more we care, the more we suffer. In fact, when the ones we love are hurting, we want to suffer. If my daughter is hurt or sick, I don't want God to make me happy or even indifferent in that situation. I would actually prefer to suffer. Thus our willingness to suffer is the true gauge of how we truly feel about another person.

Now Christ endured the ultimate suffering for us, and what can we give him back in return? Nothing. We can accept his free gift of salvation, but this is hardly a form of reciprocity because the gift benefits us so much. It is for our own good. We can also attempt to bring our lives into conformity with God's will. But this, too, is self-interest, rightly understood. God created us, and his plan for our lives is undoubtedly the best plan. Once again, recognizing this is of primary benefit to us. So, thus far, we are receiving Christ's immeasurable gift and giving him nothing in return.

We can, however, offer our suffering as a "little cross." This suffering doesn't do Christ any good. But we give it up to him all the same, not because it benefits him, but because our willingness to suffer when we follow him shows how much we love and trust him. Just as my suffering over my daughter, Danielle, would be an expression of my deep love for her, in the same way, our obedience, even when it involves suffering, is the true measure of our love for Christ and our way of thanking him for how much he suffered for us. And the greater the suffering that we offer up to him in obedience to his will, the greater the demonstration of our love. It follows from this that those who don't suffer at all are unable to relate to Christ in this powerful and unique way. Through our suffering, through taking up our own cross daily to follow him, we have the honor of walking the Via Dolorosa with Christ himself. We have the privilege of sharing in the loneliness and anguish of Calvary—as well as in the special comfort God shares with those who entrust to him their hurting hearts.

Moreover, our suffering can be turned into a blessing for others. "He comforts us in all our troubles," Scripture says, "so that we can comfort others. When they are troubled, we will be able to give them the same comfort God has given us."[9] Comfort, of course, helps us to cope with suffering; it doesn't eliminate suffering. Yet when we meditate thoughtfully on why there is evil and suffering in the world, and think back to the arguments in this book, we should recognize why these bad things can't be eliminated. Indeed when we consider that God has so finely tuned the universe in such a way as to allow us the freedom to take up our own cross and follow him and also, through that suffering, to draw closer to the divine, the suffering itself can be rendered sublime.

ACKNOWLEDGMENTS

I'D LIKE TO THANK my friend Ed McVaney, who has been a confidant and a mentor. Ed and I have worked through the main themes of this book from the beginning. I am also grateful to my friend Bruce Schooley, who has a special interest in this topic because he is in remission from cancer. Bruce is actively involved in all my books, and he is the one who helped get me on the right track with this one. Pete Marsh, B. J. Marsh, Byron Van Kley, Andrew Accardy, and all the folks at the Y God Institute are a constant help and inspiration to me. I also appreciate the help and counsel of the trustees of The King's College, especially John Beckett, Darren Blanton, Steve Douglass, Scott Ford, Lee and Allie Hanley, Kevin McVaney, and Andy Mills. Several people read this book and offered helpful comments, including Gregory Fossedal, Stan Oakes, Wayne Grudem, and Ed and Caroline Hoffman. My assistant, Tyler Vawser, is indispensable, and he has worked on all aspects of this book, from reading chapters to chasing down endnotes. My summer research assistant Joe Ford worked closely with me in brainstorming the argument, and also in getting the details right. Benjamin Wiker did a thorough critique of all the chapters, resulting in big improvements. As will be clear from the book, the atheists with whom I do public battle—Peter Singer, Bart Ehrman, Michael Shermer, and the late Christopher Hitchens—have provided me with valuable intellectual stimulation. In our debates and in this book, I work hard to defeat and refute them; yet I consider them friends rather than enemies, and ultimately I am more interested in persuading them. Finally I wish to thank the team at Tyndale, especially Jon Farrar, who first suggested this topic to me and has seen it through from start to finish.

NOTES

CHAPTER 1: AN IMMIGRANT'S JOURNEY
1. John Milton, *Paradise Lost* (New York: W. W. Norton, 1975), 7.
2. Elie Wiesel, *The Trial of God* (New York: Schocken Books, 1995), viii–ix, 54.
3. Christopher Hitchens, *Hitch 22* (New York: Twelve Publishing, 2010), 21–25.
4. Bart Ehrman, *God's Problem* (New York: HarperOne, 2008), 1–3, 5, 16, 128.
5. Philip Jenkins, *The Next Christendom* (New York: Oxford University Press, 2011), 220, 275; Philip Jenkins, *The New Faces of Christianity* (New York: Oxford University Press, 2006), 68.
6. Elie Wiesel, *Dimensions of the Holocaust:* (Evanston, IL: Northwestern University Press, 1977), 7.

CHAPTER 2: WOUNDED THEISM
1. Friedrich Nietzsche, *Twilight of the Idols* and *The Anti-Christ* (New York: Penguin Books, 1990), 175.
2. Steven Pinker, *How the Mind Works* (New York: W. W. Norton, 1997), 560.
3. Bertrand Russell, *The Scientific Outlook* (New York: Routledge Classics, 2009), 94.
4. Richard Dawkins, *River out of Eden* (New York: Basic Books, 1995), 95.
5. Charles Darwin, letter to Asa Gray, May 22, 1860, in *The Life and Letters of Charles Darwin*, ed. Francis Darwin (New York: D. Appleton, 1919), vol. 2, 105–106.

6. Richard Dawkins, *The God Delusion* (Boston: Houghton Mifflin, 2006), 51.

7. Adrian Desmond and James Moore, *Darwin* (New York: W. W. Norton, 1991), 387.

8. Gertrude Himmelfarb, *Darwin and the Darwinian Revolution* (Chicago: Ivan R. Dee, 1996), 137, 385.

9. Owen Flanagan, *The Problem of the Soul* (New York: Basic Books, 2002), 31; Thomas Nagel, *The Last Word* (New York: Oxford University Press, 1997), 130; Victor Stenger, *God: The Failed Hypothesis* (Amherst, NY: Prometheus Books, 2007), 240.

10. Fyodor Dostoyevsky, *The Brothers Karamazov* (New York: Vintage Books, 1991), 244–45.

11. Nicholas Wolterstorff, *Lament for a Son* (Grand Rapids, MI: William Eerdmans Publishing, 1987), 34, 52.

12. John Stott, *The Cross of Christ* (Downers Grove, IL: InterVarsity Press, 1986), 311; Hans Küng, cited by Michael Peterson, "Introduction," in *The Problem of Evil*, ed. Michael Peterson (Notre Dame: University of Notre Dame Press, 1992), 1.

13. As revealed in the private correspondence of Mother Teresa. See Brian Kolodiejchuk, ed., *Mother Teresa: Come Be My Light* (New York: Doubleday, 2007).

14. Rodney Stark, *Discovering God* (New York: HarperOne, 2007), 103.

15. Mary Lefkowitz, *Greek Gods, Human Lives* (New Haven, CT: Yale University Press, 2003), 12, 235; William Shakespeare, *King Lear*, Act 4, Scene 1.

16. Seyyed Hossein Nasr, *The Heart of Islam* (New York: HarperCollins, 2004), 10.

17. John Hick, *Evil and the God of Love* (New York: Palgrave Macmillan, 2010), 243.

18. *Carl Sagan's Universe*, ed. Yervant Terzian and Elizabeth Bilson (Cambridge, UK: Cambridge University Press, 1997), 148; Carl Sagan, *Pale Blue Dot* (New York: Random House, 1994), 37; Stephen Jay Gould, *Dinosaur in a Haystack* (New York: Three Rivers Press, 1996), 327.

19. Joel Primack and Nancy Ellen Abrams, *The View from the Center of the Universe* (New York: Riverhead Books, 2006), 2, 11; John Barrow, *The Origin of the Universe* (New York: Basic Books, 1994), 85, 125; Paul Davies, *The Mind of God* (New York: Touchstone Books, 1992), 16; Christian de Duve, *Vital Dust* (New York: Basic Books, 1995), xviii.

CHAPTER 3: THE LIMITS OF THEODICY

1. Robert Browning, "Pippa's Song," in *The Oxford Book of English Verse* (Oxford: Clarendon Press, 1919).

2. Blaise Pascal, *Pensées and Other Writings* (New York: Oxford University Press, 1995), 142.

3. If you're interested in these topics, you can read more about them in part 4 of my book *What's So Great about Christianity*.

4. John 12:31; 14:30; 16:11(NIV).

5. 1 John 5:19.

6. C. S. Lewis, "Animal Pain," in *The Problem of Evil: A Reader,* ed. Mark Larrimore (London: Blackwell Publishing, 2001), 331.

7. Alvin Plantinga, "Supralapsarianism, or O Felix Culpa," *Christian Faith and the Problem of Evil,* ed. Peter van Inwagen (Grand Rapids, MI: William Eerdmans Publishing, 2004), 16.

8. Bart Ehrman, *God's Problem* (New York: HarperOne, 2008), 53, 61.

9. Immanuel Kant, *Basic Writings of Kant* (New York: Modern Library, 2001), 125.

10. Timothy Keller, *The Reason for God* (New York: Dutton Books, 2008), 25.
11. Al-Ghazzali, *The Alchemy of Happiness* (Armonk, NY: M. E. Sharpe, 1991), 21.
12. Billy Graham, *Death and the Life After* (Nashville: Thomas Nelson Publishers, 1987), 68.
13. Gottfried Leibniz, "On the Radical Origination of Things," in *Leibniz: Philosophical Papers and Letters,* ed. Leroy Loemker (Dordrecht: Reidel, 1969), 488–89.
14. Peter van Inwagen, *The Problem of Evil* (New York: Clarendon Press, 2006), 69.
15. Harold Kushner, *When Bad Things Happen to Good People* (New York: Anchor Books, 1981), 147.
16. Sarah Netter and Sabina Ghebremedhin, "Jaycee Dugard Found After 18 Years, Kidnap Suspect Allegedly Fathered Her Kids," *ABC News*, August 27, 2009, www .abcnews.com.
17. Marilyn McCord Adams, *Horrendous Evils and the Goodness of God* (Ithaca, NY: Cornell University Press, 1999), 26.
18. Augustine, *City of God* (New York: Penguin Books, 1984), 454.
19. John Polkinghorne, *Exploring Reality* (New Haven, CT: Yale University Press, 2005), 140.
20. G. W. Leibniz, *Theodicy* (LaSalle, IL: Open Court Publishing, 1990).
21. Voltaire, *Candide and Related Texts* (Indianapolis: Hackett Publishing, 2000), 79.
22. Leibniz, *Theodicy*, 196.

CHAPTER 4: ATHEIST DELUSIONS

1. Peter Atkins, *The Creation* (Oxford: W. H. Freeman, 1981), 3.
2. David Hume, *Dialogues Concerning Natural Religion* (New York: Penguin Books, 1990), 114–15.
3. Sigmund Freud, *The Future of an Illusion* (New York: W. W. Norton, 1961); Christopher Hitchens, *God Is Not Great* (New York: Twelve Publishing, 2007), 103; Sam Harris, *The End of Faith* (New York: W. W. Norton, 2005), 223.
4. Ernst Mayr, *What Evolution Is* (New York: Basic Books, 2001), 252; Henry McHenry, "Human Evolution," in *Evolution: The First Four Billion Years,* Michael Ruse and Joseph Travis (Cambridge, MA: Harvard University Press, 2009), 256.
5. Nicholas Wade, *Before the Dawn* (New York: Penguin Press, 2006), 1, 11.
6. Charles Murray, *Human Accomplishment* (New York: HarperPerennial, 2003), 7.
7. Kai Nielsen, "Ethics Without God," in J. P. Moreland and Kai Nielsen, *Does God Exist?* (Amherst, NY: Prometheus Books, 1993), 99.
8. Jane Goodall, "People Primates," in *Mind, Life and Universe,* ed. Lynn Margulis and Eduardo Punset (White River Junction, VT: Chelsea Green Publishing, 2007), 28.
9. William Rowe, "The Problem of Evil and Varieties of Atheism," in *The Problem of Evil,* ed. Marilyn McCord Adams and Robert Adams (Oxford: Oxford University Press, 1990), 130–31.
10. Bruce Russell and Stephen Wykstra, "The Inductive Argument from Evil: A Dialogue," *Philosophical Topics* XVI, no. 2 (Fall 1988).
11. Walter Sinnott-Armstrong, "Some Reasons to Believe That There Is No God," in William Lane Craig and Walter Sinnott-Armstrong, *God?* (New York: Oxford University Press, 2004), 95.
12. Hume, *Dialogues Concerning Natural Religion*, 92.

13. Blaise Pascal, *Pensées and Other Writings* (New York: Oxford University Press, 1995), 62.
14. Job 38:4, 33; Job 39:27.
15. Bart Ehrman, *God's Problem* (New York: HarperOne, 2008), 184, 186.
16. Job 42:3, 6.

CHAPTER 5: FREE TO CHOOSE

1. Elie Wiesel, *Night* (New York: Bantam Books, 1982), 32.
2. Cited in Lactantius, *De Ira Dei* (Washington, DC: Catholic University of America Press, 1965), 92.
3. J. L. Mackie, "Evil and Omnipotence," *Mind* 64 (1955): 200–212.
4. C. S. Lewis, *God in the Dock* (Grand Rapids, MI: William Eerdmans Publishing, 1970), 244.
5. Harold Kushner, *When Bad Things Happen to Good People* (New York: Anchor Books, 1981), 49, 148.
6. Bart Ehrman, *God's Problem* (New York: HarperOne, 2008), 25.
7. Genesis 1:26 (KJV).
8. John Hick, *Evil and the God of Love* (New York: Harper and Row, 1978).
9. Augustine, *On Free Choice of the Will* (Indianapolis: Hackett Publishing, 1993).
10. Boethius, *The Consolation of Philosophy* (New York: Penguin Books, 1969).
11. Stephen Barr, *Modern Physics and Ancient Faith* (Notre Dame: University of Notre Dame Press, 2003), 175–89.
12. Victor Stenger, *God: The Failed Hypothesis* (Amherst, NY: Prometheus Books, 2007), 33.
13. Alvin Plantinga, "God, Evil, and the Metaphysics of Freedom," in *The Nature of Necessity,* Alvin Plantinga (New York: Oxford University Press, 1974), 166–67.

CHAPTER 6: CHOICES AND CONSEQUENCES

1. Louis Greenspan and Stefan Andersson, eds., *Russell on Religion* (London: Routledge, 1999), 101.
2. Carl Sagan, *The Varieties of Scientific Experience* (New York: Penguin, 2006), 149–50, 224.
3. Paul Davies, *The Mind of God* (New York: Touchstone Books, 1992), 195.
4. James Trefil, *Reading the Mind of God* (New York: Anchor Books, 1989), 1, 52.
5. Pierre Bayle, "Manicheans," in *The Problem of Evil,* ed. Mark Larrimore (London: Blackwell Publishing, 2001), 187.
6. David Hume, *Dialogues Concerning Natural Religion* (New York: Penguin Books, 1990), 116–19.
7. J. L. Mackie, "Evil and Omnipotence," *Mind,* April 1955; James Wood, "Holiday in Hellmouth," *The New Yorker,* June 9 & 16, 2008, 122; Christopher Hitchens, *God Is Not Great* (New York: Twelve Publishing, 2007), 100.
8. Psalm 44:23; Psalm 88:14; Psalm 10:1.
9. Richard Elliott Friedman, *The Disappearance of God* (Boston: Little, Brown and Co., 1995), 8, 14, 28, 31, 58, 69.
10. J. L. Schellenberg, *Divine Hiddenness and Human Reason* (Ithaca, NY: Cornell University Press, 2006), 3, 83.

11. Carl Sagan, *The Varieties of Scientific Experience* (New York: Penguin Books, 2006), 167.

12. Bart Ehrman, *God's Problem* (New York: HarperOne, 2008), 12.

13. Steven Pinker, *The Blank Slate* (New York: Viking, 2002), 2.

14. Jean-Jacques Rousseau, *The First and Second Discourses* (New York: St. Martin's Press, 1964), 103.

15. Pinker, *The Blank Slate*, 285.

16. Randy Alcorn, *If God Is Good* (Colorado Springs: Multnomah Books, 2009), 25.

17. Anselm, "On the Fall of the Devil," in *Anselm of Canterbury: The Major Works,* (New York: Oxford University Press, 2008), 196–204.

18. Ibid., 230.

19. Hume, *Dialogues Concerning Natural Religion*, 116; Martin Gardner, *The Whys of a Philosophical Scrivener* (New York: St. Martin's Press, 1999), 260.

20. Pascal, *Pensées and Other Writings* (New York: Oxford University Press, 1995), 57.

21. Paul Moser, "Cognitive Idolatry and Divine Hiding," in *Divine Hiddenness,* ed. Daniel Howard-Snyder and Paul Moser (Cambridge, UK: Cambridge University Press, 2002), 125–41.

CHAPTER 7: ACTS OF GOD

1. Voltaire, "The Lisbon Earthquake," in *Toleration and Other Essays* (New York: G. P. Putnam's Sons, 1912), 206.

2. Susan Neiman, *Evil in Modern Thought* (Princeton, NJ: Princeton University Press, 2002), 240.

3. Voltaire, "The Lisbon Earthquake," 204–206.

4. Amy Waldman, "Torn from Moorings, Villagers from Sri Lanka Grasp for Past," *New York Times,* March 6, 2005, http://www.nytimes.com/2005/03/06/international /asia/06lanka.html.

5. "Nature's Extremes," *Time,* special edition, 2011.

6. *Russell on Religion,* ed. Louis Greenspan and Stefan Andersson (London: Routledge, 1999), 173.

7. David Hume, *Dialogues Concerning Natural Religion* (New York: Penguin Books, 1990), 120–21.

8. Rousseau, "Letter to Voltaire on Optimism," August 18, 1756, reprinted in Voltaire, *Candide and Related Texts* (Indianapolis: Hackett Publishing, 2000), 110.

9. Barbara Ehrenreich, "God Owes Us an Apology," *The Progressive,* March 2005, www.commondreams.org.

10. Freeman Dyson, *A Many-Colored Glass* (Charlottesville, VA: University of Virginia Press, 2007), 66.

11. Peter Ward and Donald Brownlee, *Rare Earth* (New York: Copernicus Books, 2004), xii, 30, 35, 53, 194, 213, 220.

12. William Broad, "Deadly Yet Necessary, Quakes Renew the Planet," *New York Times,* January 17, 2008.

13. Michael Denton, *Nature's Destiny* (New York: The Free Press, 1998), 22, 28, 45.

14. Joel Primack and Nancy Ellen Abrams, *The View from the Center of the Universe* (New York: Riverhead Books, 2006), 213.

15. Joan Didion, *The Year of Magical Thinking* (New York: Knopf, 2005), 190.

16. William McNeill, *Plagues and Peoples* (New York: Anchor Books, 1998), 162–63, 171, 176, 212–13, 216–17.
17. Randolph Nesse and George Williams, *Why We Get Sick* (New York: Vintage Books, 1994), 180.
18. Matthew Herper, "Our Germs, Ourselves," *Forbes,* March 30, 2009, 70.
19. McNeill, *Plagues and Peoples,* 41.
20. "Bacterial Evolution," in *Evolution: The First Four Billion Years,* ed. Michael Ruse and Joseph Travis (Cambridge, MA: Harvard University Press, 2009), 440; Brett Finlay, "The Art of Bacterial Warfare," *Scientific American,* February 2010, 57–63.

CHAPTER 8: RED IN TOOTH AND CLAW
1. David Hull, "The God of the Galapagos," *Nature* 352 (1991): 485–86.
2. Annie Dillard, *Pilgrim at Tinker Creek* (New York: HarperPerennial, 1988), 6.
3. George Williams, *The Pony Fish's Glow* (New York: Basic Books, 1997), 154.
4. Charles Darwin, letter to J. D. Hooker, July 13, 1856, www.darwinproject.ac.uk.
5. Jacques Monod, *Chance and Necessity* (New York: Vintage Books, 1971), 112, 146.
6. Richard Dawkins, *River out of Eden* (New York: Basic Books, 1995), 105.
7. Arthur Schopenhauer, "On the Sufferings of the World," in *Collected Essays of Arthur Schopenhauer* (Radford, VA: Wilder Publications, 2008), 202.
8. Daniel Dennett, *Darwin's Dangerous Idea* (New York: Simon & Schuster, 1995), 521.
9. John Hick, *Evil and the God of Love* (New York: Palgrave Macmillan, 2010), 309.
10. Francisco Ayala, *Darwin's Gift to Science and Religion* (Washington, DC: Joseph Henry Press, 2007), xi, 5, 155–56, 159.
11. William Dembski, *The End of Christianity* (Nashville: B & H Publishing Group, 2009), 163.
12. Ibid., 50, 110, 169.
13. John Haught, *God After Darwin* (Boulder, CO: Westview Press, 2008), 9.
14. For a discussion of this point, see Alister McGrath, "Augustine's Origin of Species," *Christianity Today* (May 2009).
15. Charles Darwin, *The Origin of Species* (New York: Barnes & Noble Classics, 2004), 384.
16. Joel Primack and Nancy Ellen Abrams, *The View from the Center of the Universe* (New York: Riverhead Books, 2006), 219.
17. Stephen Jay Gould, *Wonderful Life* (New York: W. W. Norton, 1989), 51.
18. Freeman Dyson, *A Many-Colored Glass* (Charlottesville, VA: University of Virginia Press, 2007), 76.
19. Simon Conway Morris, *Life's Solution* (Cambridge, UK: Cambridge University Press, 2003), 307; Simon Conway Morris, *The Deep Structure of Biology* (West Conshohocken, PA: Templeton Press, 2008), viii.
20. Christian de Duve, *Life Evolving* (New York: Oxford University Press, 2002), 171; Christian de Duve, *Vital Dust* (New York: Basic Books, 1995), 299.
21. Michael Ruse, *Can a Darwinian Be a Christian?* (Cambridge, UK: Cambridge University Press, 2001), 137.
22. Rene Descartes, *Discourse on Method* (New York: Penguin Books, 1968), 73–76.
23. Dawkins, *River out of Eden,* 131.

24. C. H. Eisemann, W. K. Jorgensen, D. J. Merritt, M. J. Rice, B. W. Cribb, P. D. Webb, and M. P. Zalucki, "Do Insects Feel Pain?—A Biological View," *Experientia* 40 (Basel: Birkhäuser Verlag, 1984), 164–67; see also V. B. Wigglesworth, "Do Insects Feel Pain?" *Antenna* 4 (1980): 8–9.

25. V. S. Ramachandran, *A Brief Tour of Human Consciousness* (New York: Pi Press, 2004), 92.

26. Robert Sapolsky, *Why Zebras Don't Get Ulcers* (New York: Henry Holt, 1998), 6.

27. Darwin, *The Origin of Species*, 73.

28. Paul Brand, *Pain: The Gift Nobody Wants* (New York: HarperCollins, 1993), 12.

29. Randolph Nesse and George Williams, *Why We Get Sick* (New York: Vintage Books, 1994), 35.

CHAPTER 9: A FINE-TUNED UNIVERSE

1. Freeman Dyson, *Disturbing the Universe* (New York: Basic Books, 1979), 250.

2. H. J. McCloskey, "God and Evil," in *Critiques of God*, ed. Peter Angeles (Amherst, NY: Prometheus Books, 1997), 211.

3. Victor Stenger, *God: The Failed Hypothesis* (Amherst, NY: Prometheus Books, 2007), 144.

4. Ibid., 156; "Cretinism or Evilution," www.talkorigins.org.

5. John Barrow, *The Constants of Nature* (New York: Vintage Books, 2002), 113.

6. Joel Primack and Nancy Ellen Abrams, *The View from the Center of the Universe* (New York: Riverhead Books, 2006), 98–99.

7. Daniel Dennett, *Breaking the Spell* (New York: Viking, 2006), 69.

8. Paul Davies, *The Mind of God* (New York: Touchstone Books, 1992), 20, 232; Paul Davies, *Cosmic Jackpot* (New York: Houghton Mifflin, 2007), 5.

9. John Barrow, *The Constants of Nature* (New York: Vintage Books, 2002), xiii, 65.

10. Davies, *Cosmic Jackpot*, 146, 150.

11. John Barrow and Frank Tipler, *The Anthropic Cosmological Principle* (New York: Oxford University Press, 1986), 250; Michael Turner, cited in "Life in the Universe," *Scientific American* (October 1994).

12. Carl Sagan, *The Varieties of Scientific Experience* (New York: Penguin Books, 2006), 55.

13. Stephen Hawking, *A Brief History of Time* (New York: Bantam Books, 1996), 126, 129, 131.

14. Martin Rees, *Just Six Numbers* (New York: Basic Books, 2000), 2–4, 161, 179.

15. Carl Sagan, *Pale Blue Dot* (New York: Ballantine Books, 1994), 30.

16. Michael Denton, *Nature's Destiny* (New York: The Free Press, 1998), 372.

17. Primack and Abrams, *The View from the Center of the Universe*, 161, 177.

18. Ibid., 117–18.

19. Paul Davies, *God and the New Physics* (New York: Simon & Schuster, 1983), 189; Fred Hoyle, *The Intelligent Universe* (London: Michael Joseph Publications, 1983), 218; Fred Hoyle, cited by Barrow and Tipler, *The Anthropic Cosmological Principle*, 22; Interview with Robert Jastrow, in Roy Abraham Varghese, ed., *The Intellectuals Speak Out about God* (Washington, DC: Regnery Gateway, 1984), 22.

20. Leonard Susskind, *The Cosmic Landscape* (New York: Back Bay Books, 2006), x; Murray Gell-Mann, *The Quark and the Jaguar* (New York: A.W.H. Freeman, 1994), 212.

21. Steven Weinberg, *Facing Up* (Cambridge, MA: Harvard University Press, 2001), 238; Richard Dawkins, *The Ancestor's Tale* (Boston: Houghton Mifflin, 2004), 2.

22. John Leslie, *Immortality Defended* (Oxford, UK: Blackwell Publishing, 2007), 72.

23. Denton, *Nature's Destiny*, 253; John Wheeler, "Foreword," in Barrow and Tipler, *The Anthropic Cosmological Principle*, vii.

24. Victor Stenger, *God: The Failed Hypothesis*, 153.

25. Barrow and Tipler, *The Anthropic Cosmological Principle*, 511, 545–47.

26. Alejandro Jenkins and Gilad Perez, "Looking for Life in the Multiverse," *Scientific American,* January 2010, 42–49.

27. Stephen Hawking and Leonard Mlodinow *The Grand Design* (New York: Bantam Books, 2010), 165.

28. Sagan, *The Varieties of Scientific Experience*, 59.

29. Davies, *The Mind of God*, 190; Lee Smolin, *The Life of the Cosmos* (New York: Oxford University Press, 1997), 45.

30. Davies, *Cosmic Jackpot*, 204.

31. Stephen Jay Gould and Richard Lewontin, "The Spandrels of San Marco and the Panglossian Paradigm," *Proceedings of the Royal Society of London* 205, no. 1161 (1979), 581–98.

CHAPTER 10: CREATE OR NOT

1. Arthur Schopenhauer, "On the Suffering of the World," *Essays and Aphorisms* (New York: Penguin Books, 1970), 47.

2. Schopenhauer, "On the Suffering of the World," 47; Arthur Schopenhauer, *On the Basis of Morality* (Indianapolis: Hackett Publishing, 1995), xxxiv; Arthur Schopenhauer, *Suffering, Suicide and Immortality* (Mineola, NY: Dover Publications, 2006), 14; Arthur Schopenhauer, *Collected Essays of Arthur Schopenhauer* (Radford, VA: Wilder Publications, 2008), 196.

3. Susan Neiman, *Evil in Modern Thought* (Princeton, NJ: Princeton University Press, 2002), 207.

4. Schopenhauer, *Collected Essays of Arthur Schopenhauer*, 7.

5. G. W. Leibniz, *Theodicy* (LaSalle, IL: Open Court Publishing, 1985), 130.

6. Jean-Jacques Rousseau, "Letter to Voltaire on Optimism," August 18, 1756, in Voltaire, *Candide and Related Texts* (Indianapolis: Hackett Publishing, 2000), 112–13, 118.

7. *Why Does God Hate Amputees?*, www.whydoesgodhateamputees.com.

8. Blaise Pascal, *Pensées and Other Writings* (New York: Oxford University Press, 1995), 37.

9. Mark Ilgen, Kara Zivin, Ryan McCammon, and Marcia Valenstein, "Pain and Suicidal Thoughts, Plans and Attempts in the United States," *General Hospital Psychiatry* 30, no. 6 (2008): 521–27.

10. Life Expectancy Graph, *Scientific American* (September 2010): 44.

11. Robert Merrihew Adams, "Must God Create the Best?," *The Philosophical Review* 81 (1972): 317–32.

12. Robert Merrihew Adams, "Existence, Self-Interest, and the Problem of Evil," in Robert Merrihew Adams, *The Virtue of Faith* (New York: Oxford University Press, 1987).

13. Richard Swinburne, *The Existence of God* (Oxford, UK: Clarendon Press, 2004), 258.
14. Jonathan Haidt, *The Happiness Hypothesis* (New York: Basic Books, 2006), 84–85.
15. Philip Brickman, Dan Coates, and Ronnie Janoff-Bulman, "Lottery Winners and Accident Victims: Is Happiness Relative?," *Journal of Personality and Social Psychology* 36 (1978): 917–27.
16. R. Schulz and S. Decker, "Long-Term Adjustment to Physical Disability," *Journal of Personality and Social Psychology* 48 (1985): 1162–72; C. B. Wortman and R. C. Silver, "Coping with Irrevocable Loss," in *Cataclysms, Crises and Catastrophes*, ed. G. R. VandenBos and B. K. Bryant (Washington, DC: American Psychological Association, 1987); Samuel Bagenstos and Margo Schlanger, "Hedonic Damages, Hedonic Adaptation, and Disability," *Vanderbilt Law Review*, 60, no. 3 (April 2007): 745–97.
17. David Myers, *The Pursuit of Happiness* (New York: Quill Books, 1992), 48.
18. Daniel Gilbert, *Stumbling on Happiness* (New York: Vintage Books, 2005), 114–15, 177.
19. Patrick Marziale, comment cited in *World*, May 23, 2009, 19; Bethany Hamilton, *Soul Surfer* (New York: Pocket Books, 2004), 134–35.
20. Walter Sinnott-Armstrong, "God?," in William Lane Craig and Walter Sinnott-Armstrong, *God?* (New York: Oxford University Press, 2004), 88; Bart Ehrman, *God's Problem* (New York: HarperOne, 2008), 13; Christopher Hitchens, *God Is Not Great* (New York: Twelve Publishing, 2007), 3.
21. John Donne, "Sermon, Easter Day, March 25, 1627," in *The Complete Poetry and Selected Prose of John Donne*, ed. C. M. Coffin (New York: Modern Library, 1952),. 536.
22. John 9:3.
23. John 9:1-39.
24. H. G. Alexander, ed., *The Leibniz-Clarke Correspondence* (Manchester, UK: Manchester University Press, 1956), 12.
25. Mark 14:36.

CHAPTER 11: RAGE OF YAHWEH

1. David Lewis, "Divine Evil," in *Philosophers without Gods*, ed. Louise Antony (New York: Oxford University Press, 2007), 231.
2. Robert Ingersoll, cited by Lewis Lapham, "The Wrath of the Lamb," *Harper's*, May 2005, 7; Sam Harris, *The End of Faith* (New York: W. W. Norton, 2005), 173, 226.
3. Edward O. Wilson, *Consilience* (New York: Alfred A. Knopf, 1998), 267.
4. Michel Onfray, *Atheist Manifesto* (New York: Arcade Publishing, 2007), 163, 179.
5. Numbers 31:7, 9-12, 14-15, 17-18.
6. Joshua 6:17, 20-21; Joshua 8:22, 24-25.
7. Martin Gardner, *The Whys of a Philosophical Scrivener* (New York: St. Martin's Press, 1999), 301.
8. Christopher Hitchens, *God Is Not Great* (New York: Twelve Publishing, 2007), 206.
9. Richard Dawkins, *The God Delusion* (Boston: Houghton Mifflin, 2006), 276.
10. Elizabeth Anderson, "If God Is Dead, Is Everything Permitted?" in ed. Louise Antony, *Philosophers without Gods,* 218–19.
11. Gerald Schroeder, *God According to God* (New York: HarperOne, 2009), 185.

12. See Psalm 98:8 and Isaiah 55:12.
13. Bart Ehrman, *God's Problem* (New York: HarperOne, 2008), 70–71.
14. Richard Hess, "The Jericho and Ai of the Book of Joshua," in *Critical Issues in Early Israelite History*, ed. Richard Hess, Gerald Klingbeil, and Paul Ray Jr. (Winona Lake, IN: Eisenbrauns Publishing, 2008), 33–46.
15. James 1:17.
16. See Exodus 9:12.
17. John Owen, ed., *Calvin's Commentaries* (Grand Rapids, MI: Baker Books, 1979), 249.
18. Ibid.
19. See Genesis 18 and Numbers 14.
20. Orlando Patterson, *Slavery and Social Death* (Cambridge, MA: Harvard University Press, 1982).
21. David Brion Davis, *Slavery and Human Progress* (New York: Oxford University Press, 1984), 131, 143.
22. Walter Kaiser, *Hard Sayings of the Old Testament* (Downers Grove, IL: InterVarsity Press, 1988), 172, 174–75.
23. Paul Copan, *Is God a Moral Monster?*, (Grand Rapids, MI: Baker Books, 2011), 172, 174–76, 180.
24. John Stott, *Christ the Controversialist* (Downers Grove, IL: InterVarsity Press, 1972), 99.
25. Northrop Frye, *The Great Code* (New York: Harcourt, Inc., 1982), 79, 84.
26. Isaiah 53:5, 7.
27. Genesis 22:7-8.
28. John 1:29.

CHAPTER 12: ABANDON ALL HOPE

1. Dante, *The Divine Comedy: Inferno* (New York: Penguin Books, 1971), 89.
2. David Hume, *Essays on Suicide and Immortality of the Soul* (Whitefish, MT: Kessinger Publishing, 2004), 11.
3. Louis Greenspan and Stefan Andersson, eds., *Russell on Religion* (London: Routledge, 1999), 86.
4. Robert Ingersoll, cited in Martin Gardner, *The Whys of a Philosophical Scrivener* (New York: St. Martin's Press, 1999), 301.
5. David Lewis, "Divine Evil," in *Philosophers without Gods*, ed. Louise Antony (New York: Oxford University Press, 2007), 233, 241.
6. Gardner, *The Whys of a Philosophical Scrivener*, 301, 457.
7. John Hick, *Death and Eternal Life* (Louisville, KY: Westminster John Knox Press, 1994), 456.
8. Marilyn McCord Adams, "The Problem of Hell," in *God and the Problem of Evil*, ed. William Rowe (Oxford, UK: Blackwell Publishers, 2001), 283.
9. Rob Bell, *Love Wins* (New York: HarperOne, 2011), 107–108.
10. David Edwards and John Stott, *Essentials* (London: Hodder & Stoughton, 1988), 313–20.
11. C. S. Lewis, *The Problem of Pain* (New York: Macmillan, 1940), 119.
12. David Hume, *Dialogues Concerning Natural Religion* (New York: Penguin Books, 1990), 110.

13. N. T. Wright, *Evil and the Justice of God* (Downers Grove, IL: Intervarsity Press, 2006), 14–15.

14. Luke 16:25.

15. James Crenshaw, *Defending God* (New York: Oxford University Press, 2005), 16.

16. John Haught, *God After Darwin* (Boulder, CO: Westview Press, 2008), 54.

17. Jürgen Moltmann, *The Crucified God* (New York: Harper & Row, 1974), 274.

18. Matthew 27:46; Mark 15:34 (NIV).

19. Alvin Plantinga, "Supralapsarianism, or 'O Felix Culpa,'" in *Christian Faith and the Problem of Evil*, ed. Peter van Inwagen (Grand Rapids, MI: William Eerdmans Publishing, 2004), 25.

20. J. Gresham Machen, *God Transcendent* (Carlisle, PA: Banner of Truth Trust, 1982), 188.

21. Immanuel Kant, *Basic Writings of Kant* (New York: Modern Library, 2001), 163.

22. St. Augustine, *Enchiridion on Faith, Hope, and Love* (Washington, DC: Regnery Publishing, 1961), 33.

23. John Milton, *Paradise Lost* (New York: W. W. Norton, 1975), 35.

24. Ephesians 2:8 (NIV).

25. John Feinberg, *The Many Faces of Evil* (Wheaton, IL: Crossway Books, 2004), 439.

26. C. S. Lewis, *Mere Christianity* (San Francisco: HarperSanFrancisco, 2001), 64.

CHAPTER 13: NOT FORSAKEN

1. Richard Dawkins, *River out of Eden* (New York: Basic Books, 1995), 133; Jacques Monod, *Chance and Necessity* (New York: Vintage Books, 1971), 180; Steven Weinberg, *The First Three Minutes* (New York: Basic Books, 1993), 154; Bertrand Russell, "The Free Man's Worship," in Bertrand Russell, *Russell on Religion*, ed. Louis Greenspan and Stefan Andersson (London: Routledge, 1999), 32.

2. William James, *Writings 1902-1910* (New York: Library of America, 1987), 53.

3. Karl Marx and Friedrich Engels, *On Religion* (Mineola, NY: Dover Publications, 2008), 42.

4. Kenneth Surin, *Theology and the Problem of Evil* (New York: Basil Blackwell, 1986), 115.

5. David Sloan Wilson, *Darwin's Cathedral* (Chicago: University of Chicago Press, 2002), 176.

6. C. S. Lewis, *The Problem of Pain* (New York: HarperOne, 1996), 95–96.

7. Friedrich Nietzsche, *On the Genealogy of Morals and Ecce Homo* (New York: Vintage Books, 1989), 42–43, 65, 154, 195, 228, 272; Friedrich Nietzsche, *Twilight of the Idols and The Anti-Christ* (New York: Penguin Books, 1990), 80, 199.

8. Luke 9:23.

9. 2 Corinthians 1:4.

ABOUT THE AUTHOR

DINESH D'SOUZA IS THE president of The King's College in New York City. A former policy analyst in the Reagan White House, D'Souza also served as the John M. Olin Fellow at the American Enterprise Institute and as a Rishwain Fellow at the Hoover Institution at Stanford University. He is the author of several *New York Times* bestsellers, including *Illiberal Education, What's So Great about America, What's So Great about Christianity,* and *Life after Death: The Evidence.* His articles have appeared in major magazines and newspapers including the *New York Times, Wall Street Journal, Atlantic Monthly, Vanity Fair, New Republic, National Review,* and *Forbes.* For more information, visit dineshdsouza.com and tkc.edu.

ALSO BY DINESH D'SOUZA

The Roots of Obama's Rage (2010)

He's been called many things: a Socialist, a radical fellow traveler, a Chicago machine politician, a prince of the civil rights movement, a virtual second coming of Christ, or even a covert Muslim. But as *New York Times* bestselling author Dinesh D'Souza points out in this shockingly revealing book, these labels merely slap our own preconceived notions on Barack Obama. What really motivates Barack Obama is an inherited rage—an often masked but profound rage that comes from his African father. It is an anticolonialist rage against Western dominance, and most especially against the wealth and power of the very nation Barack Obama now leads.

Life after Death: The Evidence (2009)

Do the latest discoveries in physics and neuroscience, the most convincing philosophical deductions, and the most likely conclusions from anthropology and biology lend increasing credibility to the prospect of life after death? *Life after Death: The Evidence* presents a reasoned, scientifically based case that life after death is more than possible; it is highly probable. D'Souza argues that, indeed, life after death has far more evidence on its side than atheistic arguments about death marking our complete and utter extinction.

What's So Great about Christianity (2008)

Is Christianity true? Or has Christianity been disproven by science, debunked as a force for good, and discredited as a guide to morality? D'Souza approaches Christianity with a questioning eye but treats the skeptics with equal skepticism. The result is a book that will challenge the assumptions of both believers and doubters and affirm that there really is, indeed, something great about Christianity.

The Enemy at Home: The Cultural Left and Its Responsibility for 9/11 (2008)

In this controversial book, D'Souza argues that the cultural left and its allies in Congress, the media, Hollywood, the nonprofit sector, and the universities are the primary cause of the volcano of anger toward America that is erupting from the Islamic world. The Muslims who carried out the 9/11 attacks were the product of this visceral rage—some of it based on legitimate concerns, some of it based on wrongful prejudice, but all of it fueled and encouraged by the cultural left. D'Souza contends that the cultural left is responsible for 9/11 in two ways: by fostering a decadent and depraved American culture that angers and repulses other societies—especially traditional and religious ones—and by promoting, at home and abroad, an anti-American attitude that blames America for all the problems of the world.

Letters to a Young Conservative (2005)

In the book that serves as many students' first introduction to D'Souza's writing, he provides the next generation with a basic understanding of modern conservatism and its fundamental precepts. Addressing a fictional student by the name of "Chris," D'Souza outlines the major distinctions between the three main political positions in the United States: liberalism, conservatism, and libertarianism. Drawing on his own colorful experiences, both within the conservative world and while skirmishing with the left, D'Souza aims to enlighten and inspire young conservatives and give them weapons for the intellectual battles they face in high school, college, and everyday life.

CP0546-A

ALSO BY DINESH D'SOUZA (CONTINUED)

What's So Great about America (2003)

D'Souza argues that, more than any other country, America allows people the chance to "write the script of their own lives." This is why the idea of America is so appealing to immigrants and to young people around the world. Thoughtful and engaging, the book offers the grounds for a solid, well-considered patriotism—the sort of patriotism that America will need to sustain itself in the many challenges that lie ahead.

The Virtue of Prosperity: Finding Values in an Age of Techno-Affluence (2001)

D'Souza will surprise readers across the political spectrum with his original vision of how we can actually do well while doing good and succeed while making society better. He shows how to preserve nature, strengthen our families and communities, and expand our intellectual horizons in a techno-capitalist world. Ultimately, D'Souza reveals how we can harness the power of technology and affluence to promote individual fulfillment and the common good.

Ronald Reagan: How an Ordinary Man Became an Extraordinary Leader (1999)

Dinesh D'Souza solves the mystery of Ronald Reagan by showing how this "ordinary" man was able to transform the political landscape in a way that made a permanent impact on America and the world. Through firsthand reporting and interviews, D'Souza portrays the private side of Reagan—the man behind the mask—and reveals the moral sources of his vision and leadership. He concludes that, if Reagan does not fit our preconceptions of what makes a great leader, then we must rethink our understanding of both greatness and leadership.

The End of Racism: Principles for a Multiracial Society (1995)

Dinesh D'Souza goes beyond familiar polemics to raise fundamental questions that no one else has asked: Is racial prejudice innate, or is it culturally acquired? *The End of Racism* summons profound historical, moral, and practical arguments against the civil rights orthodoxy, which holds that "race matters" and that therefore we have no choice but to institutionalize race as the basis for identity and public policy. The book expands the range of acceptable discourse about race, offers a way out of the deadlocked debate, and sets forth the principles that should guide us in creating a multiracial society.

Illiberal Education: The Politics of Race and Sex on Campus (1991)

Is "political correctness" chilling freedom of thought and speech on America's campuses today? Based on extensive research at six major universities, *Illiberal Education* is a hugely controversial, powerful polemic that examines the most important and divisive questions confronting American education today. D'Souza argues that by charging universities with being "structurally" racist, sexist, and class biased, a coalition of student activists, junior faculty, and compliant administrators have imposed their own political ideals on admissions, hiring, curriculum, and even personal conduct, while eschewing the goals of liberal education.

Do more than simply understand
the arguments against atheism.
Meet atheistic arguments on their
own terms.

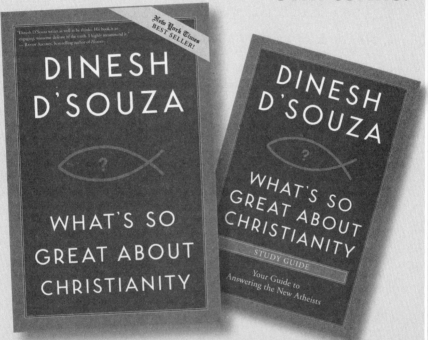

In his *New York Times* best seller *What's So Great about Christianity*,
Dinesh D'Souza takes an in-depth look at the arguments
and rhetoric in the current atheist-led debate about God and
Christianity. Along with the companion study guide, perfect for
individual or group study, this book will help you articulate

- the intellectual validity of Christianity,
- how religious belief can be reconciled with science, and
- the flaws in atheistic arguments.

Online Discussion *guide*

TAKE *your* TYNDALE READING
EXPERIENCE *to the* NEXT LEVEL

A FREE discussion guide for this book
is available at bookclubhub.net, perfect
for sparking conversations in your book
group or for digging deeper into the text
on your own.

www.bookclubhub.net

*You'll also find free discussion guides for
other Tyndale books, e-newsletters, e-mail
devotionals, virtual book tours, and more!*